N

LE

Qiryat
Shmona

GOLAN
HEIGHTS

SYRIA

Sea of
Galilee

EinGev

Haifa

Technion City
Mt. Carmel

Megiddo

Mediterranean
Sea

Herzlya

Tel Aviv

Jordan River

Mt. Scopus

Amman

Jerusalem

Ashkelon

Dead Sea

Gaza

Masada

Beersheba

ISRAEL

JORDAN

SINAI

Miles

0   25   50

Occupied Territory

Gulf of
Aqaba

OR

BY THE SAME AUTH

The Yellow Wind

Birds' Nests in Their Beards

Strike Zion!

The Bushbabies

ZANEK!

A CHRONICLE OF THE

ISRAELI AIR FORCE

William Stevenson

NEW YORK | THE VIKING PRESS

First published in 1971 by The Viking Press, Inc.
625 Madison Avenue, New York, N.Y. 10022

Published simultaneously in Canada by
The Macmillan Company of Canada Limited

SBN 670-79624-7

Library of Congress catalog card number: 71-139272

Printed in U.S.A. by The Colonial Press Inc.

Published by arrangement with Bantam Books, Inc.

ACKNOWLEDGMENTS

Excerpt from a poem by Nathan Alterman. From *The
New York Times Book Review,* August 9, 1970. Copyright © 1970 by The New York Times Company and
reprinted with their permission.

"A Refusal to Mourn the Death," by Dylan Thomas.
From his *Collected Poems.* Copyright 1946 by New
Directions Publishing Corporation and reprinted with
their permission, that of J. M. Dent & Sons, Ltd., London,
and The Trustees for the Copyrights of the late Dylan
Thomas.

FOREWORD:

THE REASON WHY

When I was a pilot in another war, my plane was catapulted from the deck of a ship. My closest friend followed. Together we climbed into dense cloud. There was an explosion. My own aircraft fell into a dive. By the time I recovered control, my friend was gone.

The burial service took place on the ship's quarterdeck. There was no corpse. The chaplain wore mittens. Rain hissed on the steel deck. The *coup de feu* rattled over the heads of men hunched in wet greatcoats. A wreath was tossed onto the gray waters and then we all raced for shelter and hot toddies of rum.

My friend was nineteen and so was I. At that age one had simple concepts of truth and honor. He died with his ideals intact; and others of my friends followed him, in much the same way.

This chronicle covers an ugly period in 1970 when a few young men and women bought time for their country in its greatest peril. In them I saw my dead companions.

The story of the Israeli Air Force has to be told in a personal way because its pilots and planes have been in the midst of a deadly conflict and few outsiders understand the desperate nature of battles fought above a region where Asia, Africa, and the Caucasian worlds all meet. Everything about this region stirs the deepest emotions. Here is the setting for great movements which have torn the hearts of men. I have had to reject an approach that pretends to weigh these current events from afar. The god's-eye view seems fraudulent, but the role of spokesman seems also an evasion of responsibility.

I write instead as someone who remembers what it is like to be part of a small group where the struggle to survive is something personal; who remembers the vows we made to build a better world; who remembers, most of all, how much the men and women who do the actual fighting in a war quite simply hate it. So much is written about war today by observers, preachers, and politicians. I thought to convey the feelings and the character of an embattled people.

To protect them I have chosen an unusual narrative form. This chronicle is not an official document and does not necessarily represent the opinion of the Israeli Defense Forces.

Being unable to inject myself into a chronicle about those who daily face dangers far greater than any I have known, I have had to create the stranger S. He could be in several places at once, watching and listening. He could bring together a number of separate incidents and make them happen on the same day. When necessary, S could create one character out of several men whose identities had to be protected for the security reasons indicated above.

I'm not sure who the stranger S really is. Myself, perhaps, and the ghosts of the dead already.

CONTENTS

Foreword: The Reason Why   v

1. Two Thousand Seconds of Silence   3
2. The Girl at the Center   23
3. Day X in Jacob's Calendar   36
4. "Thick and Fast They Came at Last"   49
5. Sand in the Killer Sky   64
6. Old Dogfights and New Tricks   81
7. A Piece of Cake for Yesnov   97
8. The Golan Dragon   113
9. In Golda's Kitchen   133
10. Treetop Raider   151
11. The Flying Guerrillas   166
12. A Phoenix from the Death Camps   189
13. Man against Missile   211
14. The Vertical Frontier   227
15. A Crack in the Wall   239
16. Phantom among the *Tilim*   254
17. Return to Masada   279
18. Jacob's Ladder   296
19. Voices in the Cockpit   319
Index   340

ZANEK!

1

TWO THOUSAND

SECONDS OF SILENCE

An old man stalked along the margin of the sea. He wore the tunic and the fur hat of a Russian peasant. His movements were jerky and lacked any apparent aim.

S, the stranger, watched him. A mad old man was useless in this emergency.

"He'll help," said the girl. She was about twenty years old. Her flying jacket was slung around her shoulders, and the metal bars on her epaulettes glinted in the misty Mediterranean sun. In this land where a name seemed sometimes to be a state secret, the stranger called her the Little Lieutenant.

"Help? He's probably deaf and certainly soft in the head," grumbled S. He turned back to the car he had hired in Tel Aviv. It squatted in sand churned higher than the axles.

The old man carried a shapeless bit of plastic to the dump he was building near a gorse bush.

"The tide's coming in faster than we're getting out," said the stranger, spinning the rear wheels, his own complaints drowned by the gunned motor, the car throwing back another shower of sand. There was a sudden cough of rage under the hood and the engine stopped.

"You need water in the radiator," said the girl after a long silence.

"I know," the stranger replied between clenched teeth.

The old man was heading their way now. He stooped to salvage another piece of junk and then he circled the car before touching his hat to the girl.

She spoke to him softly in Hebrew. The old man dropped his armful of garbage and made an answer, removing his hat and screwing it tight between his thick, arthritic fingers.

"He apologizes for his appearance," said the Little Lieutenant. "He says his hat is older than his head."

S groaned, anticipating an endless exchange of pleasantries in a language he did not understand while the sea lapped around the car and the day slid into eternity.

The old man gave a toothless grin. His arms dangled in wide-cuffed sleeves and his hands were clasped like chunks of welded rock. He might have been chipped and chiseled out of Ukrainian walnut by a wood carver from another century.

"Your car," he said in English, "is going to sink."

"Yes." The stranger took a grip upon himself. "*Unless we push it out.*"

The old man bent to examine the tire tracks.

"He says the sand is too soft," said the girl.

"The deduction of a genius . . . Look, I'll walk back to the Haifa road and flag down a car."

"He also thinks," the girl interrupted, "we should have found a more secluded spot."

"We're on official business. We took a shortcut. Tell him that!"

"There's a lovers' lane behind the dunes."

"*We-did-not-stop-because-we-wanted-to!*" The stranger roared. "And in the lane for lovers, he has his car."

"Car?"

"In which we will go and mobilize the village."

"Oh . . ."

"I have told him," the Little Lieutenant said sweetly, "to forgive your impatience. I said you were once a fighter pilot and therefore impulsive. Also that you are a writer."

The fact that S was a writer seemed to carry the most weight. The old man retrieved his driftwood. "This one is a writer too. See." He twisted the wood. It was possible to see a man's craggy profile.

Deflated, S introduced himself.

"And my name is Tolya."

S accepted the possibility. In this country perpetually at war, to which men had come under false labels by way of underground routes, he had grown accustomed to nicknames, pseudonyms, and aliases.

"No need for a *nom de guerre* with this one," said Tolya, admiring the driftwood. "He's Dostoevski."

If not mad, thought S, then certainly a crank. He helped take the old man's flotsam to the hidden car. It was a little Citroën with a broken fender and painted in two shades of fog gray. A *deux-chevaux*, as dirty and desert-stained as the rest. One saw them crawling around the country, snorting with age, relics of a time when France flirted with these people.

"Another antiquity," said Tolya, rapping the roof. "One day I will turn it into a sculpture with the rest." He tossed a lump of shrapnel into the back seat.

The stranger sat among the scrap iron, the coral, and the driftwood while the car jogged along a washboard road between hedges of fragrant mayflower. He could see how the day would end. There would be an eccentric argument among Tolya's friends on how to rescue the car. The car, of course, would meanwhile sink. The prospect gave S a perverse satisfaction. The Little Lieutenant would be at a grave disadvantage if the car vanished in the incoming tide. The shortcut had been her idea.

They paused near a cluster of houses. Red and green peppers dried on the rooftops. Onions dangled in strings under the eaves. Milk churns rattled on a horse-drawn droshky. Children raked the freshly turned earth and old ladies in kerchiefs stood in the open doorways. A group of girls beat giant sunflowers, heaping the seeds on the concrete threshing floor. Again S was reminded of a scene from Czarist Russia.

Tolya shouted to the children. "He says it won't hurt to leave the tulips and cucumbers," said the girl, laughing. "The vegetables won't spring out of the earth in an hour."

"He doesn't seem to be convincing them."

"They all know him. He's a teacher."

"That explains the sculpting. An artist—?"

"No, he's head of the nautical college. He was captain of a trawler in the Baltic long ago."

S opened his mouth and then closed it again.

The sun was low before Tolya browbeat a crew together. He had commandeered a wagon and trapped his recruits as they walked their families between cypress and hawthorn. "How would you like to be a foreigner and stranded?" he harangued them. "Come, citizens, show this Christian that a Jew can forgive. You there, Yaacov, work will be a medicine for that pot of a belly."

The men answered that they were tired. The young ones had been called for military duty. Their day of rest would begin at sundown. Didn't he know this was the eve of the Sabbath? They grumbled, but still they clambered into the wagon, abandoning wives and children on this fine Friday afternoon, but bringing with them poles and chains.

"What was that about military mobilization?" asked S.

The Little Lieutenant shrugged and pretended not to know.

When the party reached the mired car, a transformation took place. The men were past middle age but they were tough and moved like a well-drilled team.

"You were clever to pick such a girl," one of them said to S. "But you wasted valuable time."

"He's a foreigner, idiot," said Tolya with the same amiable grin. "He was on his way to the base on government business."

"Business, is it?" grunted another. "So this is where the taxes go."

"More important, is he on our side?"

"He doesn't look Jewish."

S grew restless as the light faded. Small waves creamed along the shore. The tide moved in, hissing.

"Don't worry," said the driver of the truck. "Life without trouble is no life at all."

"That's it, citizen. A cabbage leads a charmed life but it gets no further than the cooking pot."

"My wife's cousin in Rumania, for him every day was like clockwork. One day the clock stopped. Two days passed before anyone noticed he was dead and I question if he himself to this day knows his condition has changed."

"Count your blessings, stranger. If the car drowns, at least you won't be in it."

Their voices were drowsy in the dusk. They pushed boards under the rear wheels, dug away the sand, tied ropes to the bumpers, and they were still talking when they had hauled the car to firm ground.

A young man bicycled across the sand spit.

"My son," said Tolya. "He would be grateful for a lift to the base."

S was glad for an opportunity to return their kindness. But the boy looked like a teen-ager who'd been cramming for exams: pale and thin and preoccupied. "Isn't there something more I can do?"

Tolya scratched his skull under the fur hat. "My son," he said, "began his first leave in six months yesterday. Today he's wanted urgently by his squadron. If you get him back, you will do all of us a service."

The old man straightened his back. "He's a fighter pilot and we don't have all that many."

The base was scarcely visible. S had become familiar with it. Yet, approaching it by road or air, he was always taken by surprise. It lay in a great depression, in countryside that was here like the heavily cultivated soil of southern Italy. He turned a bend in the road and stopped at the striped pole which was the only warning.

The boy spoke little. He still wore the frayed shirt and corduroy trousers of a farmworker. S knew better than to ask questions. Even his father, the old man Tolya, would never ask what planes the boy flew. Now, talking softly to the guards, the boy called for an escort. A burly figure wheeled out of the bushes on a motorscooter and beckoned them to follow. The scooter was ludicrously small under its gigantic rider, bulky in air-force battle dress, wearing no hat, but surrounded by a glorious halo of black hair and red beard.

They passed the gray ghosts of Super-Hornets. The big helicopters, whenever damaged beyond repair, were gutted and trimmed; the husks became training devices for airborne commandos, who could be seen most days swinging from jump towers or working their way along the high wires. S drove under the arched eucalyptus trees lining the road and turned where an old World War II Mustang brooded on a concrete platform, its final resting place. Old aircraft dotted the base, mummified in the same way. Warplane buffs back in the States, thought S, would flip if they knew about the Messerschmidt-109s, the Harvards and Austers that were preserved as monuments to that period only twenty years ago when Jewish volunteers flew shelltorn relics against an armada of postwar fighter-bombers supplied to the Arabs by the foreign powers. Some of those early battles were fought on the Jewish side with light sports planes, against enemies sworn to strangle Israel at birth. It was the time when the present air-force commander General Mordechai "Motti" Hod, having left Palestine as Lance Corporal Fein of the British Army, returned flying a Spitfire from Czechoslovakia with just enough fuel to land near Tel Aviv and not a cent in the pockets of his borrowed suit.

The escort on his scooter wheeled right at a Piper Cub embalmed in memory of the "bomb-chuckers," youngsters who had boosted their flying hours by dropping grenades by hand on the Egyptian and Syrian armies. Some of those bomb-chuckers had died as pilots in the incessant aerial warfare that reached one peak in 1956 and a higher peak in 1967 and had grown more ferocious in each of the three years that followed. Others today held positions of command in what had become the Israeli Air Force, of which Hod was now chief.

All the bases shared the same atmosphere of unreality. The squat control towers and the angular rods above the concrete radio shacks, the hangars like deflated balloons glimpsed between the trees and embankments, gave an unearthly effect. Russian missiles, their energies expended, were twisted into grotesque shapes by amateur sculptors to decorate open spaces. Old bomb and shell casings were fashioned into surrealistic forms for visiting children to play with. There were neat roads, of course, sensibly sign-posted. But the signs were gibberish to the stranger and the roads had a way of expiring into the landscape, which might be here a desert and there an oasis of gumtrees or palms. Sometimes you followed a road and found yourself pursuing a painted line across a wilderness of tar. Bang in the middle of this black-topped desert a traffic light blinked like something in a Salvador Dali painting. You stopped on red to let a line of Skyhawks curtsey past, their jets creating a shimmering haze so that you felt the whole thing was a mirage. Sometimes there were bombs hanging from the Skyhawks. They carried their long thin noses very high and moved on long haughty legs. They had the arrogance of high-fashion models, elegant and untouchable despite their bursting bellies, swaying down the strip. Then the traffic light turned green and you crossed very cautiously indeed the runway you would otherwise never have seen.

It was dark now as S stopped the car at one of these traffic lights. Tolya's son said, "I'll walk from here. Thanks."

A light stabbed the darkness above them. The beam illuminated a patch of concrete. Another searchlight sprang out of the black sky, and then another. For a moment S felt as if he were flying upside down, above a forest of searchlights. A formation of troop-carrying helicopters moved over the field with landing lights ablaze. A shape like a prehistoric monster dropped onto the runway in front of the stranger's car and disappeared, screaming dismally into the void.

The traffic light turned to green.

The Little Lieutenant pulled her flying jacket tighter around her shoulders. "I hope you didn't mind being called 'citizen.'"

The question startled S, who was still unused to these bizarre spectacles. "God, why should I be?"

"It's a bit like 'comrade,'" she said. "It's really a compliment."

The bearded escort on the scooter weaved ahead.

"George Washington was proud to be called 'citizen,'" the girl continued defensively. "He saw himself as the leader of an army of farmers, unspoiled by the corruption of the cities. His farmers left their plows to give their lives for a new republic where the highest title was 'citizen.'"

There's no answer to that, thought the stranger. A few weeks ago, he might have bristled at being lectured by this child. He knew better now.

"You agree?" she asked.

"Of course."

"Then why don't Americans understand this is what we are doing here?"

And there was no answer to that either.

All night long the scream of jets shook the small hut where S lay sleepless on his cot.

He had disciplined himself to curb his curiosity. At first the mysteries annoyed him. He felt like a prisoner led blindfold through a guerrilla camp.

It had taken S a long time to get near this air force, where secrecy was vital to survival. He had covered most of Israel, while making a documentary film in 1967, and on the eve of the Six-Day War he drove past a few battered twenty-year-old transport planes. These were the first air-force planes he had seen. He was with the grandson of the man who had directed the Battle of Britain. Both S and his colleague shook their heads at the sight of the bedraggled old warplanes and agreed that without command of the air, Israel was finished. Neither man guessed what power lay coiled out of sight.

Within a few hours, Motti Hod launched a comparative handful of pilots against large fleets of Arab warplanes. For slightly more than thirty minutes—two thousand seconds to be exact—outdated jets sped from different bases at carefully measured intervals toward widely dispersed targets, forbidden to break radio silence until they struck at precisely the same time several hundred enemy warplanes on Arab bases between radar and rocket sites.

During those two thousand seconds in 1967, Motti Hod stood in the control room and waited. Israel had been stripped of its home defenses in the air. Not until the pilots broke silence would anyone know if the gamble had worked. "The nation's fate rested on that single throw of the dice," said one of Hod's companions.

Outsiders knew nothing of this. Few knew that the Chief of Operations was the nephew of the first President of the State, or that this man, Ezer Weizman, had planned this moment with meticulous care ("I told our generals the air force could knock out the Arabs and win air supremacy within six hours," General Weizman was to tell S later. "They thought I was nuts. Motti, God bless him, shot me down and did the job in three hours.").

The basement where Hod waited was the linchpin of Israel's organization for action information. Dim under a blue-lit roof, surrounded by dark cloistral recesses where a hundred tiny lights glowed yellow and ruby red and emerald green, the Direction Officer stood among his congregation of consoles and computers all busily calculating in seconds, meters, and fractions of nautical miles, weaving a thread of new solutions to changes in the running intelligence on enemy dispositions. Girls in summer khaki, headphones clamped to their heads, methodically marked numbers and symbols on the silvery surface of the wide transparent screen etched with a pattern of spider-web lines. Beyond them were banks of radar displays on which electronic beams swept ceaselessly round, imprinting on orange faces the most ghostly silhouettes.

One of Israel's turtle doves, whose *kruuu-kruuing* washes across the land on the soft offshore breeze, had nested in a ventilation shaft. The dove's restless movements, the scratching of claws on punctured metal, echoed in the silent control room like the tap-tap-tap of a man's knuckles rapping impatiently at the door.

Radio silence was broken by sharp exchanges between the striking pilots. To a foreign ear, Hebrew has a guttural sound. On that particular morning, even to Motti Hod's ear, the transmissions were at first bewildering. Had his forces caught the enemy with their MiGs down? Or had the Russian-built jets waited up-sun to pounce? Shouts of warning were heard, reminiscent of the big air battles over Europe and the Pacific.

"Turning left, Corsair. . . ."

"Get organized. . . . Aircraft four, above. . . ."

"I'm covering you."

"Bandits three o'clock."

"Negative, Coconut. They're ours. . . ."

It was all garbled, disjointed. It came over loudspeakers clicking with static that mutilated the words of the pilots. Then the extent of the victory became clear. The pilots began to call in their tallies. Two thousand years of Jewish history had been punctuated by two thousand seconds of courage concentrated into that single pre-emptive strike.

It took another hundred and forty minutes to destroy the Egyptian Air Force and enemy radar in the Sinai. By the end of the second day a confirmed and checked grand total of 416 enemy aircraft had been eliminated. But the few who were there remember those two thousand seconds when Motti Hod stood in silence, moving only occasionally to moisten his lips with the rim of a glass filled with water.

It was February 1970 when S finally got permission to enter the fringes of the air force. By then it had undertaken new roles. There was an immense reluctance to discuss anything with an outsider. The men were tired. The girls were protective. But they had taken him into their confidence, a stranger, at a time when the dangers of betrayal had never seemed greater.

As they gained faith in him, so they disclosed the size of their dilemma. He tried to find analogies. He thought of the RAF in the Battle of Britain. Would the English admit a neutral to their inmost councils when it was vital to conceal from Hitler that the Nazi Luftwaffe could overwhelm their defenses? The parallel was not exact. The British had been able to draw on reserves who trained in the safety of Australia, Canada, Rhodesia; Israel had no hinterland.

He considered Mao's guerrilla armies. They had revolutionized the art of war on the ground. It was fair to say the Israelis were revolutionizing the art of war in the air much as Mao had upset the West's traditional military concepts. There was no basis for comparison, though, because what Israel faced in 1970 was a combination of Maoist-style guerrilla warfare on the ground and all the scientific ingenuity of the Soviet Union in the air.

"We don't need anyone else to fight our war," General Hod had told him. "We pay cash for the weapons we buy. But nobody should have illusions. This is the cockpit where the Communists are testing their most sophisticated weapons, their technology. . . ."

Another commander had asked S, "What can a *goy* know about a Jewish air force?" "More than you might guess," the stranger replied, thinking privately that here, in fact, lay the root of many problems. To the stranger, raised in the Christian tradition, it had come as a shock to discover the prejudice against the Jews that still persisted after Hitler's defeat, the depths of which he had been unaware until his first study, years before, of Israel's story. He began to understand Israel's basic distrust of the outside world; a fear that the persecution of the Jews continued to exercise its baleful influence.

Why, he had been asked, does the West shower its most modern weapons on the Mickey-Mouse dictatorships while Israel has to beg to *buy* the means of defense? Why are the Liberation Fronts of Asia regarded as Communist-led and dangerous, while Christians see virtue in the Palestine Liberation Front, whose leaders train in Peking? Is it not significant that in the middle of 1970 we learn from the trial of the commandant of the Treblinka concentration camp that ex-Nazi exterminators fled along what was called the Vatican Escape Route?

A woman had spoken to S at a party at another base. "You must be privileged to be allowed in here," she said. S explained he was writing a book on the Israeli Air Force. "Do *you* think we've a chance?" she asked. "You're a stranger. You see things objectively." She was the wife of a senior officer. She had survived a Nazi camp. Deep in her heart, she believed nobody would come to the help of the Jews.

There were those who felt that anti-Jewish sentiment was the new equation in the attack on Israel. It was the novel ingredient in the art of psychological warfare perfected by Russia and China, whatever their private differences. The Soviet Union and the Maoists had moved into the Middle East: the first with technology, the second with Mao's "silver bullets" of propaganda.

The besieged Israelis could find no comfort in their own history as a nation. It was a tangle of broken promises, betrayals, and disenchantment. There had been an atavistic urge to find refuge in a land of their own. They had been confronted with hostility from the start. Every weapon they possessed had to be purchased and frequently smuggled. One source of supply after another had dried up until the greatest betrayal of all, by the

French. Now their last resort was the United States and here it seemed that the warplanes which were given to the doubtful democracies of Asia could not be purchased for cash by the Jews.

S knew all the arguments against arming Israel. Now he was looking at the situation purely from an Israeli point of view. Samson, eyeless in Gaza, had pulled down the temple and destroyed both himself and all around him. That story was familiar to Christians as part of the Bible. For every Israeli, it was part of Jewish history.

"We fight because we have no alternative," General Hod had told the stranger.

The words were not spoken boastfully. Hod was not that kind of man. S remembered a day when he was summoned hastily to the Citadel, the air-force headquarters in Tel Aviv.

There was a sentry who did not recognize S. And few strangers entered the Citadel. S, in a hurry, said he was late for an appointment with Brigadier General Hod. "Brigadier General . . ." The guard repeated the words slowly, looking puzzled. He called others for advice. They were bright youngsters, handling their weapons professionally, but in their manner casual and friendly. They shook their heads. No brigadier generals around here, they seemed to say.

Suddenly inspired, S said "Motti Hod. Brigadier General Motti—"

"Ah!" they interrupted with a collective sigh. They stood aside. The gates opened. "Why didn't you say so? *Motti*. Of course."

S took breakfast in the aircrew mess. The men were silent, most of them clad in flying coveralls, some wearing anti-G suits and knives strapped to their legs. One of them was Tolya's son.

The Little Lieutenant interrupted S in the middle of his second cup of coffee. She said "Motti's just landed. Would you join him at the base commander's office?"

When S got there, the air-force chief had gone again.

There was a Skyhawk jockeying on the tarmac outside, and S drew his own conclusions. He was certain by now that a big operation was brewing, if it was not already under way. He knew also that if the whole air force was to be flung into another pre-emptive strike like that of 1967, the base commander would remain true to the obligations of a good host. He was known as the Little Czar, Czareko. He had served five years in the Soviet Air Force and returned to his village in the Ukraine in 1946 to find his parents and sisters dead. "They were not killed by the Nazis," said Czareko. "They were slaughtered by what I had thought were my own countrymen. So I said to hell with Russia and let my legs carry me to Jerusalem."

His legs must have covered twice the distance of a normal man's, Czareko liked to observe, "because they're half as long as anyone else's."

Sitting behind his desk, large head balanced on a weight-lifter's shoulders, he seemed larger than life. Only when he left his chair was it apparent that Czareko had to tilt his head back to speak to most of his visitors.

"The only position where I can look anyone directly in the eye is sitting down," said Czareko. "But I can't fight sitting down. That I discovered. So I fly. And one of these days, the Lord willing (and always supposing he exists), I'll get my eye straight and level on a flying Cossack and make him pay for those, my ancestors and sisters and cousins who were hacked down by the sabers of his comrades.

"I'm not saying there is a God and I'm not saying there isn't a God, but I do say if God exists then I believe in giving Him a helping hand."

When he spoke like this, Czareko leaned back and rolled his pouched eyes upward like a child watching for the blade of a man on horseback. The eyes were blue, of an astonishing brilliance. They reminded S of the blue patches of sky at the end of a long climb through a dismal overcast. They were surrounded by black clouds of eyelids and lashes, and leathery flesh bruised by experience.

Such blueness of eye, the fresh use of words in several languages, and the small boy's walk made Czareko seem young and bright as a button. When he crouched in the back of a staff car, speeding across the base to quiz pilots back from a mission, his granite face under the peaked cap was that of a Marshal in the Soviet Red Air Force. Czareko did not crumple his cap or bend the peak in the style of others more casual. In this too he resembled the square Russian disciplinarians. The comparison always sent him into a fury, quickly terminating in laughter. "The Russians are so stupid if you kick them in the backside they think they've got bleeding piles," he would say. "In that respect, doubtless there is much of the Russian in me."

He was, this Czareko, useful for his knowledge of the Russian air force and the Russian mind. He liked to close his eyes and form a mental picture of his opposite numbers advising the Arabs.

When S had first met him a few weeks ago, the IAF was still reticent about Russian participation in Arab military operations. Israeli leaders did not want to make a bad situation worse by disclosing what they knew about Russian and other Communist experts who directed Arab military units, sometimes down to squadron and battalion levels. By April 1970, there were detailed photographs of Russian rocket sites disguised as mosques and schools. S had seen them but shared with the Israelis an unhappy conviction that, at this stage, many Westerners would dismiss such evidence as anti-Soviet propaganda.

Now, a month later, the truth was out. The Russians were constructing a defense umbrella that would discourage the IAF from attacking the bases from which Arab guerrillas launched their terrorist actions. Russian military technology was providing a variation of the privileged sanctuary in Asia. If it worked, Israel's enemies could keep biting until she bled to death.

Czareko interrupted the stranger's thoughts. "Come over to the hangars."

They walked through black caverns where the silhouettes of gutted jets looked like prehistoric insects, some beheaded and others minus tails. Those without engines were nothing more than lobster shells on articulated legs.

Nothing was wasted. For the training of mechanics, there were no sophisticated mockups. Everything was improvised from the debris of wrecked aircraft.

"We built ourselves on the French aircraft industry," said Czareko. "French aircraft are like French women. Look at these Vautours and Mirages, wasp-waisted, clean curves, and beautiful. The Americans bend their tailplanes down and twist their wings upward and hang stuff from every position. See how this slot drops when a Skyhawk makes a slow turn. Newton's at work, you see, and the slot drops and the wing shakes and the pilot bangs his head against the side of the cockpit and wakes up."

Two mechanics had dropped to the hangar floor and slept where they lay. "Poor boys," said Czareko. "They worked all through the night and fall, the darlings, like small children. You see how Newton is always at work." He shook his head. "They have to learn all about American technology, having mastered the French and before that the British and German machines. If we could catch enough Russians, perhaps we could standardize on Soviet aircraft."

Outside, a Spitfire landed. It had a red propeller boss and jet-black wings.

"No sense in hiding facts," said Czareko. "There's the Black Widow."

The Spit jogged in their direction, the Rolls-Royce Merlin farting and spitting, a frail old dowager among the jets, too proud to admit the passage of the years. She gave a final belch, the prop stopped, the canopy slid back, and Ezer Weizman climbed onto the fabric-covered wing.

For a Cabinet minister, he was dressed more than a little informally in open-necked shirt and scuffed linen trousers, his toes poking out of sandals and a strip of plaster stuck on the heel of one bare foot. Some of the crewmen gave him the thumbs-up sign. Here he was better known as Motti Hod's predecessor than as an irate Minister of Transport who had come down hard on careless drivers. Behind him a Mirage whistled into a parking space and Hod bounced out. A staff car pulled up, and the two men disappeared inside.

Czareko excused himself, and S headed back toward the crew-rooms of the Skyhawk squadron. He crossed the concrete already shimmering with the new day's heat. A captured Russian truck-trailer jounced ahead, crammed with men.

Between the iron and concrete of the base, there were squares of soil where flowers and shrubs had been planted. The air-crew huts adjoined a patch of carefully nurtured earth where tulips and roses grew. A pilot was making a screen with sticks and a sheet of muslin to redirect the hot desert wind. Another, his flying coveralls unzipped down to the navel, dropped crocus bulbs into holes made by driving a finger into the earth. The shrubbery, the young saplings on the corners of taxi-strips, the thickets of magnolia and rhododendron, the young trees shading the villas of the fliers, all softened the harsh geometry of workshops and crew-rooms. A girl with her captain's tunic slung over her shoulders knitted in the sunshine outside the squadron commander's office.

It seems so peaceful, thought S, squatting in the shade. Each base has its own characteristics, like each kibbutz. There's a poetry to all this, a symmetry of design that's almost spine-chilling. The first settlers were refugees from Russian oppression; many disavowed God and ritual Judaism; their communes asked "from each according to his ability" and offered "to each according to his need." Out of this spirit of the kibbutz grew this air force that now finds itself confronted by the descendants of the old oppressors.

"Emotions recollected in tranquillity?" asked a familiar voice.

The stranger looked up into the face of a man who had puzzled him to the point of despair, and who would always remain an enigma: the man called Jacob.

"Damn," said S. "I can't remember who wrote that."

"Wordsworth."

"You're unforgivable."

"When you're always Number Two, you try a little harder." Jacob jerked his head in the direction of the wooden huts that served here as administrative offices. "Come."

They took over the room of the Chief Technical Officer.

"We're in the middle of a war," said Jacob, shutting the door. "You wouldn't think it." He shrugged. "Well, I'm not making excuses but your presence on bases does create difficulties. We can't always keep your appointments. . . ."

His words were drowned by the passage of jets.

"Precisely," said the stranger.

"You were asking about procedures for the conduct of missions," said Jacob. "I've got five minutes and then I have to take off, too." He looked down. "I'm a bit upset. . . ."

S sat very still, afraid to lose this rare moment of intimacy. Jacob was not a man who gave much of himself. He seemed to have been everywhere and to have done everything. He had come out of some fathomless horror in Nazi Europe. In the early air-force days, his pay as a young fighter pilot was supplemented by work as a bricklayer. Each encounter with Jacob was a voyage of discovery. He was shy on the ground, as if an essential part of himself belonged in the sky. S had watched him turn into a different person whenever they flew together, as if the wings took the place of limbs and the cockpit was a protection against personal embarrassment. Jacob, thrown into a death-camp as a child, had turned himself into one of those most rare men among aviators, a scholar and linguist and skilled artisan. His stunted body and stubby arms testified to hardship. There were numbers tattooed on his wrist which he wore as proudly as some veteran Israeli pilots carried a magical four-digit figure, in remembrance of their first operational squadron, which cockily adopted the four-figure number to conceal its puny size.

Jacob, who had test-flown almost every modern jet from Sweden to Singapore; Jacob, who had bicycled around an Egyptian airbase before its capture was complete, collecting enemy ammunition for his own planes, which were running out; Jacob, who watched the young airmen with a fierce protectiveness, now said, "Forgive me if I don't concentrate very well but a child was killed today, a young girl. . . ."

He looked out of the window and his voice changed. "There are two aspects to our military operations. First: operational. Second: political. We will consider the second aspect, which falls into four elements: *target, scope, execution, timing.* The totality of these four elements is the concern of those Cabinet ministers who handle defense and security. They have to weigh the domestic and foreign reactions. So . . . what *kind* of operation we will undertake is decided by the Cabinet Security Committee. *How* is for the defense minister, Dayan, and the chief of staff, Bar-Lev, to work out. . . ."

His voice droned on, pedantic, remote. He might have been lecturing at a staff college. *Who is he?* the stranger asked himself. *He's everywhere and nowhere. Getting to know him is like unpeeling an onion, except that I don't believe you'd ever get to the center.*

The stranger felt that to comprehend the true nature of Israel he would have to listen to Jacob fumbling at the locks of memory.

"Okay, let's go!" Suddenly Jacob was on his feet.

"Can I ask where, or is that also a military secret?" asked S dryly.

Jacob smiled bleakly. It had become an old joke between them. Only today it wasn't funny. "You'll have to make your own way back to Herzlya," he said, naming the coastal town where S kept an apartment. "I'm flying to Qiryat Shmona."

His departure was no less abrupt than his arrival. It was his way, learned in the European underground, the way of the survivor, quick, unheralded, never explained.

Outside, a bent old man with a Moses-like beard wheeled a barrow past Ezer Weizman's Spitfire.

"Zanek!" "Go! Jump take-off! Scramble!" There were many ways to translate the word that now passed quietly across the base. It evoked an echo of the orders bullhorned to fighter pilots on the old Allied desert strips that once scarred this landscape. Now, the alarm was sounded so softly that the old man collecting litter beside Weizman's veteran Spitfire never heard it.

S was conscious of the stir. And driving home, he discovered the cause. The seventeen-year-old daughter of a school caretaker had been burned to death at Qiryat Shmona, a place described later by the foreign press as "a border town." To foreigners, unaccustomed to the smallness of Israel, doubtless it seemed so. Here, it had as much reason to seem safe as Jerusalem or Tel Aviv. But the guerrillas were multiplying and their attacks were bolder. The response was to strike at their bases beyond the lines where the 1967 ceasefire had long since lost any meaning. An air strike was no way to mourn the death of a child by burning, but weeping and wailing would not stop the next ambush either. That was the awful burden that weighed upon men like Jacob.

2

THE GIRL AT
THE CENTER

In Upper Galilee there was the scent of orange blossom and the squeak of wagon wheels when Yesnov awoke the next morning. He listened to young voices in the orchards. Girls with flaxen hair were there. Girls who spoke in Scandinavian accents. This was the third year that volunteers could work on the kibbutz. Before that, the guns on the Golan Heights made visitors scarce.

Yesnov drew back the curtains above his cot. Three years ago, he had been a schoolboy up there on the watchtower, studying the sheep flocking down the hillside from the Syrian guns. The sheep had been his "radar." The shepherds were Arabs and mostly harmless. He had always watched the sheep. If they broke the usual pattern of movement down the slopes, he knew gunners were moving in the trenches above his head. If he was lucky, he would have the smaller children zigzagging along ditches toward the shelters. All that should have been finished. It should have ended when heliborne commandos stormed the Golan Heights in 1967 and moved the frontier back a score of kilometers.

Someone banged on his door. He tossed the quilt aside. "*Ken?*"

"Telephone." His sister's voice was sharp.

He tied a towel around his naked waist and danced across the stone cold floor.

Ruthi pushed past him. "I'll pack your things."

He stared.

"They want you back," she said simply.

"You're not supposed to know that."

"God forbid I should know what doesn't concern me. But when my youngest brother returns from his first leave in God knows how many months, and sleeps fourteen hours like the dead, and then is ordered to fly—"

"It is still none of your business," Yesnov said gently.

Scarves of mist lay on the Sea of Galilee, so flat you could walk on it. There was only one telephone on the kibbutz. It was perhaps a kind of protest against modern ways. Then men who built here on stony soil, leaving their wives in tumbledown barracks at Haifa, had a fierce love of natural things.

And they still lived in the politics of the nineteenth century, thought Yesnov, running through a garden of flowering shrubs that stretched endlessly. Then they saw that the guns of the Golan came from Russia. So many guns, expertly sited by Russian advisors, to kill us at will. That cured their Marxist measles but it hasn't brought the telephone any closer. He stopped to catch his breath before picking up the phone. Let this be the final Zanek! Let it be another two thousand seconds of silence.

He was not particularly bloodthirsty. He had been given compassionate leave, however, because a few days earlier the school bus had been ambushed. Arabs, hiding in a clump of bushes, had fired bazooka shells directly into the passing bus, killing and maiming most of the children and teachers. The Russians, thought Yesnov, lost their heavy artillery so now they provide rockets that are handier than a knife in the back.

He had never seen his defense chief, Moshe Dayan, look so shrunken and devastated. Dayan had helicoptered down for the

mass burial, a crumpled figure who listened to those who protested that reprisal raids could only continue the cycle of violent
death, and to others who said, "If you fight a dragon there's
always a danger of becoming a dragon too, but if we don't fight
we cease to exist."

Yesnov understood the dilemma but he believed that nothing
in Jewish history provided a different answer.

Two hours later he sat in the cockpit of a Skyhawk and dropped
like a stone to study a new feature in the Syrian landscape. The
block of territory was known at the Citadel as PS-5. He saw the
muzzle-flash of an antiaircraft gun that had not been there the
day before and identified four groups of armed figures moving
slowly between stone and scrub.

He pulled 3½ G on the elevator to whistle back to his station
at 15,000 feet. "Ozero calling Stiletto. I have one cobra and four
porcupines." He gave the coded map references. "We could use
the Walrus and the Carpenter up here. Over." His nylon-sheathed
hand on the stick moved less than one inch to the side, checked,
and held the Skyhawk at the end of a snap 180-degree roll.
He flew inverted in a 45-degree descent, selecting his switches
for low-level reconnaissance.

A few miles north of Tel Aviv lies what is known to the diplomatic community as "the air-attachés' ghetto."

This is Herzlya, which is regarded rather sourly by some cos-
mopolitans as a bit too ritzy in these times of austerity. The
homes are individually planned. Parties frequently continue into
the dawn. The Cuban ambassador has an imposing—and properly guarded—residence that overlooks the sea (the better, say
some, to communicate with like-minded political friends abroad).
There are some imposing hotels, a large and exclusive club, an
American school, one or two unusually good restaurants, a discotheque run by a South African and a sidewalk café owned by
the former airport controller at Leopoldville in the Congo, a

parrot that whistles after the girls, and a pool that attracts some of the briefest bikinis in the world. Many airline pilots live here, several retired army colonels, and a former banker who now manages the local Philharmonic. There are sand dunes and moors where the sparrowhawks swoop among the heather, long stretches of lonely beach, the skeleton of an apartment-hotel for which there has never been sufficient money to complete the construction, and places where men come with horse and cart to cut the peat moss. Like so much of Israel, this small community has an astounding variety of scenery and many places of concealment. Motorists between Tel Aviv and Haifa can pick up a girl along the highway and if she is a member of the oldest profession, it is said, they can buy five dollars' worth of satisfaction within a few feet of the traffic, and continue on their way again after losing no more than the necessary time. Residents say jokingly, when giving directions, "Turn right at the second whore on the west side. . . ." It is also said that hidden in the moors is a place where agents are debriefed. Perhaps such stories are true. The stranger can never be sure in this land of wry self-deprecation.

A wooden fishing boat hangs above the highway near Herzlya. It has a stumpy mast and weathered planks of black and yellow. It looks uncomfortable up there, imprisoned in a cradle high on a cliff a mile from its native sea.

S, the stranger, passed it whenever he drove from his apartment to the Citadel. The boat had brought some of the first immigrants here, and someone had printed on a board beside it a quotation from the Bible: "They shall build the waste cities and inhabit them; and they shall plant vineyards and drink the wine thereof; they shall also make gardens, and eat the fruit of them. And I will plant them upon their land, and they shall no more be pulled up out of their land which I have given them, saith the Lord Thy God." The words came from the Prophet Amos but the stranger had difficulty in discovering the name of the boat itself.

It was a girl named Naomi in the Citadel who told him, during his first month back in Israel. She was a young captain with a desk outside a deputy-commander's office. She had long slender legs which she kept discreetly crossed, tucking one foot under the opposite ankle, her legs leaning first this way and then that, as S knew from having to sit sometimes in a low-slung Department-of-Works armchair on the other side of that same desk. He found he could watch her endlessly, fascinated by what he read (or fancied he saw) in her face and mannerisms.

She was quite unlike the other girls scooting through the corridors or suddenly assuming attitudes of kittenish abandon. Most of the air-force girls seemed to expect some headmistress to appear at any moment and clap her hands, whereupon impish faces would return to expressions of gravity. Captain Naomi never giggled, never sat on the edge of a desk with legs swinging. She spent a lot of time frowning over statistics and graphs, writing with a quilled pen, there being a shortage of typewriters. S thought there were few places left in the world where business was conducted by handwritten notes, inky copybooks, and ladies wielding quill pens. Here, business was transacted often by word of mouth, which, incidentally, provided an additional safeguard against the leaking of secrets. Voices, like handwriting, were easily identifiable and thus proof against enemy falsification. Still, any other air force would have considered it unthinkable to manage without calculating machines and all those devices that are supposed to be essential to secretarial happiness.

This girl seemed content each day to put a fresh sprig of lilac or a bunch of wild flowers in an old paste pot at the edge of the files above which her face occasionally appeared. The face was quite beautifully sculptured: rather thin with high cheekbones, which on one side were ridged by faint scars. The mouth was softer than one would expect, considering the girl's straight back and disciplined movements. Her hair was severely cut. Her eyes had an expression of sadness and although she smiled whenever

S arrived, the smile never reached her eyes, which were focused beyond that small cluttered annex where the deputy-commander's white flying-helmet hung like a skull.

S found a box of oranges beside the armchair one morning and Naomi caught his glance and said, "They're yours."

"That's very kind."

"They come from Jaffa."

"A kibbutz?"

"Yes, a kind of kibbutz. Near Jaffa—" She waved one hand vaguely and a plain metal ring on her finger caught the sunlight. "We make gifts of fruit and flowers at this time of the year." She named a festival but the word then meant nothing to S. He was encouraged by her friendliness. He had always thought she was rather shy about speaking English and now she seemed relaxed and ready to talk. She was leaning back. The window behind her was bright with the color of young trees in bud. There was a warm smell of orange blossom drifting through the open casement. She seemed wonderfully alive, in contrast to the worn furniture, the torn curtains, the battered cabinets and dusty files.

He said, "I keep passing this fisherman's boat—"

"The *Yad Hamapil.*"

"You know the one I mean." He was surprised and pleased with her quickness.

"It means 'Hand of the Immigrant,' " she said, picking up the pen with the small and elegant gesture that he knew well. She recrossed her legs and swayed to the opposite side of her chair. She was wearing a shirt-blouse with neatly stitched mends in one sleeve and above a breast-pocket. The shirt was more open at the neck than usual. He found himself admiring the curve of shoulders and throat before she bent to her papers again.

"It looks uncomfortable up there," he said. "The boat, I mean."

Naomi lifted her head and this time there was nothing impatient in the way she put down the pen again. "Perhaps it misses the sea."

"Yes. I suppose a boat is like a person. Unhappy out of his element."

"You feel out of your element." She made it a statement.

S stiffened. He was wary of these casual conversations which led suddenly into discussions heavy with significance. "I'm not sure what you mean."

"We must seem very strange to you."

"I must seem very strange to you. A stranger wandering freely inside—inside this place."

"Inside the fortress? Yes, it is unsettling."

He noticed that the deputy-commander's padded door was slightly open. There were none of the usual clerks on the other side of the glass partition where the filing was done. He sensed that the building was almost empty—because of the festival, perhaps.

She said, "You mustn't mind us. This way of suspicion. A stranger can always go, and what he takes with him may hurt us later."

"You've got to trust outsiders at some time."

She shook her head. "While the British were here, my mother worked as a teleprinter operator in the signals branch of the British Army. Her boss used to say, 'Don't worry. Trust us.' Then the British quit Palestine and left us nothing for defense against the Arabs."

She stopped abruptly.

"The Russians recognized your statehood but all you remember is their betrayal later." He took up the refrain, impatient because he had heard it so often. "The Czechs sold you fighters but all you remember is they cut you off when it became embarrassing. The Yugoslavs provided you with secret bases but all you talk about now is how they closed them down. The French sold you the backbone of a modern air force—"

She picked up the pen. "I have your pass here for the library."

His attention distracted, he took the permit.

"You see, we give you more freedom than you deserve."

"Why couldn't I get in the library before?" He made no effort to conceal his astonishment. The library had seemed a closely guarded secret.

"Because it is small, untidy, uncomfortable, and poor. Because the librarian said she was ashamed to let an outsider see it."

Duly humbled, S let the young captain escort him to this monument to alleged inefficiency. It proved to be compact. Beneath the veneer of disorder it was expertly arranged. He recognized the earmarks of a small operation where ingenuity takes the place of adequate funds. The librarian knew where everything was, because she had no assistants to scramble her files. She worked under pressure, which forced her to make fast decisions. Librarians, as a breed, have a compulsion to behave like squirrels. 'When in doubt, never throw out,' is their motto. Here, the elderly woman in charge could not indulge herself. What she kept was the quintessential stuff. There were neither the resources of manpower nor the room for borderline books and clippings. The library was extremely functional, which is to say that when a file had ceased to serve any purpose it was ruthlessly destroyed: when a pilot needed to consult some authority, he was directed straight to the source: if a document needed to be copied, there was a single ancient duplicator that had the effect of discouraging the frivolous.

S settled down to find technical information. He wanted to prove that his questions about the performance and weaponry of aircraft could be answered from data provided by the foreign press. Too often, his curiosity had caused hard-eyed suspicion among the squadron commanders. He had to demonstrate that secrecy should be balanced by a realistic awareness of the information that was published freely elsewhere on these delicate matters.

He strayed into journals such as the *International Defense Review,* distributed from the accommodating neutrality of Switzerland, and lavish with illustrations of the latest weapons for sale.

His pencil flying across his notebook, he was aware of growing despondency. At first he couldn't put a finger on the cause. He glanced up. Perhaps it was the barred windows, and the narrow space between the improvised bookshelves. Perhaps it was a kind of claustrophobia, from being hemmed about by cardboard boxes of files. Men and women from other parts of the headquarters, where work never stopped, jostled each other. The duplicator hummed and clattered. A girl corporal was forced to weave an evasive path through the throng, pushing her trolley of papers. A small group of officers had cleared a space on one table to balance an old projector. The picture of Russian jets in flight was flung against a patch of bare wall. The projector grumbled and squeaked and the Russian commentary trickled out of the battered loudspeaker like the soundtrack from a Movieola.

Later, driving back past *The Hand of the Immigrant,* he recognized the cause of his depression.

It was the contrast between that threadbare library and the slick advertisements for weaponry in the military magazines.

He slowed down enough to study the poor lampblack hull of the little fishing boat. Twenty or so years ago, it brought the survivors from Nazi Europe to this land, where, in the lunatic fashion of our times, the same British armies that stood against Hitler in the name of liberty later prevented Hitler's victims from sailing here. Or tried. This boat, and the small boats that followed, had broken the blockade with their cargoes of human freight. Little more than twenty years ago, the settlers scrounged and scavenged the world for old guns and aircraft by which they could defend themselves against advancing Arab armies. And ever since that time, the twin struggles had never for one second let up. There was the struggle to remain strong, and also the struggle to survive amidst poverty.

In his notebook were extracts from full-page spreads purchased by the manufacturers of weapons to proclaim their wares. For a moment, staring down the road, he felt the hopelessness of it all. In 1948 it had cost these people everything they possessed to buy the few Spitfires, Messerschmidts, and Mustangs to defend their skies. With each passing year, the cost had gone up.

"One man and his *Blowpipe* can stop anything from a supersonic fighter to an armored vehicle," trumpeted Short Brothers of England. "Missile and launcher complete . . . ready for action in ten seconds . . . shoots straight from the shoulder . . . the equaliser."

Out of the European massacres had crawled the builders of a new nation. Now their children were forced to study the grim shopping lists: "In this Delta jet crouches the *DEFA TYPE 552* cannon delivering a 30-mm knockout blow!!!!!"

Beyond the fishing boat lay fields of kitchen vegetables. To grow more, workers walked between long plastic covers, which kept out the wind and captured the sunshine. The plastic shimmered on small wooden hoops, and the covers had to be adjusted by hand in accordance with the whims of weather and the sun's position. To protect the young orchards, the new groves of oranges and lemons, to defend the settlements that had been built with bare hands, cheap plastic and voluntary labor were not enough. It was necessary to buy arms. If you didn't, the enemy would still receive them with money borrowed from East and West. Israel, needing every cent to make a dream come true, must pay the price down to the last nickel. In the Citadel, men watched the arms grow more complicated and more expensive. To keep pace, they must study weapons like "Type Submarine Daphné," sold by the French for the equivalent of a minesweeper fleet in 1948.

"The Super-Fledermaus fire-control equipment tracks low-flying aircraft," said an advertiser from Zurich, displaying two photographs—"before using our moving-target-indicator" (a smudge flashing across a screen) and "after installing MTI" (this time the smudge became an identifiable jet).

The irony was that within a generation the new farmers had battle-tested the latest breeds of aerial weaponry. The biggest maker of aircraft in France owed its worldwide success to Israel's development of the *Mirage* series of fighter-bombers. One of the advertisements in the *Defense Review* showed war pictures of Russian MiGs destroyed on the ground by Israeli jets, under the caption: SITTING DUCK, and a blurb for the four-million-dollar British Harrier Vertical Take-Off jet, made by "the largest aerospace group in Europe."

For Arabs looking to creep forward with new long-range guns and rockets, there was the new German defense against low-flying Israeli bombers: "Anti-aircraft field mounting, with twin 20mm automatic guns . . . up to 6,600 feet . . . by Rheinmetall."

It was silly, thought S, to get sentimental about these things. But he felt the sweat pricking his forehead. The oldest and most successful farming settlement, starting from scratch with no money and not one square inch of tillable soil, today sustained five hundred families and by exercising self-restraint (the kibbutz still paid in kind, not in cash) was producing from its small factories and freshly fertile fields about a million dollars net profit a year. That meant six years' production to pay for a single twelve-year-old Phantom jet, designed for landing on the aircraft carriers which Israel did not have.

"If Israel cannot buy these weapons," Senator Stewart Symington, the former United States Air Force Secretary had said weeks earlier, "it is only a question of time before they are going to be annihilated."

The young captain was out when S returned to collect her gift of oranges.

"I forgot them," he told Ezer Weizman. The Minister of Transport stood in the doorway looking faintly surprised at the spectacle of a stranger carrying a box of oranges. Ezer still liked to keep an eye on things in the air force.

"Be my guest," said Ezer with a mock bow.

He seemed in no hurry. "Who gave you the oranges? Captain Naomi?"

S nodded, feeling unaccountably embarrassed.

"She must like you." The minister fell into step along the corridor.

"She's a nice kid."

Ezer glanced down with a surprised grin. He wore his customary sports shirt and slacks, and between himself and any friendly stranger there was always an easy *bonhomie*. Perhaps it was a little stronger in this case because both men shared the same love of Spitfires.

"I mean," added S, "she's rather shy—"

Ezer ran long fingers through his curly hair. "A shy kid? Mmmm . . ."

He dropped the subject. S, knowing the need to catch busy men in flight, said, "Can we fix a time for our next talk?"

"About the air force?"

"More specifically, about you. I'd like to get your account of how you shot down a Battle of Britain veteran. He's now an air-commodore, I think . . . Crawford Milling?"

"Crawley? Well, it's a bit embarrassing. I mean, the chap was intruding, and we were jumpy. It was the War of Independence. A lot of the RAF types seemed to be harassing our men and supporting the Arabs—" The Minister hesitated. He had a reputation for flamboyance which concealed a good deal of humility. He had flown on operations with the RAF in World War II. Another member of the family, Michael, had died on a special RAF mission. S wondered now if Ezer might back down. This was, after all, the man who changed the spelling of his name as a gesture of independence from Chaim Weizmann, who had persuaded Britain to "view with favor the establishment in

Palestine of a national home for the Jewish people." Uncle Chaim had become Israel's first President.

Ezer walked S to the guardhouse before giving his answer. "You know where my office is in Jerusalem. Drop by whenever you've time." As S was leaving, he called after him, "Good luck with the shy kid."

Much later S discovered that Naomi had been copilot in a troop-transport dropping commandos in the 1956 Sinai campaign. Her mother had been killed in the 1948 fighting. Her husband, who had been shot down in 1967, was paralyzed below the waist and finally crashed to his death after learning to fly again with special hand controls. She was thirty-four years old and S decided, with some of the lingering glibness of a foreigner, that she was devoted to war through no fault of her own. She had grown up in one war and survived three others. Now she worked with total dedication at the heart of a powerful war machine. Doubtless there was in her a streak of fanaticism.

The day would come when Captain Naomi would shatter that illusion too.

3

DAY X IN

JACOB'S CALENDAR

Captain Naomi was in the Citadel at the time Yesnov began his reconnaissance dive on the Syrian terrorists in the area designated PS-5, 80 miles away to the northeast.

She knew when be began his dive. She knew that he was traveling fast enough at the end of it to reach Tel Aviv within five hundred seconds. This was less than the time it took her to walk to work from where she lived. Normally she allowed ten minutes to reach the Citadel from the top-floor flat that she preferred to the hotels discreetly occupied by headquarters staff.

At the other extreme of the air-war zone, dawn had signaled the heaviest artillery barrage from the Egyptian side of the Suez Canal since the installation of the new Russian SA-III missiles.

Captain Naomi knew this too. She sat at the center of an electronic web. There were duplicate webs at other centers. But for her, on this day, the center was here. She heard the orders dispatched to airbases, heard them acknowledged, heard the swift exchanges between squadron commanders and operational planners. Somewhere, Motti Hod would be hauling out the inevitable stop watch with which he orchestrated the movement of his men. Wherever the air-force commander might be, it was always certain that he was linked by radiophone with every unit. This was his strength. And wherever his aircraft might happen to be, the pilots could reach him. Less than three months ago, on Friday, February 13, 1970, Nasser had told *The New York Times:* "They [the IAF] have electronic jamming against our radar. . . . Electronic reconnaissance gives pinpoint positions of radar and rockets. We called a Soviet group to study that and to tell us a solution. They didn't believe it at the beginning, the Soviets, when we told them the Israelis had so and so."

There were other things Nasser and the Soviets might not believe. Captain Naomi flicked a switch and used the phrase which in English means QRA—Quick Reaction Alert.

The voice of Captain Naomi, who did not always sit demurely at the desk where S usually found her, was known to every squadron commander and most of the pilots. It was the self-same voice that earlier gave reassurance to Jacob, who had passed the night on the balcony of her apartment, staring numbly across the rooftops.

While young Lieutenant Yesnov was making his photographic run across the Syrians, Jacob leaned over the balcony watching the early morning traffic swirl around the Dizengoff plaza. From here to Keren Kayemet, a distance of only five blocks, were crammed the sidewalk cafés and restaurants that gave Tel Aviv its reputation for being the liveliest city in the eastern Mediterranean. At this hour the sidewalks were empty and down along the waterfront a few eager tourists began to fan out across the beaches or went in search of newsstands richly laden with airmailed editions of most of the world's great newspapers. There was no war down there in the streets. No censorship. Jacob pondered the phenomenon of tourists who could hear the distant and continuous rumble of guns without turning a hair;

who complained about the high sales taxes which helped pay
for Israel's defenses: tourists who sometimes infuriated him
even while he acknowledged the nourishment they provided a
people otherwise cut off. He knew the dangers of a siege mentality. He knew how easy it was, too, for a besieged people to
postpone a confrontation with danger. He had seen this while
still a boy in Europe. "The elders couldn't believe that from our
ghetto, people were being taken for execution," he had once
told S. "It was early in Hitler's time. Nobody wanted to believe
that in a civilized country an entire race could be liquidated."

Jacob formed a curious habit after his own father was tricked
into boarding a train to extinction. He started to keep a personal
calendar, using letters from the alphabet, taught him by his
mother, a schoolmistress. This private marking of the milestones
in his life gave him points of reference when all the external
structures of his existence had been destroyed. The day he had
been sent to a schoolboys' slaughterhouse was burned on his
memory as D; his escape was N; his rebirth, after the Jewish
Brigade found him, was P. He recognized that this mildly eccentric compulsion helped preserve his sanity. When the Six-
Day War broke out, he had reached the letter R in this small
history of his own passage through time. He had reached a point
where he felt that Israel itself was floating in some unreal world
of the imagination and needed to be nailed down with the letters
from his private lexicon. To look at him, one would think he was a
truck driver. His movements were small explosions of energy,
as if he needed to take a run at anything which required physical
exertion. There was no hint of poetry.

He ran down the five flights of stairs from Naomi's flat, although he was in no particular hurry. He found the coffee-bar
he wanted and ordered the flat bread called *pita* and a plate of
humus, a mixture of chickpeas and spices topped with sesame
paste and olive oil. He put his notebook on the table and without
any conscious thought, made an entry under the heading, *Day*
X. Perhaps he was thinking of the meeting called for this after-

noon of the Cabinet Security Committee. Perhaps he read some awful omen in the burning of the child at Qiryat Shmona. Or more probably, instinct told him that this would be another day to remember.

Later, he doodled. All his sketches feature a long hook beneath a triangle.

Giant hooks tucked under their tails, the four Phantoms waited on their ready-pans at a base near what was once known as the Wilderness of Zin. The hooks came with the jets, but not the aircraft carriers for which the hooks were designed.

Sealed inside his full-pressure suit, his blond head encased in a fishbowl space helmet, Colonel Aaron sat in the completely self-contained environment of the front cockpit. Ground crew supplied external power during this waiting period for men of the Quick Reaction Alert force. Pilots got their briefing directly from IAF commander Hod or from one of his deputies. The Phantoms were part of the "known armed presence" that could be seen to intercept enemy aircraft approaching Israel without a flight plan or who crossed into the air-defense zone without warning. If Israel had been an island, its postage-stamp size would have warranted an air-defense zone extending many miles beyond its borders. Instead, it was bounded on two sides by hostile territory from which a surprise attack could be launched and completed within minutes. For this reason, the QRA force had to be on 24-hour alert against any suspicious movement of aircraft over Egypt, Syria, and (to a lesser degree) even Jordan and Lebanon. This included the Russian jets busy at all times over Cairo and the Mediterranean. Sometimes the Russians flew around to test the readiness of the Israelis. Sometimes they listened for the signatures of current ECM (Electronic Counter-Measure) devices while others recorded Israel's radio and radar frequencies. Over and above these dangers and shadowy movements of hostile bodies in the surround-

ing skies, there was the pressing need for swift reaction to
border attacks on the ground. Woefully short of artillery, and
husbanding its resources of manpower, Israel used its fighter-
bombers as flying cannons. There were, at this time, a thousand
artillery pieces ranged along the Egyptian side of the Suez
Canal alone, seeking to wear down Israeli ground defenses by
steady bombardment in what Nasser proclaimed to be a "war of
attrition" when he broke the ceasefire.

Colonel Aaron spoke over the hot mike to his Flight Officer
Talik in the rear cockpit. "No problems?"

"No problems."

The reply was deceptively laconic. Aaron smiled. The hot
mike made it possible to talk freely, like two men on the phone.
It also fed the sound of Talik's breathing in the wires. The FO
was eighteen, half the colonel's age, and new to Phantoms. His
breathing, exaggerated by the oxygen regulator, sounded a
bit fast. His stiff good manners were fresh from flying school.
The quick breathing would pass in time but the manners would
persist. Experience would polish them. The small courtesies were
a part of discipline: a special kind of discipline that the casual
visitor never saw, because they flaked away in public.

Ten feet below the colonel stood the ground crew. They, too,
put on formality in the same way that the fliers donned their
discipline along with suits and helmets. An hour ago, all of
them had been brewing coffee and arguing about the delay in
buying more Phantoms. The price went up with each month's
postponement. Not just the shelf-price of the plane. There was
a price paid in uncertainty, lost time, wastage of expensively
trained men, and a price paid in morale. Suppose the production
of Phantoms stopped? Suppose President Nixon agreed to the
sale of more Phantoms only when the Soviet-Arab build-up of
missiles had gone beyond the point where Israel could fight
back? Where was that point? Listening to them argue, Aaron
had thought, There's no problem here of morale. Mechanics and

airmen shared a sense of closeness which one could not find elsewhere. Yet the long-drawn agony of waiting for the new Phantoms was discouraging. The mechanics were qualified to handle one of the most sophisticated aircraft in the world. Each could earn many times his pay in civilian life. Each worked brutal hours without overtime pay, sometimes sleeping out at dispersal, often away from their families.

Colonel Aaron checked the time again. His own children would be tumbling out of bed, getting ready for the bus that took them to school.

The ground-crew chief in plastic headphones looked like a doctor listening to the Phantom's heartbeat through a streamlined stethoscope. His concern was more deeply personal. Between mechanics and aircraft was a bond almost mystical.

"Zanek!"

The word jerked the groundcrew chief into action. Arm and hand signals to start engines, unplug statters, check the operation of ailerons and horizontal stabilizer. . . .

Colonel Aaron rolled forward onto the taxi track in perfect unison with his three fellow Phantoms. Selection of weapons had been made when the probable nature of the mission was first known, and Colonel Aaron felt the stomach-tightening tension which was more pleasure than apprehension when he thought of the M61 Vulcan cannon capable of firing 6000 rounds a minute. He still preferred it to all the missiles and wizardry of richer air forces where the art of the dogfight was dying. Even with the ironmongery of missiles and bombs, a pilot could clean his underside with a split-second push of a button and then it was back to the eyeball-to-eyeball scrapping that Aaron loved perhaps too well. He had learned his lesson in the war of 1956, pursuing an Egyptian Vampire in his own Meteor until he had burned too much fuel to make home base.

"Stream takeoff at five-second intervals. Full reheat followed by max rate rotation climb." The four Phantoms lined up on the runway in echelon port, each pilot briefed in detail so that radio chatter was needless.

The sensation for the FO "radar-head" in the brief seconds of maximum longitudinal acceleration was that of a smart thump in the back.

On the ground, the crew chief counted them off. Colonel Aaron already airborne, wheels tucking in: Number Two unsticking, the pilot holding her down until the speed built up: Number Three rumbling in his wake: Number Four beginning to roll. The leader had rotated now into a 70-degree climb, changing from rear-profile to planform. Eight General Electric J-79 turbojets growled and grumbled, thrusting the small task force upward toward a speed that would bring it over the Egyptian lines within a couple of minutes, and sending back the deep reverberations that lifted heads in the personnel quarters.

Esther, daughter of Colonel Aaron, heard the long roll of thunder. She knew without any shadow of doubt that her father was back at work. She was in this respect like any other pilot's four-year-old child. They could distinguish by sound alone between the many different types of warplanes in use. By some uncanny sense, they also knew when their individual fathers were returning to land. This sense of recognition had captured the interest of IAF psychologists, who remembered World War II stories of dogs waiting at the runway's end as their masters flew into the airfield circuit. The psychologists had yet to find any rational explanation.

Colonel Aaron rotated the nose up fast, using Mach 0.9* on the Mach Number-Airspeed Indicator for his speed reference, holding the nose high enough to stay at this mark, letting the altimeter unwind past 5000 feet. He could hear his FO in the rear cockpit puffing slightly. For a boy on his first ride, the sensa-

* Mach: Because the speed of sound varies with height and temperature, a modern jet's speed is expressed as a Mach Number: the ratio of the plane's speed to the speed of sound in the atmosphere through which it is traveling at that time.

tion was like no other; lying on his back, propelled by two crackling afterburners straight up into the troposphere.

The four Phantoms were in an elongated tail-chase. Colonel Aaron said to his FO: "The first time you try a max power climb and acceleration, don't feel a fool if your brains still seem back down there on the deck." Aaron was feeling good. The sustained and mounting pressure of the afterburners in his back was intoxicating. He was now blasting through the sticky drag of the low subsonic region. He said, "The first time I made a zoom-climb, I had a real grunter for an FO who yelled, 'My God!'" He paused. "Then we both heard the voice: 'Yes, my son?'"

His FO's chuckle deepened into a full-bellied laugh.

The voice at 35,000 feet had not been that of God (as Colonel Aaron explained later) but Hod's.

Now again, the commander's voice came in loud, clear, and unexpected. "Aaron, listen . . ." Hod's manner was casual and intimate. "We've got a bandit at Angels Fifty. I want you to intercept. Hand over command of the sortie to Mula." Soft-spoken instructions to Number Two followed, and the other three Phantoms peeled off.

Now Colonel Aaron's whimsy became reality. The zoom-climb was a breathtaking maneuver, steeper than anything he had shown his new FO so far, and necessary to intercept an intruder in the ultra-thin air above the troposphere. Aaron guessed the intruder to be a Russian Yakovlev high-altitude reconnaissance aircraft code-named "Mandrake." It was the U-2's counterpart and therefore capable of reaching heights much greater than 50,000 feet. It would be loafing along, Aaron thought quickly while he cranked the bird up for its new high-speed climb, at perhaps 575 miles per hour. It was on a northeasterly heading, according to Motti Hod, with about 800 miles to go before reaching the Soviet airbase at Yerevan in Armenia, the nearest republic of the Soviet Union.

Colonel Aaron would have liked to follow it all the way there and then, in full sight of the Russians, force it round and back down to a landing in Israel. Other Russian jets had been captured in this way, some hitherto unknown to foreign experts.

The voice of Motti Hod was quiet and firm. On the ground, he was in control of the situation and working out tactics in accordance with data fed him by radar, computers, and specialists. His most important consideration was to preserve the Phantom and its crew, neither of which (as he frequently observed) "grow on trees." The Phantom's fuel system is complicated. There are tanks inside the fuselage, inside the inboard sections of each wing, and in three drop tanks. The center-line drop tank alone holds 600 gallons. A pilot must have a "feel" for the location and amount of fuel at all times. He can take off with a total load of 21,000 pounds of fuel, if necessary. The Phantom by itself weighs 15 tons and can lift another 13 tons of fuel and armament. A ferry range is possible of 2300 miles, four times the normal range of the Spitfire that ex-Lance Corporal Hod long ago dragged into Israel from central Europe on auxiliary-tanks and a prayer. Hod never forgot how close he came to losing the beat-up Spit through lack of fuel at a time when the loss of a fighter plane could have meant the loss of the new state. Thus he stood now in a valley near Nazareth, telebriefed by headquarters, making his own judgments in case Colonel Aaron, 10 miles high and already tightening up for a fight, should get a bulldog grip on the target and find himself unable to let go.

First Motti estimated the best altitude for this day at which to hit zoom-climb speed in the high supersonic region. This height was a point above which the temperature would no longer decrease, a level that varied more than usual over the desert. He fed this advice to Colonel Aaron, who hit the required Mach Number and pointed the nose straight up.

Aaron aimed to get above the intruder. To reach a good tactical height would require what he called "an energy swap," which is really what a zoom-climb is. The performance of an aircraft is measured in speed and altitude, representing two different forms of energy. In an energy-swap, the kinetic energy of speed is exchanged for the potential energy of altitude. All aircraft have an envelope of performance within which these forms of energy can be traded back and forth. The Phantom, the proto-type of which first flew on May 27, 1958, is built by McDonnell Douglas Corporation, which produced two thousand in the subsequent ten years. Of these, the F-4B version flown by United States Navy pilots established several time-to-height records. For instance it took slightly more than half a minute to reach 10,000 feet from a sea-level jump. Another United States Navy pilot reached 65,000 feet in three minutes. By way of contrast the IAF's early Spitfires took nine minutes to reach 20,000 feet. The Phantom's phenomenal rate of climb to extreme altitude, in Israel's situation, was not particularly useful. It did mean that the Phantom had a more elastic performance envelope than most.

Colonel Aaron was zooming into regions where the Phantom's control surfaces slipped on the thin ice of an unsubstantial atmosphere. The engines were not getting enough air to burn fuel properly. The aircraft was carried up by sheer momentum. The energy-swap was a very sharp grab upward after a tre-mendously fast sprint. The air-breathing mechanism of a jet could starve up here. If Colonel Aaron, hot for altitude, struck for 70,000 feet, where without his pressurized suit, his blood would boil, the plane would resemble a ball hurled into the air and nearing its peak. Already he was steaming through the 50,000-foot level ahead of the unseen Russian. If he continued the zoom, the Phantom would run out of energy, power, and aerodynamic control. Then it would have "gone over the top," leaving a sensation of dropping end over end.

In the rear cockpit Talik concentrated on his function as chief "radar-head." The radar antenna scanned back and forth, up and down, in wide sweeps ahead of the aircraft, shooting billions of pulses of energy outward, where they would either bounce off a target or disappear into oblivion. Colonel Aaron had a repeater scope up front, on which he could spot a target as fast as his flight officer. Instead Aaron was watching the strange reversal of light in which the sky turned to black above and the sun's illumination radiated up from the heavier atmosphere below.

The FO, forcing himself to ignore these unfamiliar sensations against which it is impossible to warn a novice beforehand, exercised all the discipline of his past twenty months of training: the long solitary treks through the desert at night; the slow adjustment to treating the weird environment of a cockpit as a classroom; the separation of emotion from mental action. He held his eyes rigidly on the radar display and rewarded himself and his pilot with a quick shout of recognition. The Mandrake, its lonely pilot suspended on giant wings, was in range.

Colonel Aaron dropped toward the Russian. Controls which had been sloppy began to bite into thicker air again. His hands moved around the cockpit.

The Mandrake must have been proceeding through the peaks of a rampart of thunderheads, their tops flung into anvil shapes by the stratospheric winds. He seemed to be sliding along the surface of high pillars of thunder clouds stuffed with vertical winds that could tear the wings from a jetliner five times the Phantom's weight. The Mandrake was invisible to Aaron's naked eye, and he hunched down to concentrate on blind-flying dials while the FO locked onto the radar-painted target. The colonel's eyes flicked around the panel: airspeed, artificial horizon, climb-and-descent, turn-and-bank. . . . Two circuits of all instruments with the eyes every second. It wasn't necessary to hand-fly all the time but Aaron was a gunfighter and a gunfighter likes to feel his weapons. They made fun at flying school of the stick-and-throttle boys and yet the training was designed to remind a pilot that in the end he still needed the same acute sensitivity that distinguished the great fliers of earlier wars. Aaron's eyes continued their half-second sweeps: *Pull up that wing, drain off the speed.* It was like a problem in arithmetic or a session in a doctor's reaction-testing machine. Press the proper tits, pull the right knobs, get the right readings on the dials. Just an exercise in quick thinking. Nothing to do with aerial fighting. Nothing to do with killing an enemy before he kills your people. Just a series of calculations made in the class-room of the cockpit. Forget that without the pressurized cabin you'd explode at this height. Get your speed down, and rotate your eyes around that circuit twice every second.

They burst into a long canyon, the Mandrake dead ahead.

Aaron's hands moved for the guns. He had always argued that guns were better than missiles for the Middle East battleground. He knew the value of getting to close quarters. He had never made a fetish of it. Close quarters meant dogfights, where it was hard to tell friend from foe. Missiles didn't turn sharp corners. Missiles misfired. Wasting a missile was like burning a year's pay. Aaron was a top scorer but in this war there were times when you passed up a kill. That was why nobody was an ace. An ace was apt to get carried away, ignoring ground-control, which might have an overriding reason for breaking off an action. There was nothing of the flying prima donna about Aaron. He was simply delighted to be creeping up on the finest prize of all. He was beautifully situated. He had arrived at this point in space and time by way of many years' experience and the past few seconds of superb airmanship. The gun cameras whirred inside his wings. He drifted through the Mandrake's wash. The buffet startled Talik, who thought he'd miscalculated. But no, the Mandrake was still 300 yards ahead. He checked. The range was down to 250 yards. Talik had already opened fire in his own mind when the order came clear as a bell from Motti Hod far below.

"*Break!*"

Colonel Aaron's face tightened. A split-second later he would have fired. Why not say the order came a split-second late? But he broke hard to port.

Above and behind, a pair of MiG-21s saw their intended victim abandon the decoy and vanish into cloud.

Hod was reporting to Jerusalem as Colonel Aaron came cork-screwing down. A meeting was called at the Citadel to examine the gun-camera film from Aaron's wings.

In a Dizengoff coffee-bar the phone rang and Jacob took the call. Then he rejoined his visitor.

"I'm sorry," said Jacob. "I have to leave."

The visitor looked put out. He had just arrived. He liked the bliss of a business day when appointments were ticked off with relentless efficiency. His satisfactions in New York came from a crowded calendar. That's how things got done.

"When," he wailed, "will you guys ever get organized?"

4

"THICK AND FAST

THEY CAME AT LAST"

Two horsemen galloped along the beach at Herzlya and looked up when Colonel Aaron eased out his dive. They rode on, climbing the bluffs near the Sharon Hotel, and circled the plaza of little shops and apartments that formed a small village of its own. They dismounted at a sidewalk café and tethered their horses to the railing. The rumble of the Phantom still hung in the still air as the two men sat down.

For these two foreign diplomats, Day X in Jacob's diary was a Sunday—a day of rest in conformity with Western routine while Israelis begin their working week. In the relaxed mood of a morning ride on the moors, or golf at Caesarea, a good diplomat might feel he was accomplishing more in conversation with a colleague. Neither of these men appeared to have anything heavier on his mind than tonight's presentation of Clare Booth Luce's *The Women* by the Little English Theatre, a local amateur group whose leading ladies included Mrs. Mandy Shauli. The question was: Did their wives want to see the play or Mrs. Shauli, otherwise known as Mandy Rice-Davies of the Profumo Scandal that long ago rocked the British establishment?

"A gossip-mongers' paradise," grunted a journalist sitting with

Mira Avrech, an Israeli columnist. "They'll chew over the sub-
tleties of one of your paragraphs as happily as they munch on the
latest rumors of new Russian weapons." He was a Frenchman,
keenly embarrassed by his own country's official policies, and he
added quickly, "I'm sorry if that sounds flippant. Yet it's true. In
times of extreme danger, one gossips about anything and gives
it all equal value."

Mira was a vivacious and handsome girl who concealed both a
sharp intelligence and her considerable knowledge beneath her
easygoing charm. "What's danger?" she asked. "Can you have
degrees of it? A rusty old Syrian cannon seemed just as dangerous to the settlers twenty years ago as a Russian rocket today.
There are lots of ways to get killed, but you can only die once."

Leaving their table, S joined a foreign diplomat who had
recently retired, choosing (it seemed quixotically) to stay in
Israel. "I hear there's an emergency session of the Target Committee this afternoon," said the ambassador.

The stranger cocked an ear, remembering Jacob's lecture at
the base the previous day.

"You'd know it as the Cabinet Security Committee," the ambassador amended. "War councils of the kind have a long history and a variety of titles. They boil down to the same thing.
When the little guy is surrounded by enemies yelping war cries,
he has to decide if he'd better hit first and fastest. If he's got
a few pals, they decide when and where. In the days when Hitler
and Tojo seemed to hold the winning hands, we called it a
Target Committee. . . ."

The stranger listened. Target Committees were the process
by which Allied chiefs could examine the political consequences
of an operation during World War II. The ambassador had been
a naval commander, in those days, representing a small nation
whose contribution to the defeat of Hitler had been dispropor-
tionately large.

"It was a lot easier then," he said. "We didn't have to prove to
the world that right was on our side like these poor devils."

He was a kindly man with a lot of experience in Africa and Asia. Before his retirement at the beginning of 1970 he had written a blunt report to his government:

Forgive this sermon. I get the feeling you, at home, do not comprehend Israel's present mood. Let me recall my earlier remarks about the personality of the Minister of Defense, Moshe Dayan, who is regularly portrayed abroad as something of a fire-eater. I wrote at the time of Dayan's moving recital of a Palestinian poetess's verses about Jerusalem called "My City Occupied." This Arab lament read at a public meeting by Israel's outstanding general was followed by Dayan's remark that "we have to make utmost effort to establish contacts with the million Arabs with whom and next to whom we are destined to live. We have to come and understand their background, their emotional climate, whether we like it or not. I know only too well that at this stage, at first, this will be a one-way road: even if we understand them, they will not understand us. But even so, we have to go and listen to them in the hope that one day they will listen to us."

I pointed out that Dayan and other members of the Cabinet have been pragmatic and open-minded in their approach to the Palestinians, and I further quoted Moshe Dayan in a speech last year: "When I was a child I used to go with my late father for long walks. . . . My father, who came from Russia at the age of seventeen, used to say the Arabs had the look of murderers. But these Arabs were not murderers, they were simple fellaheen and because it was cold and rainy they covered their heads with their kafiya and agal and of all their face you saw nothing but a nose and glistening eyes which to me seemed dark and beautiful. My father imagined he saw through the kaffiyeh the looks he recalled from his shtetl in Russia."

Dayan and the younger Israelis are extremely sensitive to Palestinian sentiments. What especially disturbs the leadership here (which does not divide conveniently into the dove-hawk categories) is the misinterpretation placed upon the policy of measured-response to terrorism. The Arab states now contain within their boundaries large forces of insurgents. These guerrilla bands benefit from the gradual acceptance by the West of military incursions. In Asia these incursions—called seepage or infiltration—have been on a scale that once would have led to war. Arabs practice subversion supported by selective terrorism. When the Israelis respond, the Arabs switch to a most sophisticated propaganda machine to exploit 'Israel aggression.' Unfortunately, Israel is not dealing with rational enemies who will listen to reason. Consequently, retaliation is *at this stage* the sole means of dampening attacks which are damaging in a small nation short of manpower. If the Israelis were dealing with gangsters, it would be different. Gangsters are businessmen. They may blow your head off, but only if it's good for business. Gangsters do things for reasons. Knowing this, one can usually give gangsters a reason for NOT blowing one's head off. Arab actions are not motivated by the business considerations of gangsters and are therefore unpredictable and dangerous.

As ambassador, he had never written in stronger language. Now he wished he had been even tougher in the light of a meeting he had just attended. Mrs. Golda Meir, the Prime Minister, was discussing the agonizing eight months since her visit to Washington in September 1969, and President Nixon's apparent inability to give a simple yes or no to Israel's urgent request for aircraft. The following exchange took place.

MRS. MEIR: The fact that President Nixon decided not to decide now on Phantoms is a disappointment. He didn't promise me that we would get Phantoms [but] I gathered from the spirit of the conversations that I had with him that we would get them. It was a great disappointment because we are convinced that the balance of power is out of line and was so even before the SA-III missiles. The SA-IIIs are an extremely dangerous element for us.

QUESTION: Do you consider there has been a general erosion in the American position?

MRS. MEIR: America for her reasons, and we for our reasons,

wouldn't like us to be surrounded with Soviet Arab states. Soviet Arab states would not be exactly ideological Communists. They accept from the Soviet Union not Communist ideology but support for their hatred of Israel. Ambassador Rabin [Israel's representative in Washington] put his finger on the point when he called our planes "flying artillery." Because one cannot say Egypt has so many planes, you have so many planes, the balance is all right. . . . You cannot take only the element of the planes. You must take everything into consideration. And when you see the solid wall of artillery against what we have in artillery, then the only way we can fight artillery is with planes.

Mrs. Meir's words had moved the ambassador greatly. They were wrung from a woman who seemed to him the very symbol of Jewish dignity. That she, and her country, should have lived on a knife's edge for so long seemed to him an outrage. It was made worse by the indifference of other governments. He felt there had been a failure of Western nerve in the face of a challenge. The Soviet Union had moved into the Middle East with brutal efficiency, knowing the West had lost its appetite for involvement. The ambassador often told the story of the sailor who, hauled aboard a rescue ship while the rest of his mates still swam around in the wreckage of their torpedoed freighter, said, "You can pull the ladder up now, Jack. . . . I'm all right." It was the attitude of small men who preferred to preach isolationism, who would rather attack their leaders than offer leadership. The Russians had moved at a time when other nations were preoccupied with dissension at home and a general disenchantment with wars abroad. There was a lack of confidence in official statements about the state of the world, and in any case nobody wanted to face more uncomfortable decisions about intervention in a region as muddled as the Middle East.

Of course the ambassador had his own reservations about the Israelis. He found them headstrong. He wondered sometimes if they were not happiest when they felt most oppressed. He sympathized with the distinguished Hebrew professor who said, "We're all a little bit unhinged by what we've been through."

When he became exasperated, the ambassador reminded himself that he was accredited to a nation about the size of the city of Detroit. He tried to imagine Detroit as a separate city-state forced to conduct vigorous trade and foreign policies all over the world, obliged to maintain an extensive intelligence service throughout the surrounding territory, striving to reach self-sufficiency, cut off from its natural friends, fighting natural enemies of climate and terrain, defending itself against persistent attack, and simultaneously developing and extending its cultural and scientific activities so that small and equally vulnerable nations might take heart and become assured that in the age of superpowers it was possible to be different and survive. He believed that if Israel succeeded, its biggest contribution to modern history would lie in this demonstration of faith in the little man. He had served in a number of the young and weak republics such as Uganda and Singapore where Israeli advisers offered a way to fend off the new imperialists. It would be nice to think that humanity was not, after all, destined to become a giant anthill. Nevertheless, when the ambassador considered every factor in the situation, he sometimes wondered. . . . Could Detroit undertake these and other obligations and still involve a third of its citizens in war along their borders? It was insane, hopelessly romantic, foolishly idealistic, and quite impossible.

He had returned nonetheless to retire to Israel. Asked why, this ambassador of Irish stock replied, "Because war has placed the most burdensome taxes on everything in this ridiculous country except books."

"If we taxed books, we'd defeat our own ends," said the Little Lieutenant an hour later, while S leafed through the Russian magazine *Sputnik* in one of the crew-rooms. "If we stopped books coming into the coutry just because they voiced a Communist or Arab viewpoint, we'd be no better than the enemy."

She's shot me down again, thought S. He had only shown surprise at finding *Sputnik* here.

The Little Lieutenant crossed the room and spooned Israeli-made instant coffee into a mug. She followed this with just the right amount of powered milk and sugar, squirted hot water from an urn, and stirred the mixture before placing it beside S. He was suitably impressed. The girls in this country didn't give a damn about a man's rank or position. He could be Grand Panjandrum of the Institute of Bank Robbers and Money Grabbers, or champion MiG-killer. He could be first violinist in the Philharmonic or president of all the bird-watchers. If he failed to meet some secret feminine standard, he was a dead duck. The fact that the Little Lieutenant had watched his drinking habits in the matter of coffee, and had actually brought him a mug of the stuff according to specifications quite overwhelmed the stranger. He had been resigned to the fact that he compared pretty unfavorably with the dashing younger pilots. He said lamely, "You shouldn't have bothered."

She shrugged. The gesture was maternal, the smile sardonic. "It's easier than watching you struggle with the urn."

"Oh."

"You're just as clumsy as the others."

He became cautious. "What others?"

"Foreigners. If you had to milk a cow, you'd need twenty-five people."

He watched the ice sliding glacially back into their uneasy relationship. "Why? How?"

"One to squeeze the udders and twenty-four to lift the cow."

He buried his nose in the mug, following her economic movements as she made more coffee for herself and two of the ground crew. He thought, They're really quite afraid to betray any sentimentality. They're islanders. Insular. Unemotional in front of strangers.

He remembered suddenly how arrogant the British always seemed, although it was often nothing worse than the island mentality at work. "Fog in the English Channel," the weathermen used to report. "Europe isolated."

Outside the hut, the desert air had become dry and very hot.

One of the pilots blocked the open doorway. He was a slender small-boned man still clad in flying coveralls. S noted with a childish satisfaction that the newcomer was left to make his own coffee.

The pilot collapsed into a chair. He had flown a sortie already this morning and had just slipped over to the house to fix his wife's washing machine. In all the time S had known him, the man had never admitted to fatigue or attempted to glamorize his job. Now, for the first time, he looked pooped. He winked at the Little Lieutenant and then turned to S with that polite expression which S recognized only too well. It was the kind of patient courtesy which S himself, as an operational pilot, would have shown to an outsider while wishing him privately in hell.

"You want to talk?" asked S.

The pilot lifted his shoulders. "Routine stuff. We were trying to see whether the Egyptians would come up and challenge us."

And then he said something which surprised S although he had supposed there was nothing about these bookish people that could still surprise him.

"'The Walrus and the Carpenter'? Know the lines?"

"They wept like anything to see
Such quantities of sand."

The pilot nodded approvingly. "They call my wingman the Carpenter and me the Walrus. That's exactly how I feel."

The phone rang and the Little Lieutenant took the call. The pilot excused himself. He had to check out a couple of rookie pilots, he said, and it was some time before the stranger realized that operational pilots were liable to fly as instructors between missions.

S squinted into his mug.

> " 'The time has come,' the Walrus said,
> 'To talk of many things: . . .
> Why the sea is boiling hot—
> And whether pigs have wings.' "

The Little Lieutenant interrupted his memory test. "Your schedule is canceled for this afternoon."

S lit a cigarette. There was no point in cursing. The deal was that he could roam around the bases pretty much at will, but must accept the fact that priorities in appointments were not on a peacetime basis. It worked out well enough, if you didn't mind having almost every day screwed up. Again S was reminded of the awkwardness of his own position. Between himself and the air force stretched a gulf as wide as the grave. He knew the gulf well. He had been on the other side himself at one time. It was the side from which you could never run away: the side from which you regarded the rest of the world as if they were images on a screen or students above the glass dome of an operating theater. It was the gulf between the man of action with everything to lose and the academic spectator. S did not much like the role of spectator, and much of the time he could identify closely with the airmen; but there was always a moment like this one when the unseen barriers dropped. It was a moment that always made him feel suddenly old and helpless, no matter how courteously he was brushed aside. It was one of the curses of being a survivor that you would never again be eighteen and confident that what you must do was right and necessary for the salvation of your people.

He heard the Little Lieutenant say something about Jerusalem. Someone would see him here this afternoon. Someone he had asked to see about procedures for the selection of targets.

They drove together to Jerusalem. The Little Lieutenant was not pleased with the car he had rented. It was made in Israel and she said, "Camels eat this particular model."

"Camels eat them?"

"Yes," she said, more prettily solemn than ever. "Don't ever go south into the desert in one. Never ever leave one near the camel market at Beersheba."

"Why—*camels?*"

"The bodywork's made of Fiberglas and there's something in the paint the camels like to eat."

She continued to gaze uninterestedly out of the window.

Camels! S took a firmer grip on the wheel. Camels and a walrus. Didn't the Walrus eat something? Of course. The Walrus invited the Oysters to join in a feast but forgot to mention that the Oysters were the major component of the banquet.

> "Now if you're ready, Oysters dear,
> We can begin to feed."

Yes, that was it. The crafty Walrus luring the Oysters to their fate.

> And thick and fast they came at last,
> And more and more and more.

With sobs and tears the Walrus talked them into the trap, until there were none left to answer.

> And this was scarcely odd because
> They'd eaten every one.

For months now, the MiGs in Egypt had been ordered to avoid combat. Nevertheless, they occasionally ventured out into the open, where they could be shot down. It was all part of this war of attrition. The Israelis, playing the Walrus, were not eating for eating's sake. They needed to gobble up the Oysters at a faster rate than Russia was willing to provide fresh orders.

Still, it was not the kind of literary allusion one expected in the desert.

He wondered about the rumors of the Security Committee meeting. In Jerusalem. If this meant a critical decision, he would not be unprepared. He'd kept a record of events. It went back many months. In a sense, he supposed it went back to the Six-Day War. Like a lodger holding his breath for the other boot to drop in the room above, he'd waited a long time for the Seventh Day.

One cause for the Security Committee's concern, S would learn later, was the manner in which the young pilot Yesnov was shot down that morning. Yesnov had been selected, in the same way that his machine was allocated, for the kind of job at which he was likely to succeed. Yesnov was still in what would be called elsewhere an Operational Training Unit. Here in the IAF the training *was* operational. Once a pilot qualified he didn't waste time on practice ranges if he could get for himself a relatively minor mission. From such a mission he graduated under the wing of a squadron commander. Yesnov had yet to reach this stage. He was also new to Skyhawks. If he had a fault, it was that of pushing himself too hard. Experience would teach him to pace himself. There was never a second chance to learn *that* lesson.

As to the machine Yesnov had flown, it was the first of its type, the Douglas Skyhawk, that had entered production at the works in California back in 1953. The attack-bomber version was capable of carrying several hundred variations of military load including machine guns and missiles. The prototype A-4F had flown first in 1966 and when the IAF put orders in for it, Washington had questioned its suitability. But the pilots knew what they wanted. The Skyhawk was pint-sized but a mighty puncher. It would operate from small fields. It had a range with external tanks of 2000 miles ("We can tip our caps to the Vatican," as one pilot had told S). It carried two 20-mm cannons. The central rack under the fuselage could carry "stores" up to 3500 pounds in weight; two inboard underwing racks, 2250 pounds each; and two outboard underwing racks, 1000 pounds each.

But maximum speed was less than 600 miles an hour. Combat radius with 4000 pounds of arms was around 350 miles. The Skyhawk was a solid workhorse which had been rejuvenated by Israeli technical skill. Its IAF performance went far beyond the figures quoted above. It was adapted to give the pilot better gunfighting opportunities. One Skyhawk (by squirting juice from a refueling pack) could double his buddy's range. This inflight procedure was performed by the thirsty Skyhawk prodding its male refueling-probe into the female receptor of the "tanker." (A Skyhawk pilot's comment to S was, "We tried to persuade High Command to send us to Paris to learn the technique but our motives were slanderously misunderstood.") The male probe was easily dipped into the buddy-refueler's breadbasket, compared with the alternative method in which the tanker-aircraft trails a limp male hose until the customer maneuvers a female cap around it. The Skyhawk's large male probe, sticking forward from the starboard side of the blunt nose, gave it a rugged and erotic look.

This was the plane Yesnov had flown on an armed reconnaissance. It was a low-priority sortie suited to his experience. Man and machine were matched up.

He had arrived over PS-5 bank on time. He saw the group of Arab guerrillas which his job was merely to identify and photograph. Something odd had been reported about the arms they carried. But nothing to cause alarm on a busy day. Yesnov recorded on the pad strapped to his thigh the time, altitude, speed, exhaust-gas temperature, and engine instrument readings. He announced his positive identification of the guerrillas by a single click of the radio call-button. The Mobile Control Officer replied with a double click. There was no need for the precaution of radio silence. But there was also no requirement for a lot of needless chatter. IAF pilots over enemy territory, where they have been most of the time, tend to be tight-lipped.

The double click was enough to send Yesnov whistling down to make his low-altitude reconnaissance run. In the lee of a small

hill he was bounced by sudden turbulence. He saw that the
guerrillas were scattering around a fortlike position that had
not been reported before. He mused on this and then, assuming
the responsibility of a zone commander as confidently as he had
led his class on a night march two weeks ago, he called for a
strike.

He had climbed back to 15,000 feet when the planes from
across the border streaked in. They slipped across the barren
land like barracudas, silvery slim in the long shafts of sunlight.
They moved with the precision of veterans, directed by Yesnov
now that the desirability for radio silence was gone. He was
puzzled by the way the guerrillas separated into small groups
putting up small-arms' fire. He saw what seemed to be the
muzzle-flash of an antiaircraft gun hidden in a featureless bowl
of the landscape pitted like the moon. The raiders came as
swiftly as barracuda and retired with the same ghostlike stealth.
Seen from above, on Yesnov's balcony, they could have been
marauding Red Sea maneaters glimpsed through a diver's gog-
gles. The second wave ebbed and flowed and Yesnov saw that
none had caught the solitary gun.

In the lull he decided to take out the gun himself. The beauty
of a Skyhawk is the tremendous load it carries. Though geared
for reconnaissance, Yesnov's little marvel gripped bombs and
rockets too in the clawlike racks. He stooped into a dive, remembering that the Skyhawk's rapid pitch and roll responses
were great assets but also placed a burden on the pilot. It was
easy to overcorrect on rudder pedals which were highly geared.
The craft was lightly framed, like a hawk, and lacked the stolid
character of the Phantom. He flashed low across the gun's position and felt the wings juddering in the updrafts of air rising
from the burning plain. He broke left into a 4½ G upward turn,
glancing back to see his eggs laid neatly in the gun's nest. He
made a wide sweep and came back to make doubly sure. He let
the speed decay, braking into a gentle descent back toward the
smoking crater, when a flash like a mirror catching the sun sprang

from the hills. He turned sharply and suddenly his head was banging hard against the canopy, first to one side and then to the other.

He thought at first it was the leading-edge slats and cursed himself for a fool. For dogfights, the slats dropped out, changing the wing's profile for greater maneuverability at slow speeds. Each slat ran the length of the leading edge and the whole process was automatic so that a green pilot, although fore-warned, felt that God had grabbed him by the wings.

Yesnov straightened out and began to climb. The controls felt sloppy. He checked inside and out. The leading-edge slats were tucked up tight again, as they should be. He worked the rudder pedals and felt no response. *Stop and think.* How many times had he been drilled in the need to stay cool? He forced down the first tendrils of panic creeping up through his bowels. Loss of rudder control? Not entirely. He squinted into the rearview mirror. Part of the tail was gone and even while he watched, he saw something peel away. There was a sensation like drag-ging through mud, and power in the Pratt & Whitney turbojet died away. No speed worth a damn. No great lateral control. And the ground not far below and alive with guerrillas.

His seat was the zero-zero type, designed to save life at zero speed and zero altitude if necessary. That meant a pretty hefty bang once he chose to eject. He still had some response in the ailerons and a few hundred feet of grace. The nose pitched for-ward as he brought the damaged Skyhawk into a skidding turn. Just another mile would do it. Just far enough from the concen-tration of Arabs at PS-5. Just close enough so that he could hole up somewhere in the hill ahead.

The canopy gone, he felt the slipstream tearing at ears and eyes despite helmet and visor. He took the escape drill step by step. The routine, practiced so often, became automatic. Thank God for drillmasters, efficient mechanics, and the Douglas Es-capac. He slapped out into the air, a young man aged nineteen, young enough to remember schoolboy dreams of floating through the air suspended between the clouds and the mustard-yellow land below.

Perhaps the schoolboy dreams had led him here, satisfying those cravings to perch on the curve of a cloud and shout aloud in air that was clean and untouched. Swinging under the blossoming canopy, he had a sense of *déjà vu*. Hadn't he always known he would float away from the gloom of a world encompassed in death? Stay in the sky, he thought, but already disobedient hands were tugging on the shrouds.

The moment passed quickly. The shock of ejection must have disoriented him. Or so he told himself. There was nevertheless a pang of regret as his boots slammed into the rock.

5

SAND IN

THE KILLER SKY

The Little Lieutenant smoked one cigarette after another while they took the longer road to Jerusalem by way of Haifa. She had calculations of her own to make and these were curiously mixed. She would be a civilian again in a few months, at the ripe old age of twenty-one, with twenty months of military service behind her. She wanted to get a place at the university in Jerusalem but the competition was intense and the cost came high.

The car crossed a chain in the road marking the perimeter of the base. Another part of her mind noted a Dassault Ouragan fighter-bomber rising over the fields. The Ouragan was her favorite jet, old and overworked as it was. She remembered that as a child aged six she thought nothing so beautiful existed on earth or above it. Perhaps she was influenced by the fact that when she was six, the whole world seemed to be collapsing around her. It was the time of the 1956 war and she had fully expected never to see her father again. He had flown Ouragans when he was not piloting El Al airliners to New York.

The stranger followed the twisting road, astonished as always by the way the landscape changed with each bend. Here the scene was German: there, Rumanian. It depended on the place of origin of the first settlers. Already the base had vanished. Even the jets, arrowheading out of the hot valley, came and went like ghosts.

They drove past Nahalal, the first smallholders' cooperative in Israel, built in a partly malarial region in 1920 by (among others) Moshe Dayan's father. Moshe had been educated here at the Girls' Agricultural College, an unusual training ground for generals.

"You smoke too much," said S. "Everybody here smokes too much. Must be the tension."

She was on guard at once. "I don't feel any tension."

"Because you live with it all the time. There's an old Chinese saying: If you live in a fish market, you don't smell the fish."

"There is no tension," said the Little Lieutenant sharply. "Do you see street fights, drunks . . . ?"

"You've got the lowest consumption of alcohol in the world."

"Do you see kids on drugs?"

"Not the local kids."

"We've got other things to think about than the state of our nerves and the cosmos. Three months' duty on the Canal is all the trip a boy needs. A psychiatrist would starve."

"Nonetheless, you all smoke like chimneys."

"So who mourns? We have our own secret remedy for cancer. A bullet in the head. We had one American expert who wanted to warn us about lung disease. We told him, 'If you want a cure for a running nose, strip down and stay out all night.' This American said we should take things more seriously. We said, 'If you want to save us, where are the Phantoms?' "

"Are you religious?" he asked abruptly.

"Who is?"

"I'm not sure. You all deny it. Perhaps it's because the word 'religious' has a different meaning here—something formal and ritualistic. You don't seem religious in that sense, not in the air force anyway. Yet you know your own Bible backward as if it were—well, a sort of history book."

"It *is* history. Look back down into that valley." The girl twisted round. Below, cloud-shadows raced across the hummocky plains. "There's Megiddo, one of Solomon's chariot cities."

He slowed the car, thinking, I'm looking down through six thousand years of human history. It's possible that civilization was born around here. Here's where it all started. Megiddo existed nearly four thousand years before Christ. The great religions were cradled here: Christians, Jews, Moslems. . . .

"It's also the place where the final battle will be fought between good and evil," said the girl.

"Armageddon?" He'd forgotten.

"Read *your* Bible," she said. "The Book of Revelations. The last great clash of arms on God's great day."

God's great day. He felt his stomach tighten. The land below was a blaze of color. Harsh land of white boulders on craggy hillsides and knotted olive trees as dark and stubborn as life itself. Out of the desert blew the *khamsin*, that intensely hot and dry wind that seems to come straight from the blazing early morning sun. It was a wind that dried the sentimentality out of one's bones: a wind that dried the palate and discouraged conversation: a wind that left one alone with thoughts that unwound like the dark ribbon of road ahead.

"There was nothing but sand in the killer sky," wrote a World War II flier. "It could wear out the moving parts of an aeroengine in a matter of hours, turning the lubricating oil into an abrasive paste. Guns became jammed, Perspex cockpit canopies scored and scratched, food ruined by the fine desert dust. Great sandstorms would descend at any time, obliterating the landscape in a swirling fog. Life became a gritty nightmare of sand in the eyes, nostrils. . . . The violent heat of the day made most movement impossible around noon. Metal parts of aircraft became so hot that to touch them was to risk a blistered hand. At night the temperature dropped so rapidly that one shivered in thick winter clothing. Water was so short that it was used, after washing, to fill radiators. Millions of flies settled on faces and food. Desert-sores festered for months. The great wastes of undulating sand, rock and scrub were difficult to navigate over. To be forced down was to risk a lingering death."

The man who wrote that was a Canadian Wing Commander, G. C. Keefer, DSO and Bar, DFC and Bar. He was recording his own fighter squadron's part in the great air battles against Hitler's Luftwaffe. It was the continuity of the fighting that fascinated the stranger S. Most of the world had forgotten how Israel was born in a region where conflicts went right back to the collapse of the Ottoman Empire. Sixty years ago an Englishman who gave birth to all kinds of romantic and frequently misleading notions, Lawrence of Arabia, had walked on foot through this same region in preparation for Britain's bid to control as much territory east and west of Suez as she could before the hungry Russians, French, and Italians arrived with their own particular justifications of empire.

Lawrence of Arabia saw the region as the natural battleground for the aerial armadas to come. The little man with the big head had finally joined the Royal Air Force but it was only now, with the publication of hitherto secret documents, that Lawrence could be seen as the agent of British ambitions and not the leader of some vast Arab revolt against oppression. Yet millions would continue to think of him as Prince of Mecca, uncrowned King of Damascus, and not as a conspirator who wanted to put the Jews into Palestine for his own inscrutable but imperialist reasons. It was Lawrence the stoic, in his gold-adorned kaffiyeh, with his direct line to Whitehall, who brought together King Feisal and one of the founders of Israel, Dr. Chaim Weizmann. And it was Dr. Weizmann's son who died flying for the British; and his nephew Ezer who flew the same Spitfires that had given so much trouble in the desert was described by Wing Commander Keefer.

It was Ezer, still flying his Spitfire, who gave up command of Israel's new air force at the end of 1969: Ezer who regretfully helped shoot down five British fighters sent to convey to the Israelis at the end of the 1948–1949 war that Britain would tolerate no closer approach to the Suez Canal. Down all the years the fighting had continued, and there were few outside Israel who recognized that the roots of conflict reached deep into this history of imperial ambition, broken promises, cynical alliances, and changing friendships. When the State of Israel declared its independence on May 15, 1948, the Russians gave immediate recognition and arms came from Czechoslovakia in token of Soviet support. By 1956, Britain and France, which had been anti-Israel, were now supporting her in a new war because the late President Nasser's Egypt had nationalized the Suez Canal and seriously hurt British and French national interests. In 1967 the kaleidoscope fell into yet another pattern. The only consistency was that Israel never had the same ally, twice in a row.

With the passing years, Israel had grown stronger in response to the overwhelmingly larger military resources of the Arab states, themselves still in that mood of suspicion and fear which Lawrence had exploited six decades ago.

Motti Hod, now commanding one of history's greatest tactical air forces, could recall as a schoolboy envying the British pilots of antiquated Gloster Gladiator biplanes near his home in Galilee. When the first truce in the first fighting between Jews and Arabs ended on July 9, 1948, Benjamin Kagan, now one of Motti's colonels, wrote, "The United Nations proposes we live in what would be in effect a sort of ghetto encircled by Arab countries and with the Negev, Galilee and Jerusalem taken away from us."

The Jews then, as now, had to build up an image of strength. The Arab League in 1948 estimated fifty thousand mobilized Jewish troops, plus reserves, equipped with artillery, armor, and an air force. The truth was that the men dedicated to creating

Israel had at the time three thousand fully trained Palmach troops, of which several hundred were girls. There were enough weapons for less than a quarter of the men, none of whom were trained to fight at more than battalion strength. Their total arsenal consisted of 8300 rifles, 3600 Sten guns, 700 light machine guns, 600 two-inch and 100 three-inch mortars, and 200 medium machine guns. Most of these were purchased by individual kibbutzim, whose founders had come here with a socialist and pacifist ideology.

There, of course, was the irony. When Lawrence of Arabia made his first thousand-mile trek in 1909, at the age of twenty-two, he had written, "The sooner the Jews farm it all the better." And the Jews had come to settle the region in good faith and with a profound distaste for armed conflict. They, the victims of violence, became the targets of resurgent Arab militarism. The imperialist powers that had provoked Arab anticolonialism and shaped militant nationalism were gone. All that remained was Israel, whose people had arrived at this point in time when they were no longer in any mood to submit to more threats of liquidation. Arabs and Jews had arrived at a crossroads when neither was prepared to suffer injustice again.

The fearful progression of armed strength after the Six-Day War showed Israel a year later with only 270 combat aircraft. Egypt, whose air force had been destroyed, was back to a strength of 400 combat aircraft supplied by the Soviet Union.

"The logic of victory and defeat doesn't work here," the stranger S had been told once by Lester B. Pearson, the Canadian premier awarded a Nobel Peace Prize for his United Nations peace-keeping efforts after the 1956 Suez conflict. It was the confession of a well-intentioned and disillusioned former Secretary General of the United Nations.

"We can win and win," said David Ben-Gurion, "and still lose everything with our first defeat."

Nasser declared a war of attrition in March 1969. A thunderous artillery barrage began against Israelis along the Suez Canal. At the time, London's Institute for Strategic Studies* reported that the total armed strength of Israel was 22,500 regulars. Israel had the smallest military force among twenty-six nations examined by the Institute and could raise at best 290,000 reservists from a population of 2,800,000. The country had a third of the size of Sweden's regular armed forces, and Sweden was next to bottom of the Institute's list. Egypt had five million men of military age compared with half a million in Israel.

A war of attrition was therefore a clever conception. "Attrition," according to the Random House Dictionary, means "a wearing down . . . as a result of continuous pressure. Example: 'The enemy surrounded the town and conducted a war of attrition.' "

Israel was like a town surrounded. On two sides were the nations on which the Soviet Union had placed high stakes—Egypt and Syria. The governments of Jordan and Lebanon were prisoners of guerrillas trained by China's Maoists and armed with the latest weapons of terror. Every attempt to retaliate could be presented as a wicked Israeli suppression of poor natives. The Arabs avoided direct invasion and the overt aggressive actions of 1967 which turned world opinion against them. Instead, it was Israel whose reactions could be made to seem belligerent.

During another war that began in 1964, another nation armed to the teeth with Soviet weapons had attempted to crush the young and small democracy of Malaysia. Inventive as ever, the Communists had inspired Indonesia's Sukarno to call *that* war "confrontation." Nonetheless, Sukarno had sworn to crush Malaysia within the year. It was a hundred million Indonesians against ten million Malays and Chinese. The defending forces put up a strong argument for striking at Indonesia with aerial weapons. The defenders, having a pact with Britain, had to make

* The Institute has an international council and staff drawing on scholars and military officials in thirty countries and was founded in 1958 to research problems of security in a nuclear age. It is regarded as one of the most disinterested and highly informed centers of its kind and is the source of statistics here except when otherwise stated.

their case in London, but it was said that if Malaysia and her British allies struck back at all, they might win a brief military victory, only to lose a psychological war.

Sukarno's unsuccessful war of confrontation in Asia was sometimes compared with Nasser's war of attrition. But S, who had been in Malaysia throughout that other war, believed there were a great many differences. Not the least was that nobody was committed to help Israel in her defense. Furthermore, terrorists entering Malaysia could be hunted through a vast hinterland of jungle. It was not possible to conquer Malaysia in one swift blow. The country was enormous, compared with Israel; it bordered friendly neighbors; it did not adjoin its enemy at any point.

Moshe Dayan had seen very clearly that the problem in Israel was to discourage Arab "salami" slicing of his people without giving grist to the Communist propaganda mills. If it came to numbers, fewer than three million Israelis took less time to whittle down than the sixty million Arabs whose leaders promised to liquidate the Jews.

So his measured response was always carefully calculated. His warplanes—many of them seemingly unfit to dogfight against a modern air force—would serve as flying artillery. They could deliver a punch as effective as brigades of Egyptian cannon, using a far smaller number of men. And they would reserve the right to reply at a time and place of their own choosing. Surprise was still Israel's best defense. If the Egyptian barrages increased, there would be sharp responses. As a result, losses from shelling on the Suez fell from a monthly peak of thirty Israelis killed and seventy-six wounded * in July 1969 to five killed by the first month of January 1970. Within this period, Israeli pilots scored a ten-to-one kill ratio in dogfights. It was in the light of this experience that the seventy-one-year old matriarch, Premier Golda Meir, went to Washington in September 1969 to explain why

---

* When casualties reached twenty Israelis a week, it was estimated in Jerusalem that this was the equivalent of eighteen hundred United States servicemen a week in Vietnam, where the actual killing had never gone higher than 562 a week.

her air force was so vital to defense. "We are finished with gim-
micks," she said. "Finished with observers and emergency forces
and demilitarized zones and armistices. We ourselves intend to
forestall any buildup to a major Arab attack. We ourselves will
protect our troops from shells and our children from guerrilla
rockets."

Perhaps her strength seemed more like stubbornness. The
daughter of a Russian carpenter, with an American upbringing
and memories of hard times on a kibbutz, she displayed a deep
suspicion of major-power guarantees. This was hardly surprising to anyone familiar with Israel's history. She showed great
honesty: "The Arabs want us dead. We want to be alive. Com-
promise between those two views is not exactly easy."

In Washington the question was asked: Is this a siege mentality turning into a martyr's complex?

Mrs. Meir impressed S as one of those stunningly honest leaders who come along once in a very long time. She seemed far
less stubborn than misunderstood abroad. She was not stiffnecked
but outspoken. She saw no way to deal with the Arabs except
through a demonstration of the will to survive.

Whatever effect she may have had in Washington, the fact was
that the request to purchase some 125 Phantoms and Skyhawks
was shelved. An order for 50 Phantoms, previously signed, was
being met at the rate of four Phantoms a month. Nevertheless,
the IAF started 1970 with aircraft and manpower comparable
to that of the Swiss, while Egypt's air force could be compared
with that of Britain's RAF. According to the Institute for Strategic
Studies, Israel had 15 obsolescent Vautour light bombers, 48
aging Skyhawk fighter/fighter-bombers, 65 obsolescent Mirage
3C fighter-bombers, 12 Super-Mystère fighters that had flown
beyond their designed operational life, 35 Mystère 4A fighter-
bombers of similar decrepitude, and 35 Ouragan fighter-bombers
also due for the glue factory. Israel had paid for 50 Mirage 5s
from France but the French government had stopped delivery.
A few Phantoms were going into service instead. If things got

really tough, there were 65 Magister jet-trainers of some antiquity.

Against this modest force, the United Arab Republic had 100 MiG-21 jet interceptors, 120 MiG-15 and MiG-17 fighter-bombers, 90 Su-7 all-weather fighter-bombers, 30 Il-28 light jet bombers, 12 Tu-16 medium jet bombers, and 150 MiG, Yak, and Delfin jet-trainers of which some could be armed.

Syria had 55 MiG-21 jet interceptors, 70 MiG-15 and MiG-17 fighter-bombers, 20 Su-7 all-weather fighter-bombers: Iraq had 60 MiG-21 interceptors, 50 Hunter Mark-9 ground-attack jets, 45 MiG-17 and MiG-19 jet fighters, 20 Su-7 all-weather fighter-bombers, 20 T-52 light-strike jets, and 18 Tu-16 and Il-28 light bombers.

Libya, whose new Premier, Muammar Gaddafi, had just promised "to kick the hell out of Israel," had got the 50 French Mirage 5s denied to Israel, plus 30 Mirage 3Es equipped with Doppler radar for low-level and poor-visibility attacks, and 20 Mirage 3s. Algeria had 140 MiG-21s, MiG-17s and MiG-15s.

Such figures could be misleading. They dramatized, however, the Soviet Union's bolstering of Arab strength.* The Commander of the Soviet Navy, Serge Gorshkov, was reported in from Moscow as saying his Mediterranean fleet was growing in order to have a "sobering effect" on Israel. There were rumors of a Russian plan to install new electronic devices along Israel's borders, a kind of radar-missile wall over which it would be impossible to climb.

When the stranger S had discussed these reports in Washington at the beginning of 1970, he found an odd ambivalence. Military experts were ready to see the danger. For example, they pointed to the great disparity in firepower between Israel and the Arab states allied under a Joint Defense Command: the

---

* One year later, Soviet-supplied air power was to swell to the alarming dimensions described at the end of this chronicle.

United Arab Republic, Syria, Iraq, and Jordan. This, they said, was more dangerous to Israel in the long run because the Arabs had the men to feed unlimited numbers of guns.

Again the Israelis were seen as occupants of a beleaguered fortress. They had no artillery worth any serious consideration, compared with Egypt's 950 pieces of heavy artillery: 500 122-mm, 130-mm, and 152-mm guns, 10 artillery brigades, 10 commando battalions equipped with mobile rocket-launchers, and a large Missile Command. It was recalled that the toughest fighting in the Six-Day War had been against the dense Syrian gun emplacements on the Golan Heights above the Sea of Galilee, where Russian artillery pieces were sown like dragon's teeth above the small Israeli settlements.

It was also recognized that Israel's use of combat-weary aircraft was a sensible substitute for artillery. The planes were kept aloft by the team spirit and ingenuity of several thousand skilled mechanics. Nevertheless the planes had a limited life. Now was the time to utilize this frayed air force in a determined bid to stop the growth of enemy strength along the borders.

Yet the more effectively this force was employed, the less Washington's advisers to President Nixon seemed to understand. In January alone, the Star of David wheeled above Cairo's suburbs, struck at military installations in the Delta, and challenged Egyptian MiGs to come up and dogfight. Feinting here and clouting there, the Israelis publicized the visit of General Haim Bar-Lev to Suez while an armored force thundered into Jordan after guerrillas. While Mrs. Meir and Moshe Dayan diverted attention with a tour down the Jordan River valley, paratroopers scooted across the Gulf of Suez to grab a radar unit used by Cairo to monitor naval traffic out of the Red Sea.

The capture of a complete Russian-built S-12 Barlock searchradar installation on December 26, 1969, was another seemingly flamboyant exploit with very real military advantages. It started casually enough when a young IAF pilot came back from a photoreconnaissance mission. He had seen something that photographic blowups confirmed. He drove to the Citadel with copies and marched through Motti Hod's door. The brigadier general had often said that a good leader kept his door open to all comers. "Well," said the young captain, "I've come to tell you I think the Egyptians are building a decoy *here* to distract our attention from something that's happening *here*."

Hod sent the pictures for analysis. The report he got back sent him into a whirlwind of action. The captain had guessed correctly that something of value was being built near the Canal. It was lightly guarded to avoid the IAF's attention. But according to intelligence reports, it would be heavily guarded by dawn next day.

The secret installation might be the kind of valuable hardware Hod was seeking at the time to trade with the Egyptians for some captured Israeli fliers. He called for an estimate of this desirable object's weight and size. If it was indeed a Russian search-radar unit, could heliborne commandos snatch the prize?

"The request seemed fantastic enough," a leader of the expedition was to say later. "But the time we were given was impossible. There were seven hours of daylight left. We had three hours to experiment with a mock-up, and in that time we had to build the mock-up. We raided a junkyard and based our simulation on the evidence of the photographs. We found we'd need two heavy-lift choppers and we'd have to cut the object into two chunks. We had to practice lifting these chunks in different conditions of light, wind, temperature. . . . We'd expect two months for a job like this. Instead we had two hours in which to decide if it could be done. When you're up against that kind of deadline, you say, '*Yes it can be done*,' and you figure out how later."

The operational plan, with alternatives, was submitted to the Security Committee. Permission was granted on the understanding that there should be no loss of life and no direct confrontation with any uniformed Russians around the site.

Thus, within hours of the captain's delivering his pictures, the

operation was set to begin. In a bunker along the 100-mile string
of underground forts and minefields known as the Bar-Lev Line,
the Israeli chief-of-staff, Lieutenant General Haim Bar-Lev,
chatted with one of the helicopter squadron commanders during the tense moments when the first military scouts went in.
The target lay roughly 20 miles across the Gulf of Suez at an
oilfield near Ras Gharib. The enemy's strategy had been to assemble the unit at very high speed and the scouts confirmed by
radio that the Egyptians had concentrated their troops at the
decoy some miles away. The Egyptian plan was not a bad one:
the decoy would not only draw the Israelis away from the real
installation; it also meant that troops could be moved overnight
for when the new installation went into operation at dawn.

It was, the scouts reported, the S-12 Barlock. This had been
anticipated and air intelligence had worked feverishly to gather
what scant information there was on this Russian-type radar used
for the detection of low-flying aircraft. The unit's removal was
more imperative now than ever. Deep-penetration IAF strikes
were due to begin in two weeks, in an attempt to pressure Egypt
into relaxing her artillery bombardments along the Canal. The
shelling was a prelude to an Egyptian attack across Suez, or so
Cairo said.

Men with blowtorches, wire-cutters, and wrenches dropped
around the S-12 and began to dismantle it. The sky-cranes were
waved in. Hooks descended and technicians attached them to
the handily trussed packages of S-12 parts. The dissection and
packaging had not been easy. The radar was already embedded
in concrete. Consoles and antenna had to be carefully detached.
Delicate instruments were wrapped and placed into crumple-
proof boxes. While this was going on, heliborne commandos
spread out into defensive positions. Outlying pickets reported
signs of military activity on the horizon. The area was engulfed
in choking dust. Pilots and the men on the ground had to work
almost by touch. The giant rotor-blades of the choppers created

a whirlwind of sand. Flash-lamps moved eerily in the choking dust. Signals were lost or misread.

"It was a classic operation of its kind," reported one of the senior officers who had sweated it out with Bar-Lev. "As you know, the cardinal rule in our defense forces is to advance whatever the cost. In this kind of piracy, advance means you keep going with the operation despite unexpected setbacks. Officers lead, and if they fall, others replace them. Every man in every unit down to the lowliest private is trained to take over and continue the operation. That's not so easy when you have to improvise as you go along. On the other side of the Gulf we were second-guessing as best we could but the real decisions were being made on the spot."

Such a decision was made halfway home across the seaway when one of the sky-cranes sprang a leak in its hydraulic system. The hydraulically operated hoist began slipping cable. Half of a seven-ton Russian prize headed toward the bottom of Suez. The pilot managed to keep it skimming the waves by climbing faster than the load was descending. The race was unequal. In almost any other situation, Motti Hod would have ordered the pilot to jettison his cargo. But the IAF commander, as always with stop watch in hand and cigar in mouth, this time deferred to the pilot's judgment. He was sure he could just about make the crossing. He did. The cargo skidded on wet sand as the sky-crane passed over Israeli territory and the pilot released the hook. The strange cargo was retrieved later.

Back at the site, now gaping like the socket of a pulled tooth, technicians retired under cover of commandos engaged in a firefight. The last to leave were the infantrymen, who took with them a few prisoners. Whether or not these included Russians has never been disclosed.

The news of the coup swept right through Israel in a clocked time of exactly two hours, despite the utmost secrecy surrounding the whole operation. A news correspondent picked up the rumors and flew to Cyprus to file the story to London. At first the experts assumed the IAF had employed the French Sud-Aviation Super Frelon (Hornet), capable of airlifting 30 troops or 8,818 pounds of cargo over 124-mile stage lengths. Hornets had been used in commando raids before. Then it dawned on them that something like the heavy-lift Sikorsky CH-53 must have been employed, and so it was reported much later in the United States magazine *Aviation Week & Space Technology*, with the comment that Israel had not admitted receiving the CH-53.

Some foreign observers applauded this example of what they called "Elizabethan Israel's piracy." It was bound to feed the misgivings of others, however, who did not understand that Israel in reality was striking out at new dangers. The net result was that Israel entered 1970 a victim of her own ingenuity. Her friends felt she could take care of herself. Her critics said she was cocksure and intransigent. Perhaps only the Russians sensed the truth. Israel's strength was wearing down just when the West was in its most escapist mood and therefore reluctant to replace broken parts. Russia could safely graduate from a protector of the Arabs to participation in Middle East hostilities.

And Israel made an ideal victim from Russia's point of view.

The stylish execution of these operations gave a new dimension to the word "piratical," which some foreign diplomats used admiringly to describe Israel's campaign to discourage Russian intervention and outwit the Arabs. Now "piratical" became linked to other words such as "belligerent" and "hawkish." There was talk of cocksure Israelis trying to bludgeon the Arabs into passivity, a description that seemed fair enough to distant observers but was far too glib and distorted. On January 30, 1970, President Nixon said he would reply to Israel's request for more planes within thirty days. It sounded as though the Arabs were being put on probation. As it turned out, it was the Israelis who were being put on probation at a time when their own knowledge of events told them to keep up the pressure.

Those were thirty days of tension. One had to be in Israel to see the gulf between Washington's view and that of the besieged. James Feron reported in *The New York Times* on February 8, "The Middle East is at war. But it is a strange war conducted differently on each of four fronts. While the Israelis are seemingly content to conduct a defensive war on the Lebanese, Syrian, and Jordanian fronts—that is, sitting quietly until shot at, and then responding sharply—they have taken the offensive against the UAR in seeking to turn President Nasser's war of attrition against him."

At the end of thirty days there was silence from the White House and intensified action on all fronts. Arab terrorists appeared to suspend their harassment of Israel's aerial lifelines after blowing up the Swissair plane bound for Tel Aviv in which all forty-seven aboard were killed. Instead, guerrillas raided Israeli settlements, using the more refined techniques of terror learned in Asia. The front page of the *Jerusalem Post* on March 17 reported three raids into Syria, the shelling of guerrilla hideouts in Lebanon, the destruction of the forty-fifth Egyptian MiG-21 since 1967, and "an extraordinary buildup" of the Soviet fleet in the east Mediterranean. The banner headline was: STATE DEP'T TO REPLY ON ISRAEL BID FOR JETS. But answer came there none.

"A definite Sovietization of certain operational aspects of the conflict" was reported on March 29 by General Dayan. This followed several different accounts from abroad of Russian transports with Egyptian markings flying out of Yugoslavia to Cairo West with new SA-III missile units and the necessary Russians to assemble and operate them.

On this same day, the streets of Tel Aviv were alive with small children in gala costume. They celebrated Purim, anniversary of the deliverance of the Jewish people from certain destruction during the reign of the Persian King Ahasuerus. In Jerusalem priests and nuns made a Palm Sunday procession along the route taken by Christ five days before his crucifixion. Windstorms swept both cities and a cold rain lashed the coast. Two small girls were injured by bomb blasts in Jaffa. An outgoing Alitalia flight to Rome was held up while police investigated a terrorist-bomb report. Two Arab children from the Gaza Strip were on their way at Israel's expense to Holland for plastic surgery after their faces were disfigured by exploding grenades. An old woman had been killed by another grenade while terrorists distributed warning pamphlets.

On this same day, too, the great controversy over a power-plant chimney took a new turn. Citizens of Tel Aviv had launched a legal action to stop the alleged pollution caused by the chimney. A British expert, E. G. Clark, told the court that waste matter from the chimney would not add appreciably to air pollution. He said out of court that he was astonished and impressed to find anyone showing any concern at all over such a matter "at a time like this." He added that he thought the air of Tel Aviv the purest among large cities.

And it was on this day that Cairo acknowledged the arrival of Soviet missiles and technicians; Peking reported the welcome given by Red China's leaders to the Arab terrorist chief Yasser Arafat; Algiers reported the visit there of the Soviet Navy Chief; the *Jerusalem Post*'s front page headlined the news that ISRAEL WON'T GET MORE U.S. PLANES.

President Nixon was a month behind his own promise to make a decision in thirty days.

6

OLD DOGFIGHTS

AND NEW TRICKS

"Hit them now. If we wait, we'll pass the point where retaliation becomes possible. Strike now and we'll have the whole world against us. Wait, and what the world thinks won't matter."

Jacob put down the phone.

"What's all that about?" asked Jo-jo.

"Security Committee. I'm expected there this afternoon but I want them to know what I think beforehand."

Jo-jo tugged his beard. He had Jacob's sketches on the desk in front of him; endless doodles of useless hooks. Jo-jo was known as the Pogo Stick because he had turned the helicopter into a vehicle that hopped around the battle zones. It was said that he could bounce a troop-carrier from the Syrian front to Haifa to Tel Aviv to Jerusalem like a rubber ball within the space of an hour. Now he was glued to a desk, filling in as director of the IAF's technical institute, plagued with academic problems.

"The Phantoms were built for carriers, Jacob. So we get hooks and no carriers."

"I hate to see anything wasted, you know that."

"We've stripped every plane to the bone. You want us to have carriers?"

"God forbid. Give the carrier to Nasser and let him go broke."

"Artillery burns money faster. Do you see Egypt bankrupt? All they do is provide Russia with free gun practice and we're the moving targets." Jo-jo turned to the window. He could see an open classroom where a twenty-year-old airwoman held the attention of a dozen eighteen-year-old boys with an exercise in higher math scrawled across a blackboard. The buildings had once been a British barracks. Now they sprawled across marshland to runways and low-profile hangars that remained invisible to the tourists on Mount Carmel above the great port of Haifa.

Jacob shrugged. "Aaron caught a Russian spy-plane, this morning. Motti made him hold his fire."

"Why?"

"A pair of MiGs were waiting to jump Aaron. The Russians get bolder while we run out of time and allies." All night he had wrestled with the problem, out there on Naomi's balcony. Now, with his meeting in Jerusalem still hours way, he had stopped at this school where inventions flowed almost as fast as new mechanics.

Jo-jo played with a piece of elastic, stretching it so that he could inspect the writing, which diminished to a blur when the rubber went slack. One of the teachers had confiscated the crib from a boy taking an exam in electronics. There was an entire cabinet of cribs beside his files: miniature scrolls of mathematical formulae, watch straps with tiny diagrams on the inside, trick pencils, false bandages. If anyone could find a use for the Phantom's tail-hook, designed for deck landings, that person was likely to be here.

"Jacob, did you know that a hundred million years ago there was a kind of flying reptile with wings twenty-five feet across?"

"I'm not one of your pupils."

"Patience. We know about *Pteranodon* from skeletons. It weighed forty pounds and in the light of modern scientific knowledge it had no capacity for flight. Yet it flew. It dominated an age of dinosaurs."

"A reptile dead a hundred million years, so we have to talk about it?"

"Yes. Because what all the clever scientists overlooked was that in that era, the *Pteranodon* did not have to flap its wings to fly. Winds above fifteen miles an hour were common. All it did was spread those wings and the wind made it soar."

"I still don't see . . ."

"The tail-hook seems useless to us because its job is to hook the plane down to the deck of a ship. We're stuck with that idea. What's wrong with looking at it differently? We lose planes *after* they land because of burst tires, damaged undercarts, running off the runway at high speed. . . ."

"So we buy mid-runway arrester gear and add to our bills?"

"Not *buy*, Jacob. Make our own. A wire across a runway, weights to hold back a damaged Phantom . . . Even if we have one accident in a thousand landings, and even if the arrester gear worked only once in a thousand of those accidents, wouldn't we come out ahead?"

Jacob scratched his head. "How?"

"It's done. We rigged an arrester system at Aaron's base. We can't afford to experiment. We probably won't know if it works until someone actually does have undercarriage trouble, but it's there."

"I wish people would tell me these things," Jacob began, and then stopped. Jo-jo's face was alight with enthusiasm.

"Nobody knows everything in this air force," said Jo-jo. "Things happen too fast."

"Would it strain your resources to tell me who created this particular device?" Jacob asked.

"The Instrument Basher."

The Instrument Basher dwelt in a cramped wooden hut near the playing fields. He got his name from a period of service in the RAF, where specialists are given peculiar and not altogether respectful titles.

Jacob strolled in his direction, enjoying for the moment the sense of pride and reassurance he got whenever he came here. Cadets moved at the double between classes. There were gooseneck paraffin flares along a runway whose end vanished in a thick sea-mist. Worn rubber tires were used to protect flares and other fragile devices on the taxiways. There was an air of improvisation wherever Jacob looked, and this always pleased him. He never came here without feeling heartened. Before the 1956 Suez conflict, a few hundred youngsters trained here. Now they came in their thousands. They came often as dropouts at sixteen and there was something exciting about the way veterans like Colonel Jo-jo transformed them into self-respecting and competitive men. Out of Israel's thirty-six thousand dropouts in the previous year, the technical institute had garnered about one-fifth of all the boys. The day's routine was tough, starting at six a.m. and continuing often late into the night. Yet discipline was administered with a light hand. Natural rebels became cooperative and lively. Perhaps it was the proximity of hangars where Russian equipment underwent conversion. Perhaps it was the evidence on every hand of the careful husbanding of resources: there was not a single training device, from jet engines to the smallest electronic gizmo, that was not either rescued from crashed aircraft or improvised in the workshops.

Jogging along the perimeter of the playing fields came the chief physical-training instructor. In white track suit and flying blue cape, he reminded Jacob of an American cartoon belatedly in vogue among the students. But more heroic than Batman was the PTI, who had been a frogman until an underwater explosion damaged his lungs. He kept as fit as he could and left the heavy work to his girls. One of them was entering the changing rooms now: a graceful girl in tight sand-gray skirt and open-necked shirt, white bobby socks and black flat-heeled shoes, her blue sweater with silver lieutenant's bars slung over her shoulder.

The girls taught physical training to boys only a year or two younger than themselves. Yet they kept full command. Was it,

Jacob wondered, because of a traditional respect for women? Or simply that the kids realized these girls were trying to do men's work, to release the men for combat duty?

Whatever the reason, there was never trouble from boys protesting against taking orders from the girls. Perhaps there was somewhere an unconscious identification with Mother? He remembered when the 1967 war started, Jo-jo saying, "I'll send the lads back to their Mamas until it's all over." To a stranger it might have seemed an odd remark, coming from a burly commander whose chief job was to bring schoolboys off the streets and turn them in double-quick time into hundreds of disciplined technicians, skilled in some fifty different trades, yet individualistic enough to take responsibility. Some of the kids who were sent home to Mama were today improvising new bomb-release mechanisms in the field.

A giant of a colonel emerged from one of the hangars—Elephant Moses. When the air force sold off its last Spits to Burma, he'd gone there to help reorganize Burma's air defense. He lumbered over to Jacob with his usual shy grin. "I hear there's another flap."

"You've got long ears."

"No, just a niece driving around with a stranger."

Jacob grinned. It was a small family all right.

S, the stranger, had encountered the Instrument Basher on his first visit to the technical institute. Elephant Moses, who was host to S, showed frank envy of the young pilots flying the Phantoms.

"You had your turn fourteen years ago," said the Instrument Basher. He was a grizzled man of late middle years with a London Cockney accent. He wore a woolen cardigan in the sticky heat on the theory that if you wore heavy clothing to conserve the body's temperature in winter, you should conserve it against hot weather too. The fact that sweat dribbled along the crevices of his face and blurred his spectacles did not deter him. The cardigan itself was all that the Instrument Basher had salvaged from the bombed ruins of his home and watchmaker's shop during what he called "the Nasties' Blitz." He told S, "Moses here flew Mustangs is the '56 war. We didn't have jet bombers. The Mustangs were driven by copies of Queen Victoria's original treadle sewing machine. What a load of old iron! But better than 1948 when we stole what we could from the junk heaps. People forget. The kids flying our jets today weren't even born then. And the commander of our first Phantom squadron was ten years old when Elephant Moses here flew in the '56 bit of nastiness. We still hold some of the bloody planes together with baling wire—"

The Instrument Basher never stopped talking while he worked in the wooden hut crammed with devices. Models of new wing-shapes hung from the rafters. A crude wind-tunnel blew wood shavings across a corner of the room. A sophisticated system of glass-walled chambers gurgled and splashed with fluids pumped along plastic pipes. Workmen bent over scarred benches, engrossed in testing equipment. S had an over-all impression of a frenzied hobby shop spewing out lunar modules or the technical extravaganzas in a mad professor's potting shed.

From time to time Elephant Moses had tried to interrupt the Instrument Basher during his absent-minded discourse with the stranger. He might as well have tried to distract Marconi from the first wireless telegraph. The old man's fingers were busy with tools and instruments while his tongue wagged on. S had an uneasy feeling that the Instrument Basher had never stopped talking since the day in London's East End when the bombs fell on the Jews that Hitler missed. He had in fact poured ideas and inventions in a compulsive stream through all the wars and skirmishes; sucking up information on the one hand and regurgitating this technical knowledge in the form of modifications and conversions to whole stables of aircraft and engines whose points of origin covered Europe and North America.

The Instrument Basher was a man of quick and sparrow-like movements although he measured a good six feet in the thick-soled boots he always wore. When the Dorniers flew up the Thames estuary to set fire to the oil farms and pulverize Surrey Commercial, the East India, and the Royal Albert docks on a bright September day in 1940, he was on duty as a Special Constable and saw the early Hurricanes and Spitfires tangle with the big bomber formations. His part of London took such punishment that he was away from home for three days working in the chaos of wrecked and burning buildings. He returned to find his street demolished, his wife and three children buried beyond salvation in the rubble, and his shop destroyed. His fingertip skill as a watchmaker was well known and he had no trouble offering his services. The Air Ministry cut through the red tape and in short order he found himself installed in a large country house with a mixed bag of men: a couple of notorious safe-crackers, several other ex-convicts with credentials as forgers and confidence tricksters, a few scholars from European countries already overrun by the Nazis, and others. Most of the others seemed to be Oxford dons or scientists. The Instrument Basher was selected to work on explosive devices and anything else he cared to dream up. He was moved to Bletchley in North Buckinghamshire, where he was in daily contact with agents either going into or coming out of Europe. He slept very little in this period and became known for the way his mind would leap across logical processes of thought to arrive by a kind of mad genius at the solutions to difficult problems. There seemed to be no limit to his capacity to absorb technical information. Senior men would ask him questions that seemed far beyond his competence as an Aircraftsman A/C-2. When it was necessary to drop agents into neutral countries by more diplomatic means than a parachute, he designed a capsule that could be released at the end of a runway by a transport plane, looking as innocent as you please, just at touch-down.

He was, and insisted upon remaining, what sergeant-majors call "the lowest form of human life." He wanted neither rank nor privilege. His leisure was spent with technical handbooks. He spoke or understood several languages because his parents had come to London from Central Europe. He made two trips into Europe in a way that these parents of his would have never foreseen. On both missions he was in pursuit of scientific documents, and it was his watchmaking skill again that came in handy. He was brought out each time by a spy-collecting aircraft, the Westland Lysander, whose special characteristics for rough landings and short takeoffs he studied. He never became a member of the inner circle of defense scientists, the British boffins, because he lacked the sheepskins testifying to his academic worthiness. He had left school at fourteen and he was that most completely humble figure, the British artisan. He was uneasy in clubs, awkward in any social situation, and uninterested in people. The view was widely held that the Instrument Basher had become a work maniac to blot out the memory of the blitz. The truth was stranger.

Just before Germany collapsed, he was received by Churchill's scientific advisers, who asked him bluntly what it was he wanted from life. Some of his inventions would have earned big royalties in peacetime. Would he like money to start a new business, or a medal, or one of those vaguely defined jobs sometimes awarded to loyal British subjects?

The Instrument Basher said he would just as soon sign on for another period of RAF service. If, by chance, he should be posted close to his Jewish homeland, so much the better. A year later his friends sent him to Cairo. Two years later he was in Haifa assembling the first of his Hammacher Schlemmer–type gadgets.

"There was a time," the Instrument Basher told S, "when we had to cut telephone lines between the Port of Suez and the Mitla Pass. That'd be in the Sinai Campaign of '56. We built a device to put under the tails of the Mustangs. A hook, it was.

Four Mustangs we fixed up this way. I could quote you numbers and names even now, only I suppose it's still secret. But all of us remember these details, see. I mean, all the blokes know every single one of our aircraft like it was an individual. Any aircraftsman can tell you when such-and-such a plane went down, where, why, and who was in it. So among us, within the family as you might say, we know about these four Mustangs. They took off on October 29 in 1956 at 1400 hours and their job was to hook up the Egyptian communication lines. In the end they had to use propellers—"

At this point, Elephant Moses interrupted the flow of words. "You wanted to try out the Phantom?"

The Instrument Basher raised his head, adjusted his position at the bench, peered over spectacles that were taped in the middle where the bridge had broken, wiped his hands on his cardigan, pursed his lips, and said *"Oh ah?"*

"Because I've got a flight for you at noon."

The old man straightened his back. "I suppose this'll mean another baptism. Every time I go up in a new plane, the blokes dump me in the water tank afterwards. Last time, I was doing a study on a Russian plane we captured. When I got down the little blighters chased me and I tripped over an oil drum and cut my nose. Proper bashed up, I was. I tell you, I'd sooner be in the air than on the ground any old day. . . ."

S had asked both Elephant Moses and the Instrument Basher about the procedure for modifying aircraft or introducing new devices. They both snorted with laughter. "Procedures?" The big colonel looped an arm around the aircraftsman in his baggy cardigan. "He talks to me, I talk to him, we all talk to one another."

This turned out to be literally true. Ideas or proposals were born on the bases, where pilots flew as many as five combat missions a day. Ground crews worked at a dizzy pace. At one fighter base there were one hundred and thirty thousand different types of spare parts always in circulation, and these were tracked by central computers by which any tool or part could be located at any time. Under pressure, the men generated ideas that drifted like fog over the land, sometimes to be examined at scientific centers, sometimes to be solved on the spot.

"It takes thirty-three men to manhandle the Phantom," the Instrument Basher pointed out before his baptismal flight. "We can't spare men just to push and pull the machine around the hangars. So one of the pilots suggested some kind of mechanism like the power controls on the big new planes where muscle-power is supplemented. Someone else picked up the idea and produced this trolley. One man gives it a push, a small half-horsepower electric motor goes into action, the trolley engages the landing gear, and we don't have to waste thirty other men to push and shove."

"What's the point of *you* flying?" he was asked by S.

"We all try to get some of the feeling of the fliers, so we can understand their problems, know what they're talking about. Also because a lot of the new planes are too sophisticated for our needs. Take this Phantom; it's built to fire missiles and nobody else bothers to dogfight it. They think we're crazy. It's got servo-mechanisms and push-button controls and a bloke could sit like he was in an office and never really strain hisself. We reckon a pilot needs feedback all the time from his controls. He must *feel* his way through a fight."

When the Instrument Basher talked about flying in this way, there was an expression on his face that the stranger saw frequently among the thousands of IAF ground crew who would never themselves handle a plane. Without being too fanciful about it, S thought the skies over Israel provided its people with an extra dimension that offered escape from the suffocating effects of isolation.

"Into the air is a logical way for us to go," agreed Elephant Moses. "Only who would have predicted it twenty years ago? *Flying Yids!*"

They had watched the aging Instrument Basher kitting up.

They followed his stiff-legged progress to the Phantom and heard the friendly mocking of other mechanics and students.

"I know it sounds daft," said S, "but is it conceivable that a nonflying man like the Instrument Basher might—well, *invent* or improvise some new flying maneuver?"

The suggestion was offered hesitantly. S himself could think of almost nothing drastically new since World War II. There was Jan Zurakowsky, once the world's best-known test pilot, whose "Zurabatic" was evolved in 1953 in the Avro CF-100 twin-jet fighter. Zurakowsky had taught the maneuver to S, who flew with him in the prototype. Otherwise the art of aerial combat had developed into one electronic device against another.

"In a sense, air warfare *is* tightly tailored these days," said Elephant Moses. "Once the operational details are decided, then your 'suit' is stitched around you, and a very tight fit it is. You know where to break, when, at what altitude. . . . *But—but— but!!!!*"

He removed a tattered beret and scratched his head. Then he became aware of what he was doing and laughed, holding the beret between his two big freckled hands. "Regulations say we have to wear caps—peaked caps. I can't stand them and most of the time I don't even put this beret on my head. I screw it up and stick it under my shoulder lapel. It sets a bad example and if the general caught me, he'd say so. But the general? He still lets us call him Motti."

He swung round. "You want to *see* what I'm driving at?"

"Sure—"

Elephant Moses grinned. "I'll take you up, shake you round a bit. I'll show you a maneuver that's not in the book. Somebody worked it out on the ground, in theory—"

"Our own invention," said Elephant Moses, standing the jet on its tail.

The stranger gave a strangled cough. In his bone-domed helmet, plugged into radio and oxygen, mask clasped over his nose and mouth, cramped into the rear cockpit with a clear view of his pilot's head in front, he fought back an urge to grab the duplicated controls. The plane climbed vertically, the sun splintering against the sea-green visor.

The stranger saw the air-speed indicator drop to zero and again his hands stretched instinctively for the controls. *No speed, for petessake!*

"It's the quickest way to reverse direction in a dogfight," Elephant Moses explained pedantically. "We climb vertically, check pitch so we don't lose direction. Now, a sharp turn through ninety degrees. Check. Still going straight up but we're balanced on the jets like celluloid balls at a fair. Back with the stick. Pull back. Keep pulling. Let the nose fall into the dive. So . . . straight down. A vertical dive and keep it absolutely vertical!"

S felt his vision return to eyes popping like organ stops. A small settlement came racing up to meet him. "That's a kibbutz," said Elephant Moses, interest quickening his voice. "You can tell the difference from a cooperative because all the buildings are centralized, you see what I mean?"

S could see only too well. The kibbutz was coming up like an express train.

"So . . ." Elephant Moses returned to the work in hand. "Now we turn again another ninety degrees. That means we turned ninety degrees counter-clockwise going up, and completed the half-circle coming down."

S watched the doll's-eye indicator measuring the flow of oxygen. *Slow your breathing. The man in the front cockpit will think you're in a panic.* The doll's eye turned white when he breathed in, black when he exhaled.

"Now pull out," said Elephant Moses. S felt the lead pour through his veins and into boots. His eyes swiveled to watch the wings shuddering under the high G-forces. The manufacturer's date on the throttle beside his left hand was old enough to give him the shudders too.

"We're flying in the opposite direction," said Elephant Moses. "Same speed. Same altitude. For a long time the Immelmann Turn was impracticable for high-speed aircraft. Stalled turns were the thing. This variation is an offensive maneuver to bring our boys right tight on the enemy's tail."

His voice droned along while the stranger recovered his wits.

"Want to try it?" Elephant Moses asked companionably.

"Explain the theory first," S suggested.

"What made Immelmann turn?" Laughter rattled the earphones. "Max Immelmann tried it first in 1915 in a Fokker monoplane. He was jumped by an Englishman and Immelmann climbed into a loop. The Englishman followed the German into the loop and then lost his victim. What Immelmann did was to push the stick over 180 degrees, while inverted at the top of an inside loop, so he rolled out flying in the opposite direction. Then all he did was fall into a dive for the kill from six-o'clock high. Our maneuver's a big departure but it can be adapted in a number of ways. For instance . . ."

They went into a dive. "Imagine there's a MiG dead ahead," said Elephant Moses. "We get speed to overtake because he's faster than we are. If the guns jam on the first pass we climb, roll over. . . ."

Upside down, hanging in the straps, S tried to fix on the matter-of-fact voice up front. "Let's say the MiG decides to fight. He turns in, meeting the attack. But he can't find us. We're above him. So-o-o-o we half-loop into another dive. Speed builds up and here we are making a second pass at him from twelve-o'-clock high."

They pulled out of the dive.

"You've got control," said Elephant Moses. Gingerly at first, S tried a few gentle turns. Their aerobatics had brought them some distance down the coast. He tightened his steep turns while a northerly wind pushed the jet toward Gaza.

"Where did you learn about Immelmann?"

Elephant Moses' head bobbed. "He was the first dogfighter.

Fifty-five years ago. And frankly nothing has changed in basic tactics. Max Immelmann of Feldfliegerabteilung 62 in his 80-mile-an-hour Fokker is our spiritual father. His weapons were primitive. One machine gun and no ailerons, no vertical fin, no stabilizer. But he had dash and imagination. No parachute but he felt everything through his backside. Today Americans and British let the plane fly itself. As for the Russians, all their battles are won by artillery. But the last battle will be won by fighters who fly."

"Were you born in Germany?"

"No," said the muffled voice. "Poland."

"Why do you pick the German Immelmann?"

"He was a real airman. God knows I could pretend otherwise. My father and my mother were doctors and the Germans killed them. I cannot connect these things though. Even myself, a graduate from Auschwitz."

"No resentment?"

"Against any world that obliges me to waste this life fighting, yes, of course I have resentment. My parents, may they rest in peace, left nothing but me. I could have been a great surgeon perhaps. Or a philosopher. Out of all the generations I am left to instruct young puppies, 'Go in so close for the kill that your wings come out the other side black from the enemy's explosion.' "

Elephant Moses stopped.

S had become absorbed in measuring the jet's rate of turn by using a building below as a point of reference.

The brown landscape revolved under the wingtip.

"Why do you circle here?"

"It's the edge of Gaza. . . ." S began.

"And you look for the place where Samson pulled down the temple and destroyed everyone?"

"Is *that* where it happened?"

Elephant Moses grunted.

On the way back he said, "Forgive me for talking about myself."

"I'd like to hear more."

"Remember what Nietzsche wrote? If you fight too long against dragons, you become a dragon yourself?"

Much later they sat in the dining hall used by pilots and class instructors. A very old man served their table. He wore white overalls and a small white cap, and his gray beard flowed grandly like the thick roots of a gnarled tree. He pressed a menu of eggplant and roast beef on the stranger, fresh vegetables, new small potatoes, fragrant spices. It was a pleasure to see, said he, someone from outside. He wished S a good appetite, blessings upon his house. . . . And what did the stranger think were Israel's chances of survival?

Elephant Moses said to S, "You *were* thinking about Samson as we drifted between Ashkelon and Gaza?"

"Really, I wasn't. But since you bring it up . . . Would Israel pull down the temple?"

"If we had to, yes."

Suddenly, again, S felt a chasm between himself and the men who had arrived at this table by so many strange routes. Here was Colonel Jon, late and rushed, a bearded uncle who treated the students as children. Near him, a wiry little figure with a burned face: once a Mosquito pilot, part-time librarian, insisting his books must include modern novels, Marx, Lenin, and the works of the philosophers. The chief supply officer: a wizard at improvising new tools or finding substitutes for costly foreign-made equipment, who had outfitted the stranger and observed wryly, "Don't worry if none of the flying overalls fit—this air force has more tailors than airplanes." These were all dedicated men, without the grim humorlessness of an elite or the obsessive professionalism of career officers. None of them wore medals because medals had no place in their tradition. Doubtless most of them, in Immelmann's company, would jingle with Knight's Crosses of the Iron Cross or a Deutsches Kreuz in gold. With such chunks of metal and colored ribbons other men bolstered their courage and paraded their prowess. Here nobody talked big. Just once in a while, there came an echo of that remark by General Tal: "To save my children I am ready to destroy the world."

S stirred his coffee. "I've just remembered the second part of that thing by Nietzsche," he said to Elephant Moses. "If thou gaze too long into the abyss, the abyss will gaze into thee."

The old man from the kitchen cocked his head.

Colonel Jon spread his arms on the table. "We're not quite so desperate. Remember the story of the scorpion who begged a ride across the Suez Canal on the back of a camel. The camel said, 'How do I know you won't sting me along the way?' The scorpion said, 'If I sting you, we both drown.' So the camel saw the logic of this, and began to swim across the Canal with the scorpion on his back. Halfway over, the scorpion stung him. Just before they drowned, the camel said, 'Why would you do a stupid thing like that?' And the scorpion replied, 'This is the Middle East, stupid.'"

There was a roar of laughter around the table.

The old man from the kitchen leaned over the back of the commander's chair. "Two thousand years we wandered over the face of the earth and the only thing that sustained us was our faith. Don't you think we should be hard as rock now?" He clenched his fist, looking as fierce and old as an olive tree. "Yet I will tell you something. We do not cook or heat food on the Sabbath and God knows how many of our forefathers died for obeying this law. Still we are a practical people. We have more sense than either the scorpion or the camel." He patted S, the stranger, on the shoulder. "We do not send out boys on the Sabbath to fight at 60,000 feet on a cold boiled egg. . . ."

7

A PIECE OF CAKE

FOR YESNOV

A distant radio played "The whole world is against us/ But we don't give a damn," the words evaporating in the noonday sands.

The partition at Major Zee's elbow slid open. The colonel's face in the hatch was that of a gray-haired schoolboy: plump cheeks with tiny scars instead of dimples; a snub nose scorched by sun and bracketed by deep lines; china-blue eyes in pockets of fatigue.

Major Zee jerked his combat boots off the desk.

"Sorry to wake you," said his baby-faced commander.

"No problem." Zee brushed aside the apology along with the sand under a plastic model of the squadron's insignia: a Super-Hornet helicopter surrealistically imposed on the Hebrew letter approximating S, the whole design thrusting like a dagger.

"The old man's calling an inquest on today's op."

"Now?"

"Well . . . Certainly before he takes tea with Golda."

"Security Committee?"

"Could be." The colonel hesitated. "Yesnov's bought it."

Major Zee's chair swung upright. "Dead?"

"He ejected. Someone saw him take cover but he seemed hurt."

"Name of thunder!" Zee rubbed his face. "I used to date his sister Ruthi. We're from the same kibbutz."

"I know. The irony—" The colonel shrugged. "We yanked him off leave early this morning. Now he's back just a few miles from home but on the wrong side."

"So he's in the Golan. What the hell happened?"

"He spotted a guerrilla formation, photographed it, and was Air Controller for the first attack. Then the Syrians moved tanks and troops at about 1100 hours and the fighting's spread. Yesnov couldn't direct anyone to the gun that started the trouble and between waves he went down and bombed it himself. He was hit by a new kind of missile."

"Russian?"

"It's possible. Aaron intercepted one of their spy-planes over Tel Aviv and two MiGs were on his tail. One of our patrols was challenged near Port Said by a Russian flight of twenty-ones."

"You think the balloon's going up?"

"Has it ever been down?"

"I'd like to get Yesnov out."

"I thought you might. I'll get you Doctor Golden."

Thus began the role Major Zee would play on the day marked X in Jacob's diary. Outside the fiberboard walls of his office the radio still played: ". . . All those who are against us/ Can go to hell."

Doctor Golden was much admired by his lady patients as a cuddlesome old teddy bear. He was a furry blond with button-bright eyes. He moved with the economy of a large man. He said little. Rescue-pilots liked to take him on helicopter missions because he was fast and unflappable, handled a gun with the steadiness of a surgeon, and improvised a repair-job as handily as he applied a tourniquet. He used to fly Mustangs, Me-109s, and Spitfires.

On this day Doctor Golden was driving through honking lunchtime traffic between pizza parlors and ice-cream shops, bookstores and sidewalk cafés, apartment blocks and hotels that line four miles of the Mediterranean shore. With him was an air-force colonel in mufti. They were trying to reach an airbase beyond the marshes north of the Yarkon River. If military planes rose out of the base in accordance with normal procedures, there would be times when their flight pattern would take them over the Hilton and Sheraton hotels. But discipline and discretion are such that few tourists even know the base exists.

The colonel, a few minutes earlier, had run from the Citadel to Doctor Golden's clinic and explained that a young Skyhawk pilot named Yesnov was down behind Arab lines. Doctor Golden had visited the few pilots who were returned after being captured alive. So he was not the least bit sorry to have canceled all his appointments, although his stomach tightened (as it always did) at the thought of another run into territory where a prisoner may be tortured.

"There's fighter cover," said the colonel. "But the whole front's blown up in the last hour. The Egyptians started a major artillery barrage along the Canal which seems to be synchronized. Anyway you've got Zee. . . ."

"Good, good."

"And of course Yesnov has priority."

"Of course," Golden acknowledged. Nevertheless he knew that in the heat of battle an injured boy's priority is reduced by events, not human decisions.

The doctor's white Volkswagen was blocked by an old Citroën angled across his path. The driver of the other car was convinced the doctor bumped his rear fender, and an argument began. Traffic in four directions was stalled while the doctor pointed out the impossibility of the Volkswagen striking the Citroën from this particular position. Finally he showed his driver's license, promised to get in touch, and claimed exemption from any further discussion at this stage because he was a doctor on an urgent case.

"An urgent case of lunch with your mistress," mumbled the other motorist as he walked away. The colonel wanted to get out and punch him, but contented himself instead with a few graceful curses, adding, "This driving from the Citadel to the planes gets crazier."

"It's our craziness that confuses the enemy," said Doctor Golden in his best bedside manner.

The wreckage of Yesnov's Skyhawk was spread down the hillside. Above it circled a French-built Dassault Mirage 3 with a wingman above and astern to keep his tail clear.

The wing leader was a twenty-eight-year-old veteran known as the Confectioner. Like all the pilots, he had studied every foreign publication on aviation and aerial warfare. His special interest was the defense of Malta, that island in the Mediterranean which in 1942 was Britain's "unsinkable aircraft carrier." He regarded Israel as playing much the same role, except that *this* carrier held all his people's hopes and fears. He had been flying since he was eighteen, and with all the wisdom of 3000 hours of combat in ten years, he reminded the newcomers that "there are old pilots and bold pilots, but no old-bold pilots." It was a piece of advice he'd borrowed from the defenders of Malta. Another of his favorite quotations was "It's a piece of cake," meaning that an operation was unlikely to be any tougher than apple pie. If this seemed to contradict his cautionary advice, it was because he lived in an atmosphere where "bold" was a relative term. What an average citizen might regard as dangerous, he took to be routine. This was pure habit of mind. He had lived in the wartime atmosphere of the airbases throughout that decade in a man's life when adolescence has ended and maturity unfolds, when the course is set and ambitions fixed upon. He had astonished S once by stating that in seven years' military flying he'd taken only one month of unbroken leave, and the weapon which he knew as intimately as an insurance salesman knows his own car was the Mirage.

When S had flown a Mirage, in another place and at a time that now seemed so long ago, to try to get some inkling of the minds of the men who fought with them daily, it was the French 3CJ training version supplied to the Royal Australian Air Force. He got an impression of a gigantic jet engine on which the wings had yet to be attached. This was because the Mirage's delta wing has a 60-degree sweepback. On the ground, this dartlike wing simply lacks any visible contours. It filled S with the most profound misgivings. He got into the rear cockpit and was warned not to grope around with his left hand while sorting out the levers and switches. If his left hand hit the wrong tit, he stood a sporting chance of disembarking vertically with a 20-times-the-force-of-gravity bang in the ejector seat. It was a sobering start to the test run of a plane that more than any other, is associated with Israel's survival in the 1960s. (According to *Jane's All the World's Aircraft*, France sold 72 Mirage 3s to Israel in 1963. By 1970, the number was down to 60, including replacements, according to Washington reports.)

On the runway, S opened to maximum dry power and released the brakes. He gave the bird full reheat and the airspeed shot up to 130 miles per hour. He rotated to 10 degrees nose high. By the time he'd lifted the gear, reduced to maximum dry thrust, and let the speed build up to 400 mph, the Mirage was already above 20,000 feet. Near the speed of sound, S lifted the throttle for medium reheat. There was a slight change in engine note, the altimeter needle twitched, the Machmeter read 1.0, and S was flying supersonically at 45,000 feet, which is well above dogfighting levels.

The flight gave S some notion of the weapon that Israelis feel they developed into one of the most effective combat planes for its time. He found that control effectiveness is reduced above Mach 1 when he turned into a steady 45-degree bank without altering his throttle setting. The speed decayed slowly until it became subsonic, as happens in a maneuver. Immediately below sonic speed, the elevons became fully effective again and the turn tightened up without any control movement by S. This, and other differences in performance, helped S to understand and check the Confectioner's later accounts of dogfights. He found it impossible to stall because delta-wings suffer a slow decay of speed instead of the abrupt drop of conventional aircraft. He found too that the speed at which level flight could be maintained with a 10-degree nose-up attitude, without reheat, was 190 knots (a knot is a unit of speed equal to one nautical mile or 1.15 miles per hour) at that particular height.

Such technicalities are vital, of course, to fighting a thoroughbred like the Mirage. When S flew at low speed, the delta-winged aircraft was well on the back side of the drag curve. For precise control of the aircraft in these conditions, S discovered that it was best to make small movements of the throttle and keep altitude or adjust the descent gradient with the control column. The technique was not unlike landing aboard an aircraft carrier and S brought the Mirage down at an approach speed of 190 knots with the nose 7 degrees up to obtain the required 3 degrees downward flight path. When the Confectioner told S that landing the Mirage at night was difficult, S appreciated what he meant. The high angle of attack puts the pilot "in the land of the blind," as the Confectioner described it, "where the one-eyed fool is king."

Measured against the MiG-17s supplied to the Arabs, the Mirage has certain advantages. "I'd say the Mirage behaves much as the American F4U-Corsair did against the Japanese Zero," said the Confectioner.

He was a small-boned man who talked with S in the aircrew reading room at a fighter base. He wore his anti-G suit, the customary knife strapped to his leg, the coveralls unzipped to his waist because of the heat. He had the pallor of men who spend most of their time in the cockpit with the canopy sealed. He looked very young. His hands were very fine, the fingers long and as delicate as a musician's.

After one conversation, which turned into a kind of debriefing, it dawned upon S that the Confectioner must be one of the world's top killers of MiG-21s and -17s. "I suppose you're right," said the Confectioner, the color creeping into his thin cheeks. Just after this, an extremely pretty girl joined them. It was raining hard outside and the Confectioner asked S if he would mind giving the girl a ride into Tel Aviv. Then, even more diffidently, he requested a lift for himself to the base. He was very apologetic but he didn't feel like running through the rain. His pay as a major was 1200 Israeli pounds a month (roughly the equivalent of $80 a week in the United States). Half of this sum was deducted for income tax, to the extent that he couldn't afford his own car. Later, the girl admitted to being the Confectioner's younger sister. But her conversation was very guarded and she would not let S drop her at their parents' home. It was the automatic protectiveness of a girl for someone she loved dearly. She knew what had happened to other pilots in Arab hands and did not want her brother to be identified, even by accident. This concern for each other's safety, of course, is and always had been Israel's great strength. It is almost as if everyone thinks on two different levels. There is a level of concern with national security, which means the security of each other, and is therefore apt to seem secretive to the stranger; and the other level is one of spontaneous friendliness in which visitors are often surprised by the frankness of speech that is perhaps a compensation for the enforced silence on other matters.

Another time, when the Confectioner explained his nickname (it came from this habit of describing a fight as "a piece of cake") the reading room was packed with men watching a television set, wired through the chimney of the open hearth. There was a large fishtank along one wall (most bases kept aquariums,

which were said to have a restful effect, although the crews were
more interested in breeding tropical fish for export). The Confectioner took S into the canteen, beyond television's range, and
said, "*The Forsyte Saga* keeps everyone out of circulation for an
hour every Friday night." So while the men watched the latest
segment in the BBC version of John Galsworthy's novels, the
Confectioner talked about dogfighting.

"The Russians' MiG-17 is rugged and takes a lot of punishment.
I've hit a -17 in the wing-root and it still didn't explode. But a
MiG-21 will blow up in your face. The trouble for them and us,
in any big encounter, is that in a straight chase at the usual combat height of 30,000 feet, both jets are about evenly matched. So
if I'm chasing a -21 and he won't turn and fight, I can't overtake
him straight and level.

"It's wrong to think we're flying guerrillas, although I understand what you mean. We are unorthodox, yes. But the Mirage is
a sophisticated aircraft and you don't just stick chewing gum on
the windshield and aim that way. I agree we have simplified,
and there's a lot of improvisation all the time. The dogfights have
developed their own characteristics too. For instance, two of us
got into a fight with four of theirs. So two more of ours joined in,
and then four of theirs. Pretty soon the sky is crowded. When
I've been evaluating aircraft in the United States, I've tried to
explain why we want cannons installed instead of missiles. It's
because these are very tight dogfights and you can be sure of a
kill with a cannon. But the Americans find it hard to imagine—
they think we're living back in the days of Billy Bishop and Max
Immelmann."

After some prodding, the Confectioner recounted some typical
dogfights. He was not being mock-modest. He had gone over the
details of each battle with other pilots at the big "inquests" when
performance is examined in the cold mood of postcombat *tris-
tesse.* These inquests are very thorough, and some battle may
be re-examined several times so that lessons can be learned and

tactics developed for new emergencies. It is difficult to describe all over again a battle that you have already put under the experts' microscope. As the Confectioner said, "When you've dissected a cadaver for your fellow physicians, the corpse is already very cold indeed."

The *MiG-versus-Mirage* dramatization of Middle East aerial combat is a simplification that the French would like to encourage because Israel's experience has been good for the sale of Mirages to Israel's enemies. (The Mirage was the brainchild of Marcel Dassault. His factories earn for France many millions of dollars in the production of later versions of the Mirage.) Nevertheless most of the Confectioner's fights did involve MiGs against Mirages.

"We became the proving ground for new combat planes. My first encounter was with a MiG-21 over a Syrian base which we'd already bombed on the first day of the 1967 war. I cleaned my underside but one of the reserve tanks stuck and I went into a bad sideslip as I attacked. My first burst of cannonfire missed except for a couple of bullets in his right wing. Then I saw I wasn't properly coordinated. The -21 got away so I turned on his wingman. Again I missed although the range was okay, speed 500 knots, altitude low. He'd gone into a turn, though, and I got a second chance at 400 meters. Then I overshot him and saw the pilot was dead at the controls.

"There's a lot of nonsense about secret weapons. Look, on the first of the Six Days, our mission was to destroy the Arab air forces on the ground. It's elementary. Knock out the enemy's air power by catching it asleep. Observers said later we must have had a secret device to get such accurate results. We'd practiced and practiced low-level attacks and we knew where to put the bullets. If aerial photographs later showed every MiG bursting at the same point, it's because that's the point where the fuel tank is—yes? We didn't claim victories for planes destroyed on the ground and we don't claim now for any plane that isn't seen to crash. But we do claim a victory if we maneuver an enemy plane into the ground. That's a special technique and someone else should explain it—not me.

"Dogfights vary a great deal in time. Some are over in two minutes. I remember once though where everyone got into the scrap and it drifted over the Nile Delta and far inside Egyptian territory. You learn a lot from these battles. For example, never stick on a target for long. There's too much risk of someone getting onto your own tail. Some fights begin with both sides approaching each other at two or two and a half times the speed of sound. I prefer fighting at top speed.

"You become what you'd call a cool cat after long enough. But in the first battles I made some bad mistakes. . . .

"Lately we've had excellent interceptions under ground-control guidance. I was vectored onto four MiG-21s on their side of the Canal. I launched a missile. (I should say the early generation of missiles, in 1967, were for bombers flying straight and level. Even today a missile's really only hundred-per-cent sure if you sit on your opponent's tail at some enormous distance. I like to get in close and make absolutely sure with the 30-mm's.) Anyway this missile was a good one. It went straight for the target and hit him behind and slightly to one side. There was no fire but big pieces flew out. His formation was breaking left and up, and he was going down and right. I got behind another and then I saw my wingman slide past. He'd overshot on his first pass and now he'd got a MiG on *his* tail. We were all traveling very fast and I had to make a quick decision because one of the MiGs had crossed into the Israeli sector. He saw me and turned into me, so we passed head on.

"It was turning into a circus. More and more from both sides kept joining in. We were ten to fifteen miles north and west of Ismalya, and as the battle progressed, conditions became excellent for dogfighting—low altitude, high G-forces, and high speed. Four of ours fell in this fight and eight of theirs. No, I don't think we make mistakes in tallies because don't forget all this is watched on radar and we've developed a technique for cross-questioning and rechecking which is very thorough. Sometimes, as in this battle, you have to give the victory to someone else. I'd got on the tail of a -21 but held fire until I closed the range to a thousand feet, which was dangerously close and stupid anyway because my friend shot him down from farther behind.

"That sounds like bad discipline. It wasn't really. Some dogfights just grow and suddenly we're like wasps around a jampot. The most important thing for me is to have a wingman who'll keep my tail clean.

"We fight in pairs and the leader is still the gun and the wingman his eye. . . .

"I've done some foolish things. But since '67, we've all learned a lot. We *do* improvise a lot, even in using the gunsights. I'm familiar with the arguments between the missile-shooters and the gunmen. But here we try to stick to basic principles of air fighting so if anything goes wrong, we're not victims of the machinery.

"An example? Well, if you go by the book with a computerized gunsight you stick the radar diamonds (reflected on the windscreen) onto your target. Now that's okay if the enemy doesn't see you or is lazy, or is at too slow a speed to go into a really violent turn. But if he takes violent evasive action, then we improvise.

"In battle the fuel flow is horrible. It's like opening the floodgates. So you've got to worry all the time about how much fuel you've got left."

What impressed S about such discussions with the Confectioner was his professional detachment. There was also a curious echo of the past. The Confectioner sounded like all the great fighter aces from Oswald Boelcke to Marshal of the RAF Viscount Trenchard and Major General O. P. "Opee" Weyland, who directed USAF operations against the earlier MiGs in Korea. Furthermore, the Confectioner knew about such men in detail.

"The most effective defense is to use fighters offensively, just as Weyland and Trenchard used to argue. For us, this has meant sweeps into Arab airspace. I can't talk about range, but you know very well how the American Sabers in Korea found that a combat of eight minutes was about all they could afford if they were to return home from a dogfight deep inside Korea's Communist airspace. They found that high stick forces made aiming the gunsight so difficult that the average pilot could get only one good burst of fire.

"There's nothing the Russians would like better now than to push us onto the defensive, and make it seem like an Arab accomplishment. Whatever they think up, we'll find an answer. But there are two things always to remember. First, the Americans in World War II and in Korea always kept on the attack and pushed their long-range fighters as far from home base as possible to contain the much larger enemy forces. It was Lord Trenchard's dictum for the RAF and it goes right back to the first air engagement, where an aircraft looked for a fight and conducted it according to plan. I'm talking about Boelcke in July 1915. Perhaps it seems strange, fifty-five years later, to draw lessons. Yet if you think about it, the air is an element very recently entered by man and everything that has happened in this half-century represents all the accumulated wisdom of aerial warfare. There's nothing like this in naval or military experience.

"This is why, when you say Israel is working out new forms of air warfare, I say yes and no. Yes, because all forms of air warfare are relatively new and so we cannot help adding to human experience. No, because Boelcke in the world's first recorded air battle shows us all the basic ingredients of dogfighting or any other kind of aerial conflict. He won because he used his keen eyesight, his skill, and his patience. He spotted his target before the pilot saw him. He had the skill to lure the Frenchman into a poor tactical position. He was patient in the long stalk that made the fight possible. In the fight itself he kept the upper hand, even though his own biplane was awkward and inferior, by maneuvering with greater skill. He kept a sharp lookout for other enemy planes during the entire fight and he pressed home the attack until his enemy was exhausted.

"What is the biggest challenge to our ingenuity now? To prevent the Russians from constructing a shield over the Arabs which will enable ground forces to destroy our homes and withdraw into the sanctuary of Russian air defense. And that means we must keep up the offensive, whatever our critics abroad may think. We haven't any way to explain our strategy to a world that won't listen. So we choose survival and to hell with what the world thinks."

Put down in cold print, this may convey a sense of arrogance. S, however, with his own memories of the peculiar *élan* that characterizes all fighter pilots, saw in the Confectioner certain other qualities. There was the genuine shyness in requesting a lift for his sister and a ride for himself in the pouring rain. There was also the remoteness of men who live a strange life, alternating between periods of intense excitement in the air and spells on the ground when they become normal human beings and have to conform to the routine of family life. There was the added burden that such men could not communicate with their wives or friends any of their feelings aloft. A rigid system of security, all the more effective because throughout the Israeli Defense Forces it is applied by the youngsters themselves, meant that the Confectioner had to split himself into two people. Once in the air, such men have always had the gift of becoming part of their fighters.

On one occasion, the Confectioner told S that he never discussed his missions with his wife. "She knows when something is about to happen because she senses it. But she never questions me and I never tell her."

S asked the wife how she could live with this. "He's an extension of myself," she said without pretension.

She was diffident about discussing her husband's profession. Later, when confidence had been established, she told S, "We become so accustomed to restraining ourselves. It's a tremendous relief to talk with someone from outside. We can't open our hearts to our mothers or friends outside."

She was an attractive girl of twenty-three, with two small children, and she seemed to accept the stranger, S, until he was reminded of the underlying guardedness when she said, as he left her villa, "Are you on our side?"

The question illuminated a large area of what had been the encompassing darkness of the stranger's relations with the airmen and their families. They live on the razor's edge. Experience has taught them to question the motives of self-proclaimed friends. Their self-censorship, even in everyday contacts, is puzzling and frequently has the effect of a sharp rebuff. Again and again, S was to hear stories from foreign observers—especially United Nations' officers—about the way their good will began to sour because of Israeli secretiveness.

Thus a wrong impression has been given abroad. The Director of Information and Research of the Scottish Conservative Central Office in Edinburgh, Ian McIntyre, made this comment in a BBC broadcast:

I encountered none of the aggressiveness that one often hears ascribed to the Israelis. There is pride, certainly, but words like "cocksure" are wide of the mark. I was told one story about a flying-school cadet who asked the air-force commander, "You teach us how to be good pilots but how do we become Jewish pilots?"

The general replied, "Before you leave here you will be sent up alone in a jet. You will climb to ten thousand feet but you will receive orders not to look down. You will climb to twenty thousand feet and then to thirty thousand feet and only then will you be allowed to look down at the earth below. At that height you will observe a clear dividing line. On one side of it you will see sand, scrub and stagnation. On the other, green fields, good roads, and other marks of civilization. That is the point at which you will become a Jewish pilot."

While the Confectioner circled the downed Skyhawk pilot inside Syrian territory, Major Zee clattered around the tall chimney stack just north of Tel Aviv and picked up Doctor Golden. Zee was flying an old Sikorsky-58 helicopter of the type known in the United States Navy as the Sea King. It had been hastily converted from a commando-carrier to perform the task of casualty evacuation in the brief time Major Zee required to get his map coordinates and a quick briefing on the battle raging in the region.

"We may be busy," he told Golden as the doctor squeezed into the seat alongside.

"Anything short of a transplant we seem to be expecting," Golden mumbled. He had seen the litters and the medicine chests left by the orderlies in the cabin. It looked like an operating theater. He watched Zee check instruments, one hand on the cyclic-pitch stick, boots working the yaw pedals.

"Don't you miss *flying*?" he asked as the machine tilted forward and danced out of the small space between hangars.

Major Zee grinned. "I tried to land backward in a Fouga-Magister yesterday. Didn't work."

"What do you expect from a jet-propelled French whore?"

"Some unusual positions." Zee glared at the warning panel and a red light faltered and went out, like a drunk dropping his gaze. They were crossing the Country Club and he cast a speculative eye at the tennis courts below. But the warning light stayed shut and none of the ninety-odd buttons, knobs, controls, and switches seemed to be out of place. He said, "Anyway the French whore's a faster piece than your Czech pig."

Golden folded his hands over his round stomach. "Ach . . ." The Czech pig was a Messerschmidt-109 he'd ferried years ago from Prague. He thought for a moment, searching his memory for a suitable retort. "The helicopter does with great labor only what the balloon does without any labor at all."

"Who said that?"

"Wilbur Wright."

Zee chuckled softly. The sky ahead was dark. It could be battle-smoke blending with the hot day's haze. About eighty miles away, either within that black curtain or beyond it, young Yesnov was waiting. Three years ago, it would have been wise to detour around the artillery of the Jordan Arabs, whose borders at that time came within ten miles of Israel's opposite frontier, the sea. Now, there was no need to run the gantlet. He set a course that would bring him over one corner of the kibbutz where Yesnov and he grew up as children—the village at the foot of the Golan Heights.

8

THE GOLAN DRAGON

"The Golan Heights appeared to me like a dragon all through my boyhood," Major Zee had once told S. "They crouched over us, spitting fire. If you count the total number of shells landing in my kibbutz from the time I started kindergarten to when I joined the air force, you get an average of one explosion a week, which doesn't seem all that much. But when you can't predict the position or the timing of the explosion, and when you live with this uncertainty all through your schooldays, you develop a certain attitude. . . ."

This escarpment rising a thousand feet above the Upper Jordan Valley had been sewn with dragon's teeth by 1967. The Syrian Army dominated the valley with guns. The steep cliffs rose to a plateau that stretched eastward to Damascus and beyond. The plateau was fortified to a depth of ten miles with a continuous zone of wire, minefields, trenches, gun emplacements, pillboxes, and tanks.

This is how the Institute for Strategic Studies described it in the *Adelphi Papers Number Forty-One:* "Constructed under Russian direction, it was a masterpiece of defensive fortification and suitably equipped with artillery, machineguns, anti-aircraft batteries and rocket launchers. Viewing the ground afterwards, it seemed impossible that any army in the world could have taken it, except by a campaign lasting for weeks."

The Golan had assumed a great strategic as well as symbolic importance by mid-1970, in much the same way that the Suez Canal came to represent a vital defense role in Israeli minds. The Canal was the grander concept: a line across which the Egyptians must never again be permitted to move aggressively. But the Golan was something more intimate: here the Arabs vented their hatred against simple farmers and their wives and children.

"When I was told to go to my own kibbutz and pick up paratroops to storm the Golan," Major Zee told S, "I was stunned. It was the fifth day of the 1967 war, I think. By then I was punch-drunk with flying day and night in the few helicopters we had at that time. Everything was a dream. Still, even in my wildest dreams, I never thought a time would come when we could kill the Golan dragon."

Major Zee was twenty-seven at the time, and his wife's pregnancy had reached its full term. She was walking through the center of the kibbutz, in what people called the village square, when her husband's helicopter fluttered down between the eucalyptus trees.

She had no means of identifying the chopper but she was certain he was flying it.

He told S, "The paratroops hadn't arrived and I was perched up in the cockpit feeling scared because we'd lost a lot of men already. The Syrians were banging away and everyone was supposed to be in the shelters. Then I saw my wife. I climbed down and went to her. She said, 'I think the baby's due.' Then the paratroops arrived and she said, 'I'll have the baby when you come back.'"

During the rest of that day, she counted the helicopters flying into the fighting zone above the cider-apple orchards and she checked the number that came out again. The Israeli General

"Dadu" Elazar struck at eleven thirty a.m. on Friday, June 9, and it took three hours and seven hundred casualties to reach the crest. The following evening at nine o'clock, Major Zee returned to find his wife.

"At nine thirty she said, 'Take me to the hospital.' I got a jeep and drove her there just in time. I don't know how you explain these things. Perhaps it was the shock of seeing me with a beard and matted hair that stopped her giving birth earlier. I'm not a religious man. Nevertheless I thank God that the little boy who ran from the Golan guns grew into the man who did something about those same guns. And I'm glad that the gift of a child came in such a way. 'Hod doesn't give us medals but God gave me a son' is what my wife says."

Among many anxieties that weighed on the Security Committee in mid-1970 was the rearming of the Syrians and their urge to regain the Golan Heights by military action. The tactical use of helicopters in 1967 had made it possible to land troops and capture positions along a line roughly parallel to the old frontier but twelve miles inside Syria.

"The map would look different if it wasn't for the helicopters," one squadron commander told S. "Our machines were regarded as insects before 1967. Afterward, we were able to expand and now it's impossible to imagine war without them."

For the settlers at the foot of the Golan Heights, it was equally impossible to consider a return to the situation that had existed for nineteen years: domination by Syrian forts along the ridge running north from the Sea of Galilee, and persistent shelling.

"All of the Golan Heights is about two per cent of Syrian territory," Major Zee had pointed out. "The territory is absolutely meaningless to them but it's life or death to us. Yet I don't know anyone in the settlements who would oppose some agreement which would let them reoccupy the land *provided there was a watertight guarantee of no more shelling*. But whom can we deal with? When you talk about Syria you talk about whatever group is in control. You know, the evidence has been placed before the whole world that three years ago, Russian-built artillery was directed by Russian advisers. Their artillery charts, which we captured, pinpointed every single one of our settlements. We recorded one woman Soviet adviser losing her temper on the radio when the gunners were off-target. 'No, damn you! Bad, very bad!' Yet nobody in the West protests against Russian terrorism or all the years of shooting at our children. The protests only begin when we hit back."

Major Zee was similar in character to the Confectioner, the Mirage pilot. They were both trained to go looking for a fight, and yet neither man had the chin-out attitude of a brawler.

"I went back to farming for two years," said Major Zee. "But when you cut corn with a combine your speed is four kilometers an hour. I'd got used to something a hundred times as fast. When you sow seeds, you wait for them to sprout. I'd become accustomed to faster results. Like everyone, I flew fighters and at flying-school you just might as well forget about getting to be a pilot unless you were good at dogfighting. I could go back, of course, to fighters. But heliborne operations have become highly specialized.

"The chopper pilot is really a lone wolf. You have to fly low, fly at night as much as possible, fly always with the knowledge that if the enemy sees you, you're nothing else but a fat tank passing through the air. It takes two years to make a good helicopter ship's commander."

When he talked to the stranger, Major Zee would lean forward, his bare arms folded, his eyes fixed intently on him. He gave the impression of controlled tension. If an alarm sounded, he moved with disconcerting speed. None of his movements was made without calculation. He might have been mistaken for the prototype of a modern mechanical man except for the swiftness with which he picked up ideas outside the field of professional discussion. At one stage, for instance, he was explaining that as a youth he had been a Marxist. He shrugged. "George Bernard Shaw, I think, said if you were not a Communist at seventeen—you had no heart. If you were a Communist at forty—you had no brains.

"Our first combat formations of helicopters go back to the 1956 war. We had very few then, of course. I began piloting choppers—when? In 1963. I've put in about three thousand hours on them.

"A lone wolf? Well, because I have to land alone in terrain I've never seen before, perhaps in the night. I have to make my own calculations about wind and obstacles. I go on rescue missions. One area that sees a lot of me is around the Dead Sea. Beautiful canyons where you can get landslips and men get injured. The only way to get an injured man out is with a hoist, and flying inside a canyon at night can be pretty hard. You're cut off from the Center's radio at the bottom of a canyon and nobody hears you.

"I'm sorry. I talk about *me*. It's the difficulty of language. I mean, this is true for any helicopter pilot. Most of his time is spent flying, trying to find the limits of his experience. He spends his spare time studying foreign textbooks, working out new ways to use the machine.

"The weak link in any helicopter force is the pilot. Really. The machine can do almost anything. I feel as much a part of the helicopter as I used to feel when I was a boy driving a tractor with a special shield of armor-plating against shrapnel.

"I don't think we're overworked. I've had five days' leave since the 1967 war. But what would I do with longer vacations? Now, I can go with my wife and babies to our kibbutz at Friday lunchtime. I take some sleep at my parents' house. Then relatives come. I have a brother who is with the paratroops (another one I lost in Syria). We have tea at five o'clock. We exchange gossip.

"You know what we did last Friday night? We have a book-reading club. My wife read extracts from Balzac and the rest had to guess the author, and the name of the book.

"No, I don't manage this every week or even once a month.

But it's nice when we can do it. I'm back at the base the next evening. I feel as if I've been away a month and I'm already anxious and looking for work.

"This sounds funny, but the best thing about going to the kibbutz, for me, is lending a hand harvesting, picking fruit, working in the kitchens. It gives you physical contact with others, and with nature. Also it makes you feel *reassured*."

This last remark was a surprise. A few weeks earlier, S had flown back to Tel Aviv with the relatives of newly graduated pilots. In the plane was Gila Almagor, one of Israel's outstanding actresses. She said, commenting on the flying display, "I like to go because when I see these boys all my fears vanish and I feel reassured."

S mentioned this to Major Zee, who laughed and said, "If you have one leg and I have one leg, we lean against each other. I suppose that's Israel."

The Confectioner's wingman yelled, "Break, you damn fool! Break!"

His leader pulled the stick into his stomach as the Syrian MiG swept past.

"Did you see . . . ?" asked the Confectioner, rejoining his Number Two.

"Yes."

No further conversation was needed. The MiG had made his single pass and moved on. What both Mirage pilots had recognized was the model: a MiG-21J, the most advanced interceptor in the series.

The Confectioner searched the sky hungrily. He had flight-tested a MiG-21C captured from the Egyptians. (It had been talked down by an Arabic-speaking flight controller.) Even the -21C proved more maneuverable than the Mirage and the Phantom, and the later -21J model was, in addition, supersonic at sea level. So far as anyone knew, only Soviet pilots were flying the

-21Js and used them only on defense missions. So what was this one doing over the Golan?

Perhaps the Syrians were flying them? There was one way to find out.

The Confectioner spoke rapidly to his wingman and the Center. Although the language was Hebrew, it was made more difficult for eavesdroppers by the use of code words.

Back at headquarters the intelligence section went to work.

In the air, the Confectioner dropped away from his wingman. He leveled out at 5000 feet and circled. His Mirage, in its present air-superiority configuration, carried two 30-mm cannons, a Matra-530 missile, and two Sidewinders. Somewhere unseen lurked the MiG-21J with an external 23-mm gun in a centerline pod, and two Atoll infrared guided air-to-air missiles.

The trick was to convince the MiG pilot that the Mirage was a sitting duck. In a sense it was.

In the Citadel they located Captain Naomi. She listened to the piped tape of a conversation between the MiG-21J pilot and Damascus. "Yes, he's Russian." She translated the recorded exchange and then asked, "Why?" She knew there were others as fluent in Russian as she was.

"Because among the Russian controllers in Damascus there's a woman," came the reply.

The Center intercepted Jacob on his way by car to Jerusalem. His talk with the Instrument Basher had been profitable and his mind was still on nothing more exotic than the hook under the tail of a shipborne plane.

"We've got a new mark of Fishbed in the net," said the man at the Center.

"New?" Jacob stared straight ahead, the radiophone hard against his ear. For weeks he had predicted that Russian pilots would not be committed to combat until the latest interceptors were assigned to Egypt.

"A MiG-21J. We're playing with him, now. Motti wants to have your estimate. Do we try to talk him down?"

"Who's flying it—a Russian?"

"Affirmative."

"Has anyone engaged him?"

"The Confectioner's trailing his coat."

"Try talking him down," said Jacob. "If that's not possible, tell the Confectioner to destroy him *without using guns or missiles.*"

Motti would weigh the advice along with that of others. But in the case of a hung jury, Jacob's opinion would tip the balance. He wanted the Russian intact if possible. If not, there were ways to maneuver him to the ground. Jacob was the man with all the facts in his possession: the Arab military state of readiness, the changing day-by-day Russian commitments, the political strengths and weaknesses of each separate Arab leader, the latest reports from Moscow on Soviet manipulation of Nasser. Driving in the stinking wake of a diesel-powered *sherut,* the kind of collectively hired hearse-like taxi that always seemed to be steered by tank-corps reservists, Jacob let the new information float around his mind. He was convinced that Soviet air chiefs were pawns in a much larger game of psychological warfare. If he was right, Russian pilots would avoid any clash that resulted in news stories reflecting badly on Soviet intervention. Their war aims were pitched further ahead than that. Somehow they'd have to be made to consider the risk of nuclear war. Already the mood in Israel was that of the Zealots at Masada whose fall two thousand years ago ended Jewish independence until Israel's birth. The ultimate battle could end in nuclear catastrophe. The warning was clear in this year's edition of *Jane's All the World's Aircraft*: "It is suggested that Israel will have suitable warheads of its own design produced in the Dimona reactor and nuclear centre near the Dead Sea."

Well, let the foreign experts keep guessing. And let the Russians understand there would no meek submission to force. Jacob accelerated past the *sherut*, ignoring the anguished cries of other motorists. No wonder foreigners mistook the word for *cheroot*. That's what the ugly monsters looked like—long, black, stinking cigars. He'd have to talk to Ezer about the pollution these taxis caused. His mind wandered back to a more practical and immediate question.

Someone had suggested to the Instrument Basher that a pilot could be snatched out of the air when he was forced to bail out. The idea came from an airframe mechanic whose cousin had parachuted into the Arab lines and never survived. A pilot would release a balloon attached to the top of his chute canopy. Then a burner at the balloon's mouth would ignite, fed by a tank of propane strapped to the pilot's back.

"Is it possible?" Jacob asked.

"Some of the lads experimented," said the Instrument Basher. "They reckon the balloon could hold a pilot at 5000 feet, out of range of ground fire, for maybe twenty minutes or more. Then if we adapted a tail-hook like the Phantom's, the bloke on the end of the parachute could be towed into our own airspace."

The Center reached Major Zee as he took the helicopter across the flat calm of the Sea of Galilee.

"They want us to wait on Pad Four," he told Doctor Golden, naming a strip near his own kibbutz. "We'll drop in. . . ."

"*Drop?* Land me like a gentleman. A tourist attraction I'm not."

Zee grinned, sweeping around the big settlement of Ein Gev, internationally famous for its music festivals and at this time of year a center of tourism. Pad Four would avoid the foreign hordes.

He passed under the crest on the Golan escarpment where recent diggings had unearthed more of the city of Hippos among the Byzantine and Roman ruins. All this region, right to the 1967 border with Syria, had blossomed in the past eight decades. Acres of fields neatly cultivated. A network of detachable pipes sprinkled water on corn and cotton. And for soldiers who must march in the shade, there were roads lined with tamarisk and carob, the Aleppo pine and eucalyptus. He found a grove and saw the sheep scatter as he made his descent.

The Confectioner's wingman spotted the two Sukhoi Su-7B ground-attack fighters coming from twelve-o'clock high. He shouted a warning and the two Mirages turned to meet the new threat.

Both the Su-7Bs barreled on down. They were the standard Russian "Fitter" class of about the same vintage as the Mirage. They swept low across the hill where Yesnov's Skyhawk littered the slopes. Puffs of smoke marked the passage of rockets. The two intruders pulled up into steep chandelles, seemingly without spotting either the Confectioner at 5000 feet or his wingman "sitting on the balcony" at ten.

The Confectioner went onto afterburner and rolled onto the the first Su-7B's tail as it began another diving attack. He glimpsed his wingman pulling into a similar 180-degree turn onto the second Russian-built jet. The thought flashed through his mind that these were Syrian pilots. Their procedure was bad, for one thing. And they seemed unaware of the Russian radio chatter between Damascus and the unseen MiG.

The Confectioner's quarry must have seen the Mirage moving into range behind. He broke hard to starboard, leveled out, and turned in to meet the attack. Like the Israeli, he carried 30-mm cannon. Describing such an encounter to S, the Confectioner had told him, "The Su-7 in its strike role moves at about a thousand miles an hour at 36,000 feet. Fighting at low altitude, it has very good maneuverability. If it has cleared its underbelly, it has a tight turn and you have to be careful how you hang on the tail."

This one had disposed of its 500-pound bombs and got in a sharp burst of cannon fire. The Confectioner felt a jolt but nothing showed on instruments, and his controls felt normal. He would guess later that he'd flown into a blindly launched stream of gunfire. Now, thinking in split seconds, he knew he had to get inside the Su-7's turn.

They were down to the level of the hilltops. The Su-7 vanished around a slope and reversed its turn as the Confectioner swept out over the plateau. Experience told the Mirage pilot that the new turning radius was too tight. Brown earth and blue sky changed positions as he flung himself back onto the Su-7's tail. But the G-forces were too high; the enemy pilot was either an ace or a fool. The Confectioner decided he was a fool, relaxed, and gained a little height. He glanced automatically astern. "Don't get carried away. Your tail's clean but you've no wingman to keep it that way." He'd lost his Number Two for the moment and turned his attention back to the Su-7. It seemed to have gone into the kind of desperately tight turn that indicates a panicky pilot. He followed it, keeping his own turn looser, and holding his advantage of height. The moment the enemy pilot stopped hauling on the stick, his wings flashed in the sun and the Confectioner was on him. A puff of black smoke hurtled past the Confectioner's wings in that moment when one senses rather than sees or feels the discharge of cannon. The Su-7 leveled out, a small fire blossoming red below the left wingroot.

The running fight had followed the 1967 ceasefire line. Now the Su-7 hugged the ground in a dash for Damascus some sixty miles to the northeast. The fire seemed to be all in the belly. A good pilot could still shut down the engine, drop his gear, and land. The scrap had lasted four minutes and in the final thirty seconds the enemy pilot must have been either stunned by the prolonged strain of holding such high G-forces or shattered by the encounter. Still, there was always the risk that he might try a belly landing. The Confectioner drew closer. The range dropped from 200 yards to 150 to 100. At the back of his head lurked the knowledge that this was getting dangerously close, but some deeper fighting instinct kept him boring in *Phrrrooommm!* The Mirage reared back. The canopy was engulfed in darkness. The Confectioner felt the elevons jerk the stick inside his gloved hand. Hitting a brick wall in a racing car would have been less of a shock. He remembered the rule that if one committed a massive trespass upon a Mirage's flight characteristics, if one tried to roll or reverse turn at slow speed, the plane kicked back like an outraged thoroughbred horse. He struggled to keep her on an even keel and then he was out of the range of the Su-7's exploding tanks, his own wings black.

Captain Naomi was engaged in a different battle of wits. The Syrian-based Russian controller, having caught Tel Aviv's dirty-tricks department trying to feed wrong information to the MiG-21J, handed his mike over to a woman. The new Russian controller warned the aircraft, "Beware of another voice. . . . Don't be misled by the Jews. . . . In the name of General Raznikov you are ordered back to base."

The MiG pilot became uneasy. This woman's voice speaking in the Russian General's name might be a piece of Israeli deception in the endless war of radio jamming and counter-jamming, false orders, and other bits of chicanery.

While he dithered, Tel Aviv "controllers" switched Captain Naomi onto the Russian's wave-band. "Stay where you are," she urged the Russian pilot. Bewildered by the two women, each claiming to be the true voice of Soviet authority, and confronted with the spectacle of the dogfighting jets below, he decided to stay on patrol.

The real controller in Damascus became angry and swore.

Naomi in Tel Aviv said, "The Jew is using abusive language now! Beware. The Jew is swearing."

In a frenzy now, the Russian controller shrieked "It is *not* the Jew who is swearing. It is *me, me, me!!!*"

Back over the PS-5, the dogfight ended when the Confectioner's wingman launched a Matra-530 at the second intruder, which —to his surprise and secret sorrow—promptly disintegrated. The wingman was a gunfighter and disliked push-button devices. They made violence and death too palatable. He looked forward to challenging the MiG-21J but the order was "Come home."

What about Yesnov, awaiting rescue, already being hunted by Syrian troops? What about the MiG-21J circling about? The order was firm to the Confectioner and his wingman. "Return to base." Fuel tanks were almost emptied by the fury of the fight. (The Mirage's combat radius of 745 miles at 36,000 feet and Mach 0.9 had been considerably extended by IAF ingenuity, but it gulped kerosene at a ferocious rate in a scrap.) Besides, all serviceable aircraft were needed for a "rhubarb." Some 60 Mirage 3Js, 42 Phantoms and 48 Skyhawks* had to cope with land and air battles raging on three fronts. This required an incredibly fast turnaround, so that the effect was to multiply the number of strikes far beyond the number normally to be expected from a small air force. Skyhawks, for example, could be refueled and rearmed in six minutes. The United States Navy's turnaround time was geared to the urgent necessity on carriers to keep all planes moving fast. Clearing the flight decks at a speed and with a dispatch unknown to most land-based air forces meant that the carrier's period of vulnerability was reduced, and helped each aircraft accomplish the work of several operating from distant fields. For similar reasons the IAF's pilots "flew their eyeballs off," as one foreign air-attaché described it.

Pursuing the analogy, the MiG-21J hanging around PS-5 was rather like the enemy spy-plane circling a convoy. In quiet times, planes might be launched to pursue him. When things got hot, defending pilots were far too busy with more pressing dangers.

* Figures based on official United States sources.

So it was now. The air around Israel was erupting and no combat planes were immediately available for what had become a low-priority target. Naomi's job was to keep the MiG-21J in the area until he could be dealt with.

A day such as this one could develop very swiftly into what seemed like organized chaos to the stranger. Planes and crews rushed off in all directions. "But it suits the Israeli temperament," the novelist Wolf Mankowitz told S. "There aren't many of them but they're all moving around like mad, each doing eight different jobs at the same time." Less poetic was the explanation of the former air commander Brigadier General Dan Tolkowsky: "We've improvised and improved upon the theory of aerial warfare that's fifty-five years old—Lanchester's Law." Tolkowsky, a meticulous little man from Britain's Imperial College of Science and Technology, was explaining to S the evolution of IAF operational research. "Clever chap, Lanchester—initials F. W. What this Englishman said was that if five of your planes come up against seven of the enemy's, you must divide the seven baddies into two groups of four and three. Then you attack first one group and then the other. In other words, $5^2 = 4^2 + 3^2$."

Calculations of a more complicated kind, but basically similar, were in progress while the Confectioner and his mate dashed home for more fuel and arms.

Why had the Russians risked an overflight by the Mandrake spy-plane? Why the sudden appearance of the Su-7s over the Syrian front? Were the Russians opening a second front with other Su-7s and Ilyushin Il-28 bombers already pounding the Suez line?

Were today's aerial assaults the start of a new campaign to divide the IAF's strength and wear it down?

By midday, with their figuring done, the veteran pilots at IAF headquarters were on a fresh tack. The bigger-bang-for-a-buck philosophy, forced upon them by their slender financial resources, encouraged the use of fliers on a variety of assignments. One plane could be made to perform the work of two or three. So, too, one pilot could undertake four or five wildly dissimilar missions in anything from a jet interceptor to a behind-the-lines helicopter raid.

So it was no surprise to the jaunty commander of the IAF flying-school when he got an urgent request to switch two of his flying instructors to combat missions in training aircraft.

The mission would be flown in jet-trainers because all combat aircraft were in use. When Colonel Ditto, deputy to the flying-school commander, heard what was required, he volunteered to take on the MiG-21J himself. He was called Ditto because he specialized in making duplicates of captured Russian weapons. He also helped to capture them. One of his prizes was a MiG-21.

The captured MiG-21 was given the identification number 007 in respectful memory of the late James Bond and it was then test-flown by Ditto. Since it was the most serious challenge to the Mirage to date, IAF fighter pilots were put through courses of handling the MiG-21. A consensus of opinion was that:

> Despite the mediocrity of its exterior, due to negligence in finishing, the MiG-21 is an excellent high-altitude fighter. Unlike the Mirage, whose fuselage is smooth and fine, the outer surface of the MiG is sprinkled with thousands of rivets. The Mirage attains an effective speed of Mach 2.15 to Mach 2.2 whereas the MiG is incapable of exceeding a speed of Mach 2. Firing rate of the MiG's gun is about 600 × 30 mm cartridges a minute which is almost half the firing rate of our own guns. But the MiG is permanently armed with Atoll air-to-air missiles with infrared guidance mehanisms whereas the Mirage is not necessarily armed with comparable missiles. The ignition system of the MiG is based on gasoline, which increases the autonomy of the aircraft so that it may take off without the need for auxiliary ignition. But it necessarily involves the terrible danger of explosion in flight if the ignition gas tank is hit by a shellburst.

That was the early version of the MiG-21, than which J in the series was faster and in every way more formidable. It had started to go into service with Soviet bloc air forces and a Mirage pilot needed to have his wits about him to tackle it. "A Fouga-Magister pilot needed to have lost his wits altogether," said Ditto, "in pitting his 440-mile-an-hour trainer against the supersonic J." Nonetheless it was possible to goad the MiG-21J into a low-level and frantic dogfight in which the much slower and therefore more maneuverable Fouga-Magister would cunningly and unobtrusively tighten his turns (if he lived that long) until the Russian threw caution aside and maneuvered himself into the ground. This would have the added advantage that it met Jacob's injunction *not to* shoot the Russian down. A fight with live ammunition over Syria, ending in the midair breakup of a Russian interceptor piloted by a Russian, could cause an international uproar. But if the Russian simply flew his own rotten wings off . . .

It could be made to happen in a cold-blooded flirtation with the Russian. And Ditto had flown so many chase-me-Charlies with or in MiGs that he was a natural choice. The tail-chases demanded every ounce of pilot skill and his mark was on the flying-school where practice dogfights left the cadets wet with sweat and limp from exertion. Ditto had helped develop these very tactics in which a superior enemy could be tricked into using his own strength and speed against himself. But it was his own skill in teaching the craft that weighed against Ditto's request to take on the MiG-21J. He was told he could not be spared.

His commander was a bullet-headed man who presided over the concrete pyramid which resembled Expo 67's Habitat in Montreal. The likeness was no coincidence. The base was sprinkled with such buildings. The Commander, with his flying jacket slung across his shoulders, looked like a young Pharaoh scooting through the sand-colored chambers.

"When the Russians come up with a new weapon, we have our answer," he had once told the stranger. "For a long time it was the A.B.—*Ain Brera*—No Remedy."

"It was a way of saying we had nowhere to go and no remedy

but to stand and fight," Ditto had added. "Now we have a new secret weapon against their latest—the A.B.C.—*Ain Brera Clal* —No Remedy Whatsoever."

The A.B.C. reply to the threatening MiG-21J was, on this day, the Fouga-Magisters—beautiful as powered gliders to fly, and almost as slow. One would challenge the J. The other would drive off Arab guerrillas around their fallen comrade, Yesnov.

The two men, who worked perfectly in tandem, were the Walrus and the Carpenter. They had flown the morning mission and were doing their stint in one of the bomb-proof underground classrooms. Two jet-trainers had been taken off the line and were being armed.

The commander had a queasy sensation in the pit of his stomach. Three years ago the Fouga-Magisters had been thrown into battle in this way, and he still kept framed in his office a captured Egyptian air-force flight-schedule presented by the pilot who had brought him armaments taken from an Arab air-base. The enemy's arms had arrived just in time to keep the Fouga-Magisters operational. Their pilots had suffered the highest casualties of the '67 war and it was difficult for any commander to order his men to fly the same jets against an even tougher enemy.

The Walrus piloting the lead Fouga-Magister was given a precise fix on the MiG-21J prowling over the Golan.

He saw the smouldering lines about twelve miles east of the old frontier. There must have been a tank battle.

His wingman slid ahead to launch a pair of rockets. The Carpenter's job was to persuade the Russian that this was an orthodox air-strike. If he fired the rockets in pairs, rather than in fours or sixes, he could make them last longer.

The Walrus turned lazily near PS-5, where Yesnov early that morning had pinpointed the guerrillas. The surrounding air at this altitude of a thousand feet was thick with smoke. There was no horizon. It was like skin-diving off Sharm-el-Sheikh when the tide was wrong and the water cloudy.

And like a Red Sea shark, the Russian pounced.

The Walrus had been quartering the sky, turning his head first to the left, then sweeping ahead and glancing into the rear-view mirror before swivelling to starboard. He was naked without his wingman, helpless in this under-armed, under-powered trainer, but still with a trick or two up his sleeve.

Now he watched the Russian coming in fast at a steep angle. The 21J was clear against the sky. By contrast, the Israeli with its topside tiger-stripe camouflage was probably hard to discern against the scrub and smoke.

The Walrus waited until the Russian seemed to be committed. He knew from long study of the Soviet Air Force that pilots had no combat experience since 1945, and little taste for dogfighting at any time. If he was lucky, the Russian would go for a missile shot. He held a steady course, inviting the Russian to try it. At the last moment, instinct made him break hard.

The Atoll missile was unable to follow his turn, and burst harmlessly a long way off. The Walrus continued his turn but relaxed the stick. He was down to ground level and he had the advantage of knowing the Golan plateau from having marched over it during his cadet training.

The Russian made a wide sweep, almost losing him in the smoke rolling eastward from brushfires started by the border skirmishes. Number One continued his lazy turn.

Another missile went the way of the first. The fool. Now he's got to use his guns. The Walrus dipped into a shallow valley. Astonishing how like a shark this Russian even looks. And I must seem just the ideal bait. Here he is now, air-brakes out, no doubt, hauling back his speed, moving up on my tail for a nice clean burst. Tighten the turn just a shade. Watch the deck! Watch it! Wingtip brushing white boulders. Here comes the hill. Not too tight. Let him think he's got time to settle down astern. Damn, I've lost him.

A column of black smoke drifted across the far side of the hill. The Walrus reversed his turn. There'd be time later to take cover. He broke into clear air along the bottom of the valley and saw the 21J whip into a steep descending turn again. He pulled up into a vertical climb, turned through ninety degrees, let the nose fall, turned through another ninety degrees, and leveled out, flying faster now and in the opposite direction.

The Russian screamed along the rim of the valley and followed the Walrus into a bowl-shaped depression.

The Walrus suppressed his laughter. Already he was inside his opponent's skull. The Russian would be angry. And careless. How many times had both the Walrus and the Carpenter fallen for the same trap, scrapping with older instructors? He knew the Russian was hooked. Once you got on someone's tail, you lost your senses. Anything he can do, you can do better. Except that a Russian in a MiG-21J is playing in a sandbox with a very high-powered toy which performs best against an equally sophisticated opponent. He would try to follow the Israeli through turns that were too tight for a jet built for supersonic speed. He would cross the limits without noticing, so long as the Walrus stayed calm. He could imagine the Russian's frustration, trying to bring his guns to bear, chasing a shrimp that was always turning just a little bit too much inside his own circle so that even the hairiest deflection shot was beyond him.

A white cliff-face came up abruptly ahead. The Walrus pulled the stick back and heard a familiar crackle along one wing. Heard or felt. He was so much part of the machine, the thud of 23-mm shells seemed to hit his own skin.

He maintained the steepness of the turn without trying to check the damage. The Russian must be trigger-quick to have caught him in that split-second when his configuration altered. Suddenly his wings were shaken by a series of shock waves and the stick rocked under his hand. He pulled through another ninety degrees. A crimson-bellied pillar of oil-black smoke rose from the hillside gouged by the Russian's tail.

He waited, hovering along the perimeter of turbulence. He waited until he was certain nothing remained and then he called the Carpenter. They rendezvoused above the eastern shore of Galilee and flew swiftly home.

Sitting in his helicopter outside his village, Major Zee heard the tally.

Later he joined Doctor Golden sitting on a stone wall and dangling his feet above a fishpond.

"It's going to be a night mission after all."

Golden sighed. "And we don't even get overtime. Why can't we nip in now? It's only over the ridge."

"They've just lost two Su-7s and a MiG-21J 'just over the ridge.' They'll swarm back for a return match before dusk."

"Who got the MiG?"

"The Walrus and the Carpenter."

"Took a day off from instructing?"

"Brought their own Fouga-Magisters too."

"They got a 21J with *those* old shagbats?"

"Flew the Russian into the ground."

Doctor Golden lit a cigarette, his teddy-bear face buttoned against the flame. "Some days you fish and everything bites." He used the half-Arabic phrase from his own fighter-pilot days. "*Yom Assal—Yom Bassal!* One day many fish. One day, none."

It was two thirty in the afternoon of the day marked X in Jacob's diary. When Jacob heard the rescue mission had been delayed until dark, he shuddered. But the tactical situation in the air was darkening faster than Yesnov's prospects of escaping alive. Jacob allowed himself a bitter smile. At least Yesnov, if he wasn't getting his balls torn off, would know that he wasn't just an item in the computer. The IAF used computers but the final decisions were still made by the human beings now gathering in "Golda's Kitchen."

9

IN GOLDA'S KITCHEN

Left alone, the porcupine
does not look for trouble but goes
its own way. When trouble threatens,
the porcupine turns its back and protects
its weak interior with a bristling
array of barbed quills. When danger comes
within close range, a dozen or so quills
are discharged: and more, if the danger
is acute, until all the quills may be
driven deep into the attacker.

The female of the species, this nature note might have added, is deadlier than the male. The article on the habits of the porcupine, written by an Israeli general concerned with saving wildlife, appeared on Day X, when it had just become apparent that the rate of casualties had been dramatically reversed by the Soviet Union's intervention. By the exercise of air superiority, Israel had reduced the number of citizens killed by Arab shelling to a minimum. The introduction of a complete Soviet air-defense package was followed by the highest weekly rate of Israeli casualties since the 1967 war.

The Israeli porcupine was female in its reactions. What puzzled the stranger was the process by which it arrived at a decision to discharge all its quills. There was a collective instinct for danger which, in a nation, was hard to explain. The country was sick of war. There was no military dictatorship, nor any sign of those campaigns to hate your enemy that diminish democracy in wartime. Yet the whole community could react as sharply and as ferociously as any female animal protecting its young. Women seemed central to this decision-making process, although it was hard to see where and how they exercised their influence. The Suez defense system carried a man's name: Lieutenant General Haim Bar-Lev, who devised it to frustrate President Nasser's attempt to wear down the Israelis by bombardment across the canal. Then came new supplies of Soviet antiaircraft missiles. The numbers of Soviet-built guns multiplied. Egypt was able to lob such a tonnage of shells into the Israeli lines that *Aviation Week & Space Technology* reported "a slaughter."

The men in the tanklike forts along the Suez waterway took the punishment. Their wives and mothers suffered the torments of uncertainty. This was the cause of tension that made comparisons with United States losses in Vietnam unreal, for the conflict here was open-ended and the sense of isolation almost complete. Total losses since the end of the Six-Day War had now reached 670 killed, almost as big as the 1967 casualty list, and comparable to 57,600 U.S. servicemen killed-in-action. But here, each death was known within hours. Every family had someone on the nearby battlements. No parent or child could be sure that in any particular day's incident, a son or father might not perish.

"Far worse, in a way, are the consequences of serious injury," a young social worker told S. She had been in the air force and now worked among destitute Arab families. "To put it bluntly, a man who has lost a limb or an eye is a positive liability."

The girl's mother tried to explain the subtle way in which the country somehow arrived at a decision to strike out. She had been an underground schoolgirl-soldier in 1946/8 and thought that many mothers like herself shared the extrasensory perception of danger that this experience had given them. "Just before the 1967 war," she told S, "the women became alarmed by the faint-heartedness of the government. We were mostly mothers of men who would have to fight, so we were hardly likely to lust for blood. It was a spontaneous movement among women who wanted action beyond merely digging holes for the burial of the dead, which was all we could see happening while the Egyptian armies poured into the Sinai. In every neighborhood, groups of mothers began to demand the return of Moshe Dayan."

Within 48 hours of General Dayan's return to active service, the Israeli porcupine discharged its quills.

This empathy between the women and the menfolk, of whom all were trained to fight, was that of a closely knit family. General Bar-Lev flew his own plane, which gave him some idea of air-force problems. Every pilot had to train as a paratrooper. Every girl served at least 20 months in the armed forces. At the height of the 1970 crisis, Dayan was seen in a restaurant dining with a columnist, a poet, and a painter. "Imagine General Westmoreland, in the middle of a battle, discussing it with Ann Landers, Andy Warhol, and Grandma Moses," commented an American observer. "*And* listening to their advice!"

The subtle absorption of military facts and the arrival at a national decision was beyond any formal definition. Some high priest of political theology could talk pretentiously about ideas flowing up from the ranks of womanhood and back down again from the leadership, but it was nothing so simple. The Israeli Defense Forces provided a textbook illustration of the principles of war: *surprise, concentration, security, information, offensive planning, and superior morale and training.* There still remained an additional ingredient: the profound sense of family loyalty rooted in the stony soil of the past.

When Mrs. Golda Meir called on everyone to stand firm "in a grim, savage, and perhaps long war," she spoke as Premier, but her authority was that of a mother. She had already asked for self-sufficiency in aviation, a seemingly impossible target for any small nation in today's world. Yet progress had been made in that direction. One armed-forces jet was in full production. Other combat planes could be modified to the point where at least one interceptor was almost unrecognizable to the original designer. A flat-trajectory supersonic weapon was in operation, guided by both radar and heat-seeking systems, and designed and built in Israeli workshops: against it, no defense appeared to exist. These accomplishments were possible while wives tolerated long periods of loneliness and small amounts of housekeeping money, and mothers learned to live with their unspoken fears. The men acknowledged these sacrifices in their own gruff way. S, the stranger, had seen the air force close ranks around a newly widowed girl. Within their own limited resources, pilots and ground crews made sure that the dependents of a dead flier would be guaranteed shelter and food. But beyond this, there was an expenditure of time and energy by senior commanders who worried about the psychological consequences of sudden bereavement.

Curious about the eccentric working hours of one senior pilot, for instance, S found that one week broke down this way:

Sunday: Flying from dawn to breakfast . . . four hours' staff work . . . two afternoon sorties. . . . Evening discussion of day's operations, ending in work on staff and welfare problems. *Sleeping time: 6 hours.*

Monday: More of the same except for an evening discussion with a young widow requiring work, but with three children under school age. *Sleeping time: 6½ hours.*

Tuesday: Staff work before breakfast. . . . Operational conference. . . . Three hours' flying on instruction and combat missions. . . . Meeting with parents on base to discuss extension of kindergarten. *Sleeping time: 7 hours.*

The rest of the week went in much the same way. By North American standards, this senior pilot could have claimed about nine hours' overtime every day. A good proportion of this was spent in dealing with human needs. In fact, the take-home pay—the "clear salary"—of a pilot after he paid taxes was never more than the wages of an American dishwasher. General Hod, the highest paid general in the country, received the equivalent of $250 a month after tax deductions.

"Airmen will note with professional approval," declared the Institute for Strategic Studies* "how the Israeli Air Force was employed (in 1967) first to gain command of the air by destruction of the enemy forces, then to take part in the ground battle by interdiction of enemy communications, direct support of ground attacks, and finally pursuit. . . . Methods likely to be studied for years to come."

Stated that way, it all sounds like a masterpiece of planning. It overlooks such eccentric influences as former underground-fighters who became mothers and wives.

"Golda's Kitchen" exemplified this in mid-1970. This was, more often than not, where the Cabinet met informally: in the kitchen of Mrs. Golda Meir. It was about as close to being the headquarters of the Security Committee as any place was ever likely to be. Mrs. Meir herself, when she became Prime Minister at the age of seventy-one, was asked if it meant Israel was finally being run by a Jewish mother.

One of her friends exploded: "She is the absolute antithesis of a 'Jewish mother.' . . . She's a mother, sure, and she cooks chicken soup and keeps a spotless house and has children that she dotes upon—but she's not a 'Jewish mother'!"

She was reputed to have bitterly opposed General Dayan's joining the Government before the 1967 war; yet she had him cooing—if not like a dove, at least with affection. "She carries a natural personal authority," wrote William Rees-Mogg, editor of the *Times* of London. She could handle the fighter-pilot thrust of such men as Ezer Weizman and Motti Hod, and balance their ebullience—"boisterousness" is the word she used to one visitor—

* *Israel & The Arab World: The Crisis of 1967* by Michael Howard and Robert Hunter (London: Institute of Strategic Studies).

against the political advice of internationalists such as Abba
Eban. She stumped about the business of being Prime Minister
in built-up orthopedic shoes, carrying a grandmotherly handbag,
dressed in the fashion of the 1930s, her ear very keenly tuned to
all voices within the besieged State. She had once said she was
sure the Jews would forgive the Arabs for killing Jews when
peace came: it would be harder to forgive Arabs "for making us
kill Arabs." The mother of a dead Israeli soldier wrote, "How
can you say that?" Mrs. Meir, according to a close friend, was
dreadfully upset and tried to contact the woman. What she had
meant, she said, was that the Jews who came to Israel were
idealists but had to become soldiers and killers—"and *that* won't
be easy to forget."

This, then, was the woman presiding in "Golda's Kitchen" or
whatever alternative and pretentious titles one may wish to
bestow upon an assembly of experts. "We are all involved," she
had once said. "Mothers and fathers and wives and children and
grandmothers and uncles and aunts . . . worried about our
loved ones, hating war and united by it." She knew all the arguments that haunted Zionists. Some opposed the use of arms because it seemed a denial of their Jewishness. Others insisted that
Jewish communities were destroyed in the past because of a
refusal to arm.

And so the old dilemma recurred, now grown to nightmare
proportions. This was not a ghetto in Russia, though. It was not
a shipload of migrants seeking a country that would let them in.
It was not a camp where the Star of David marked one for
chimneys belching smoke. It was Israel, where the young refused to be burdened by fear of the past.

When Jacob arrived at Golda's Kitchen it was Day X on his
calendar as a result of his own intuition. Others far away recognized that a significant moment had arrived. President Nixon
would later compare it with the Balkans in 1914 when the superpowers were drawn into a war nobody wanted. He warned
the United States it was on a collision course with Russia in the

Middle East and added somberly: "Once the balance of power shifts where Israel is weaker than its neighbors, there will be war."

The facts presented in Golda's Kitchen would never leak out. The stranger could reconstruct the situation from outside sources. "As a veteran of the Cuban missile crisis," former Under Secretary of State George Ball was writing, "I am alarmed by the well-orchestrated leaks from East European embassies to the effect that Soviet activities in the Mideast will confront Americans with the equivalent of another Cuban crisis and that this time the U.S. will back down. Viewed from the Kremlin, such a prospect is both tempting and plausible. If our Cambodian decision is seen—and the Soviet Union is likely to see it this way—as broadening the combat theater while implicitly extending the geographical scope of our commitments and widening the fissures in our national life, the Russians may well conclude that no United States government could command the national attention and will to intervene in the Mideast, even though the continued existence of Israel were threatened." *

Russia had now taken over the complete operation of three Egyptian military airfields and controlled three others; delivered 80 low-level surface-to-air SA-III Goa Missile launchers and 160 Goa missiles to Egypt; built 15 T-shaped Goa concrete shelter sites at 7.5-mile intervals along the Suez narrows which permitted a range overlap for the SA-IIIs; deployed Tupolev Tu-16 strategic reconnaissance aircraft to Aswan to watch the Red Sea; stationed an electronic-intelligence warship off the Sinai coast; accelerated air- and sea-lifts between Communist and Egyptian ports to a point where deliveries were now the heaviest since 1967; and was continuing to increase the number of seasoned Russian airmen and ground troops in Egypt.

Air photographs published in Western technical magazines showed that Soviet aircraft were now installed within 450 cam-

* Article in *The New York Times Magazine*. June 28, 1970.

ouflaged and hardened shelters in Egypt alone. A total of 150 MiG-21J interceptors and about twice that number of Russian pilots had been assigned to Egypt's air defense. Hangarettes built of reinforced concrete, holding up to five jets, were dispersed to prevent a recurrence of 1967, when the Egyptian air force was caught on the ground and destroyed.

Russian specialists were now responsible not only for the operation and maintenance of jets and Goa missiles but also for managing search radars and artillery positions. Two kinds of Russian low-level radars were now in Egypt, code-named Low Blow and Flat Face.

The Soviet air fleet was going on alert whenever Israeli aircraft penetrated Egyptian airspace. The fleet consisted of "fighter regiments" of 36 Russian-piloted jets divided into 12-aircraft units. Egypt's tactical combat air force had grown by a further 55 MiG-21Cs, 44 MiG-21Ds, and 73 helicopters.

A master training center for Arab pilots was planned for the Libyan base which the United States had just vacated at Wheelus. With Libya drawn into the alliance of Arab states against Israel, new factors had to be considered, of which the most important was that the conflict thus extended to Northwest Africa. Suddenly, without involving any Russian territory, the Soviet Union had made it difficult to strike at the source of Israel's troubles. Rear divisions of Arab guerrillas and airmen were now withdrawn still further to points in Libya that lay as much as twelve hundred miles from Tel Aviv. With Algeria adjoining, a continuous land mass was available to Arab irregulars openly armed and trained by specialists from the Soviet bloc. Libya itself had persuaded France to divert 108 Mirages from Israel to the new revolutionary Libyan government and the Russians offered the "Mongol" version of the MiG-21 to train Libyan pilots. For Israel to maintain and fly one hundred Mirages, a total of four thousand highly trained technicians would be needed. By Arab standards, the figure would be three times as high—twelve thousand (an estimate based upon detailed knowledge of the degree of Arab training). It was assumed Egypt would control a Libyan-based air force.

The Soviets and Arabs now deployed 1280 fighter-bombers and bombers in the Middle East against about 330 Israeli planes, of which half were scarcely fit for combat.

This demanded a reappraisal of Israel's air strategy. This was based fundamentally on keeping the ceasefire lines quiet. Deep strikes at multiple targets had started on January 7, 1970, forcing the Egyptians to thin out their missiles and artillery along the Suez front. In late April the deep-penetration raids were suspended after a Russian-speaking Israeli pilot reported hearing a conversation in Russian between pilots of two MiG-21s: for wider political reasons, Israel wished to avoid a confrontation that might set the stage for a general war. But the immediate effect was a sharp rise in Israeli ground casualties; a multiplication of terrorist attacks along all borders; and the massing of two hundred and fifty thousand Egyptians along the Suez front, with thirty thousand troops in reserve, against thirty thousand Israeli troops. Syria and Jordan were bases from which terrorists made forays and strikes, dividing Israel's few resources.

Military observers did not believe Russia wanted to be directly involved. They could explain some Russian moves by pointing to the need to protect Soviet military and economic investments in Egypt worth about three billion dollars (including 934 aircraft and what little was left of 300 SA-II Guideline missiles after IAF strikes). There were larger aims which the West was forced to recognize: Russia was on the way to controlling the Suez Canal, the Red Sea, and the oil-rich defenseless states bordering the Persian Gulf.

Meanwhile Israel had to fix its eye on the one question of survival. The remaining ten undelivered McDonnell Douglas F-4 Phantom Mach 2 fighters, out of the original order placed in President Johnson's time, were reconfigured to incorporate an optical gunsight fire-control system so it could be used as an interceptor. Steps were taken to fit some Mirage 3CJs with United

States-built engines (General Electric J79 and the Pratt & Whitney J52) in view of a French embargo on the Mirage's original Snecma Atar 9. There was no lack of ingenuity. But ingenuity was not enough.

The cost of defense ate up two-thirds of Israel's 1968–1969 tax revenue and by 1969–1970 had reached $900 million or 20.8 per cent of the country's gross national product (compared with 9.2 per cent in the United States). This was a staggering jump from the 1966–1967 figure of $360 million or 9.4 per cent. But worse was to come. Defense costs began to escalate so that projections for 1970–1971 were $1430 million, or four times the figure for the year of the Six-Day War. The sum total of foreign contributions, by contrast, never exceeded 70 per cent of the cost of absorbing new immigrants, and it could be argued that, in reality, Israel shouldered these staggering defense costs alone.

On the other hand, Israeli resilience had to be kept always in mind. The G.N.P. had increased by more than 30 per cent since the end of the Six-Day War and in 1969 had reached $443 billion. One hundred thousand new immigrants had settled despite the war and heavy taxation. And if the war was costing Israel a shocking proportion of her income, Egypt's defense expenditure had doubled in three years to about 22 per cent of G.N.P.; and this was in addition to the hidden costs of the Soviet Union's "free" supplies of arms.

All these figures held little meaning for the average Israeli because the horrendous aspects of the threat lay in its endlessness. One said he felt like a victim in John Wyndham's *Day of the Triffids*, barricaded against an inferior but multiplying enemy, using flamethrowers to fight off insensate and therefore unheeding armies whose numbers would outlast the jets of burning fuel.

With four times as much territory to defend as in 1967, servicemen found it harder to hitch-hike home at weekends. The cry of "Quiet—news!" preceded the hourly newscasts so that one might hear of new casualties (and then find out who they were through one's own channels). The newspapers carried an almost daily burden of passport-type photographs showing smiling youngsters suddenly dead.

Over all this stretched a blanket of cheerful activity, even exuberance. Tourists were coming in record numbers and bowled across the countryside in growing fleets of air-conditioned buses, oblivious to the grim continuity of the fighting (except for the occasional coy note inserted in guidebooks, such as: "Please exercise proper caution in visiting new areas").

A Tel Aviv lawyer described it as "a war-by-turns." Its slogan: "You guard the country today while I have a good time inside, and tomorrow I'll stand guard."

Israelis, as S had discovered many times, hate poor-mouthing. Colonels whose take-home pay, even with danger-money for flying, left them unable to buy luxuries would nevertheless go to great lengths to be hospitable and conceal the meagerness of their resources.

A bold example was that of Colonel Uri Yarom, who landed on the United States aircraft carrier *Wasp* because he was running out of fuel. No navy in the world likes to have foreign warplanes drop casually onto its decks. The *Wasp*'s commander chewed out Colonel Yarom, who flashed a disarming smile and said, "Sorry, I thought it was one of ours." It was a bitter little joke. The cost of the aircraft on the *Wasp*, let alone the carrier, would have put Israel into bankruptcy. But the colonel insisted at least on paying for his tankful of gas.

A Spitfire used to seem expensive at $50,000. Now $4.5 million was one quoted price for the Spitfire's modern equivalent, and training and supplies were liable to cost as much again.

All these considerations and many more haunted "Golda's Kitchen." It seemed like 1967 all over again, when Israel decided it could not wait to be worn down. In those days the Israeli High Command assumed that, before outside pressures compelled a ceasefire, it would have three days to complete the task of destroying the threatening forces encroaching upon its fragile borders.

What was the task in 1970?

As Mrs. Meir explained it, "to protect Israeli soldiers; to bring home the consequences of the Arabs' own declaration of a war of attrition; to forestall the buildup of a major Egyptian attack."

To perform this mission, the IAF needed more planes. There were difficulties of very high-speed strikes, and the camouflaging of Russian-built installations to resemble Arab schools and mosques so that "atrocity stories" could be circulated to the outside world. The IAF had been nevertheless remarkably skillful in avoiding attacks that would alienate the general public. S had himself seen the dangers that pilots ran in order to avoid hitting civilian targets. All the same, before President Nixon's speech on the eve of the Fourth of July 1970, the Russians had successfully played for more time by first shocking the West with the boldness of their moves into the Middle East, and then presenting a peace plan that would sow confusion. President Nixon had been expected to demonstrate the support for Israel which seemed psychologically so vital. Russia had never been known to respond to conciliatory moves and it seemed important that the President announce the sale of the 25 F-4s and 100 A-4 Skyhawks, which in any case would arrive so late that the promise of future delivery would be more important than their arrival. As it was, the Russians had employed an old principle of Communist strategy, restated by Chairman Mao in Peking: "Frighten the patient and then prescribe the medicine." The West *was* frightened and the medicine was a Russian peace plan that would help the United States stay uninvolved. For the fact was, in the words of the former Under Secretary of State George Ball, "Disenchantment over Vietnam has been translated into suspicion of all military commitments overseas. It has led us dangerously close to pacifism and isolationism." He was afraid that any suggestion of America risking another foreign war to preserve Israel's national home "could not arise at a worse time." Furthermore, the fears of another Vietnam might lead to the ugly reflex of a frightened people—"lunatic charges that we are being led into the danger of a world conflict by the Jews."

The tragic dilemma seemed best expressed in the Institute for Strategic Studies' Adelphi Papers on the 1967 war. It acknowledged that the Israeli Air Force had won professional approval, that leadership at all levels and great flexibility had been vital, and that the peak of excellence had been reached without the aid of drill sergeants and the barrack square. But, the study went on:

> . . . Israel observed a principle which appears in few military textbooks but which armed forces neglect at their peril: the Clausewitzian principle of Political Context which the British ignored so disastrously in 1956. The Israeli High Command knew that it was not operating in a political vacuum. It worked on the assumption that it would have three days to complete its task before outside pressures compelled a cease-fire. In fact it had four, and needed five.

The margin was so narrow that the United Nations call for the 1967 ceasefire came before Israel had time to deal with the last of its major torments, Syria. The offensive against Syria went ahead nonetheless. Western reaction was curious and confirmed the feeling of Israelis that outsiders either did not understand or did not want to understand the nature of their long travail. This reaction was one of general disapproval although the Israeli offensive was strictly limited, and designed to destroy the complex of Russian cannons on the Golan Heights and to push the disputed border a few miles back to provide a few settlements with a better margin of safety. Involved was a barren waste representing less than two per cent of Syria. The action was fought with such courage that it elicited the tributes of military experts. Nevertheless it was condemned by the self-righteous among United Nations delegates and other world agencies. Nothing had been said by these same voices, prior to June 1967, about the incessant shelling of the settlements by the same Syrian guns now removed. It was this double standard that disturbed Israelis and made them so cynical about promises of foreign help. They had voluntarily restricted their own offensive, holding enough territory to provide the physical barriers which previously did not exist against the destructive forces that frank and official Arab statements had promised would erase Israel at one blow.

These threats, however, were less precisely stated in English-language versions. Lord Rothschild was obliged to point out, late in 1970 when the world had forgotten again:

> The liquidation of Israel is still a possibility. . . . The Palestinian National Council's revised National Covenant, adopted in Cairo . . . is the basic political document of terrorist organizations. Article 6 is important in the context of intended Jewish genocide: "Jews who were customarily living in Palestine until the beginning of the Zionist invasion will be considered Palestinians."

Lord Rothschild pointed out that the new Covenant in fact intended to accept the existence of one or two thousand Jews who might be descended from those in Palestine before the "Zionist invasion," i.e., 1917 and the Balfour Declaration. "So," wrote Rothschild, "there are some 2,400,000 Jews to be got rid of. . . . No Arab state or organization has as yet formally disavowed this new and equally horrible plan. As for cost-effectiveness, it is well to remember that it can be applied to battle as well as to genocide." *

S, the stranger, as an observer in the Middle East and Asia during the 1950s and the 1960s, had noticed that non-Jews almost always preferred the Arab terrorist organizations' more moderate propaganda in Western translations (probably because few could read Arabic). As a non-Jew himself, he was aware of an inclination to dismiss the danger and the explicit threats to liquidate Israel as somehow fictional. Thus Hitler and later dictators could describe exactly how they proposed to bury their enemies,

* *The New York Times*, August 20, 1970.

and then caught everyone by surprise when they embarked upon this enterprise.

If the past was anything to go by, Israel could expect the double standard to prevail. Nobody in the West seemed ready to intervene. There were several recent examples of the gap between Western protestations of virtue and Western willingness to act. Biafra was the tragedy most often quoted by Israelis, whose engineers had been working on aid programs in that part of Nigeria. It was recalled too that Russia had walked into Czechoslovakia without any more serious opposition than a few blowhard threats of retaliation from comfortably distant places.

The Institute for Strategic Studies report had gone on to say:

> The lesson is clear. So long as there remains a tacit agreement between the super-powers to cooperate in preventing overt conflicts which threaten international peace and security, a nation using open force to resolve a political problem must do so rapidly, if it is to succeed at all. Once it *has* succeeded, the reluctance of the Great Powers to countenance a second conflict means that it is likely to preserve its gains. The lesson is a sombre one, placing as it does a premium on adventurism and pre-emption.

Three years later the Russians had made it possible for their Arab clients to set sail upon such an adventure. A pre-emptive strike against Israel would be over long before anyone could act; and it would be final.

Never ones to tolerate an impossible situation, habitués of "Golda's Kitchen" looked for new solutions. Forty years ago, Jewish settlements had been separated from each other with hostile Arabs between; and the solution then was to utilize light planes masquerading as flying-club machines.

Unorthodox uses of old and heavily doctored aircraft were again the solution when the survivors of Nazi concentration-camps were stopped from entering Palestine. Immigrants were smuggled through a British blockade in planes taken from post-

1945 war dumps, sometimes using the flag of a legitimate air-service, often flying under cover of darkness, occasionally helped by sympathetic governments, and on one occasion launched by the Panamanian government in a moment of aberration.

Again an admittedly ramshackle air force came to the rescue when Arab armies attacked from all sides at the time of Palestine's partition in 1947. This was the time of the "bomb-chuckers" dropping grenades from sports planes; the time of training young pilots in underground schools around Europe; the time when a small fleet of veteran fighter-planes escaped British law by participating in the shooting of a nonmovie and (while filmless cameras rolled) flying straight into the wild blue yonder, never to return.

The challenge to the air force always expanded. By 1956 Egypt had seized the Suez Canal and Goebbels former Nazi Jew-baiter was broadcasting from Cairo his daily promise to destroy the Zionists.* This time the Israeli Air Force faced Russian-built jets as well as squadrons of Western-made fighters, bombers, and transports. The aerial fighting was fiercer and the Israelis still had to fall back upon one of World War II's oldest training aircraft, the North American Harvard. They nevertheless possessed the first of the French Mystères and Ouragans which were to form the backbone of their future jet fleet of interceptors and fighter-bombers. The need for strong air support, however, was accompanied by a lack of confidence in the IAF's ability to handle the enemy's combined air forces alone. Hence the Anglo-French intervention. Later operational research showed the IAF could have acted alone, and would have been politically wise to do so. Confidence in Israel's own air force was growing.

How that air force would cope with different kinds of military threat had been discussed regularly since 1954. "Sixteen years'

---

* Dr. Johannes von Lehrs. He told S in Cairo in 1956 that eventually Egypt would be swallowed up by the Soviet Union but "it doesn't matter so long as we destroy the Zionist plotters in Israel. "It was this fanatical old man who helped convince S of what had seemed incredible: that the war to exterminate the Jews continued despite the defeat of Hitler.

experience went into the first eighty minutes of the 1967 strike," General Hod was to say later. That pre-emptive strike gave the IAF its final credibility.

By Day X of 1970, the air force had graduated from the delivery of illegal immigrants to the capture of military prizes deep in the enemy's heartland; from the impromptu scrambling of gypsy fighter-squadrons to tight operational control of tactical aircraft; from mercenaries and swashbucklers to coolly scientific pilots who "buttoned themselves into tailored suits of operational orders, with precise measurements on where and when to attack or break off an action." Behind each pilot stood a small knot of specialists who could absorb new information quickly, integrate it into existing plans, and convey new orders to pilots already airborne. This organization was not all in the head; but very little, nonetheless, got onto paper for hostile eyes to read.

From "Golda's Kitchen" through the labyrinth of this tightly structured force passed the question: *What now?*

Every airman knew in his bones that the solution must come from Israel's own resources. Foreign indifference seemed to be exemplified by the inane *aide-mémoire* circulated in the spring of 1970 among diplomats stationed in Israel: "The Ambassador of Liberia, Dean of the Diplomatic Corps, presents his compliments to Their Excellencies, the Ladies and Gentlemen, Heads of Diplomatic Missions, and has the Honor to inform them that the Ambassador of Sweden, His Excellency Bo L. Siegban, has expressed the desire that his tray should be engraved on its back instead of on the front, as is usually done. Therefore the Ambassador of Liberia, Dean of the Diplomatic Corps, hereby submits this matter to Their Excellencies, the Ladies and Gentlemen, Heads of Diplomatic Missions, for their reactions. . . ."

While the diplomats shuffled their tea-trays and groused about the contempt with which they felt themselves to be treated by men now preoccupied with a life-or-death decision, a newspaper cartoon was pinned up on military notice-boards. It showed a very small soldier sitting on a rock and resolutely ignoring the vultures overhead. The caption was a quotation from the Bible: "For from the top of the rocks I see him, and from the hills I behold him: lo, the people shall dwell alone, and shall not be reckoned among the nations." (Numbers 23:9)

10

TREETOP RAIDER

High-speed low-level attack
Is the greatest threat from the air
In modern warfare.
Not so long ago
There was no effective answer.
Ack-ack is powerless
To cope with the fast
Treetop raider.
He has had it all his own destructive way.
RAPIER has changed
All that.
Now the man on the ground is master
Even of the supersonic striker. . . .
Each low-cost missile is only US $10,000
(In rough figures)
Orders now exceed
Two hundred million dollars.*

The words danced absurdly in Jacob's head, chopped
into lines of free verse by the rhythmic *chomp-chomp-chomp* of
the chopper's rotor blades. He looked again at the full-page ad

* From a 1970 advertisement in *Flight International* by the Guided Weapons Division of the British Aircraft Corporation.

under the cockpit dome-light and wondered how many readers could afford this "exceptional lethality." Certainly not Israel. Still less her enemies. But Russia would lavish such missile systems upon her clients and collect payment later.

For two months, thought Jacob, we've pummelled the sites and tried to stop the wall from growing. Every day hurling ourselves against their steel. Every day risking our treetop raiders, our high-speed low-level attackers whose purpose is to prevent the wall from rising higher. Soon, perhaps, we'll have to switch tactics. The question had come up this afternoon in Golda's Kitchen. Motti Hod, who met his pilots as they landed from missions or watched the intensive debriefing later, had reported something odd about the way Yesnov had been brought down. Had the Russians introduced a new device into Syria? One way to find out was to ask Yesnov. If he was still alive.

Jacob's pilot flicked the artificial-feel switch. The bubble-helicopter floated over the domed and spired city bathed in an unreal sunset glow. "Jerusalem—my chiefest joy!" The words and the aerial photograph taken in June 1967 could be seen in every squadron office. For Jacob the picture often seemed more vivid than the reality and looking down he felt a familiar stab of fear. He needed Naomi to reassure him, to tell him to forget the past, to shake off these suspicions and intimations of betrayal. He wished he had Motti Hod's confidence which came from being born here, instead of this awful sense of being in a dream-Israel that would evaporate with the first kick of the block-master's boot. Naomi alone could calm him. His only other refuge was physical action. He clenched his hands. The thought of another wall going up, another barrier to make another ghetto, aroused in him the most violent emotions.

"Lord," he prayed. "Make me an instrument of Thy peace." A Christian had taught him the words in prison. He wasn't sure about a God who permitted such things to happen but the words had saved him before from sudden and futile anger.

Major Zee and Doctor Golden were eating an early supper

when he joined them. Two of the kibbutz girls had brought food to where they waited behind the orchard. One of the girls was Ruthi, sister of Yesnov.

"Does she know?" asked Jacob, out of earshot.

Doctor Golden shook his head quickly. "She may guess but she doesn't know."

The girls were sheltered under the trees from the turbulence created by Jacob's machine as it rose and tilted away, leaving Jacob with the larger Sikorski and its crew.

"Are you coming with us?" asked Major Zee.

"No," Jacob rubbed his elbow. "*Ruthi?*"

She came to meet him. She wore a white kerchief over glossy black hair tied back like a schoolgirl. She had done her time in the army and she walked with the proud gait of someone who can shoulder a rifle, her shoulders back, her thin red blouse partly unbuttoned in the heat, the blue skirt tight around the narrow waist and ending high on bare thighs. She crossed the meadow, past the reservists guarding Zee's rescue-helicopter. Behind her, silhouetted against the Sea of Galilee, was a bronze statue of a woman shielding her child. The statue by Hanna Orloff conveyed the same sense of granite strength that the girl Ruthi seemed to conceal within her lithe form. She never took her eyes from Jacob's face; and when she reached him, she said, "It's my brother?"

"I'm afraid so . . ."

Doctor Golden threw down his cigarette, shocked by the stark brutality of the reply.

Jacob cut short his protest. "We need you, little one," he said, putting an arm around her shoulders.

When her brother Yesnov was recalled that morning, a computerized air-defense command and control system (ADCC) was already spewing out facts and figures that hinted at the troubled day ahead.

The system consisted of military radar stations with three-dimensional long-range and underground detection and control centers. At the heart were general-purpose high-speed computers. A master computer was the nucleus of this electronic nervous system. It established the speed, heading, and altitude of potential intruders together with updated information on the weapons available, their launch ranges, velocities, armament, limitations, and time-to-kill.

Because of Israel's peculiar defense problems, the system watched the air and ground for a considerable distance away from the 1967 ceasefire lines.

Display consoles gave a constantly changing picture of events in the surrounding skies. Back-up systems were distributed around the country in case master control should be knocked out. Any threatening activity projected onto the banks of display units was reported instantly to Motti Hod or his acting commander. He, or his deputy, could dispatch electronic requests to interceptors or missiles to hunt down any potential intruder.

Fed into the basic nervous system, instantly available in the Citadel and in the bunkers along the Suez line, and repeated at duplicate ADCCs near other front lines, were the latest, continually updated intelligence reports.

These reports and the activities visible around Cairo and Damascus caused the recall signals to go out to young pilots such as Yesnov. Some might be part of the Dizengoff crowd but most on their one- or two-day passes went home. The decision to bring them back, never lightly taken by commanders who themselves knew the hidden strains, was taken in this case by Motti Hod, who was in the position of an aircraft-carrier's captain. Like a carrier's captain, he could not afford to let an enemy attack develop and must therefore maintain patrols and warning systems against sneak raiders. Unlike a carrier's skipper he did not have flanking escorts, a protective screen of fast destroyers, or the means to send up a curtain of steel against any raider breaking through outer circles of defense. But what he had, he used with economy and skill, driven by the knowledge that it needed only a single well-placed torpedo to sink the ship.

When a threat seemed to be developing, there were strategic computers to present a list of the defenses available at that particular moment. Hard decisions followed the listing of vital facts: how many IAF combat planes were ready; what other aircraft could be pressed into service; the precise location of every single plane and pilot and ground crew man; what pilots and planes were on Quick Reaction Alert pads; and a cold assessment of each pilot and plane.

Soon after leaving his sister that morning, Yesnov was suited-up and "on the hose"—breathing oxygen—he had changed from a boy at the kibbutz to a vital statistic, clamped into the Escapac seat of a Skyhawk while others were studying the day's prospects and the human resources at hand.

At such moments, the essential humanity of Israel's defense forces becomes plain to a stranger. There was a sense of wonder which S had seen many times on the faces of army and air-force men, no matter what their vintage. It was an enchantment at the reality of Jewish fields of grain, Jewish hens laying (such is this childlike pleasure) presumably Jewish eggs. And with this, S had seen also with some emotion, went a great caring for Jewish soldiers. Others have said that this feeling, this guardianship, is a consequence of those many centuries when the people were imprisoned in a petrified faith and lived on familiar terms with the supernatural and with external dangers. The green meadows of Israel, it has been said, are born of the desert without water and the desert of the people's past. The concern for the young is born of a past when families ran the steady risk of sudden and final division. This may be so. But when an Israeli-born man such as Motti Hod was making his decisions on a day like this, he was balancing in his mind the directions suggested by the computers against his knowledge of his own crews. He knew the capabilities of each pilot and the state of combat-worthiness of every plane, and the difficult love of a good father was something the stranger glimpsed in more relaxed moments. It was the love that protects and yet does not possess, and to live with it while dispatching your sons into danger is an agony too private to share.

Jacob pieced events together for Yesnov's sister. There was little point in withholding the bare facts because he needed Ruthi's help and the more she understood the better. Major Zee stared at his thick farmer's hands, listening and saying nothing. Doctor Golden's expression was that of an angry teddy bear, for he was not like the others who could conceal their distaste for involving a girl in danger. Girls did the work that released men for the front lines. Girls did *not* get themselves exposed to violence.

"We think the guerrillas are getting a Russian off-the-shoulder missile," said Jacob. "It would explain how your brother's tail was damaged."

Doctor Golden looked up. "How does it work?"

Ruthi smiled. She was the least worried among them. She had always been very close to Yesnov and she knew, *she insisted upon believing*, that he was safe. She smiled to reassure Golden; and because the doctor never could curb his curiosity when it came to technical matters.

"One man can carry it," said Jacob. "It weighs less than fifty pounds, including missile, launcher, and aiming unit. The missile is supersonic and it's designed exclusively for airborne targets."

"Sounds like a Russian version of the British Blowpipe," said Zee.

"Exactly."

"Our margins get smaller," muttered the doctor.

"Or the surrounding wall gets higher, depending on how you look at it." Jacob squeezed his elbow. There was an evening mist in the trees. The birdsong was dying away. A warm smell of sweet new-mown hay drifted across the meadow.

"Will Yesnov have seen this weapon?"

"Probably. He's had fighter cover, on and off, all day. We think he's lying low, dead-center of the main guerrilla groups. He would have seen the launchers."

Ruthi shivered. Major Zee called his flight engineer. The man emerged from the Sikorski. It looked in the fading light like a giant dragonfly perched for flight. The flight engineer carried a padded and fur-collared jacket which he put around Ruthi's shoulders. She said, "The first Russian missiles, the SA-IIs, were good above three thousand feet?"

Jacob nodded.

"We flew through the gap between sea-level and three thousand," said Major Zee. "Then the SA-III's came along and the gap became very narrow."

"How narrow?" asked Ruthi.

The major glanced at Jacob, who shrugged. "Three hundred feet."

"That doesn't leave much room," the girl said softly.

"In a Sikorski it's room enough," replied the major.

"At the speed of a tractor, of course." Ruthi pulled the flying jacket tighter around her shoulders. "At the speed of sound, you cover three hundred feet in half a second."

Doctor Golden stirred uneasily.

"At the speed of sound," Ruthi continued, "you have five or six seconds to recognize an enemy gun position—"

"If you're flat on the deck," said the doctor.

"If you're flat on the deck, as you say." She watched Jacob with slanting eyes. "Is this what we've accomplished? A tiny space under a fence, through which we can slip if we're lucky?"

"It's not that bad," protested Major Zee.

"It could hardly be worse though, could it?" the girl said, carried forward by her own remorseless logic. "This—this portable missile launcher . . . It plugs the gap under the fence, then?"

"We've had to find answers before, and we'll find answers again," said Jacob mechanically.

"Do you know what they say back there?" Ruthi demanded. Her kerchief had fallen back and she pulled her ponytail of hair over one shoulder, stroking it. "They say you create the problems that demand these complicated answers."

They fell into an uncomfortable silence. A flock of Egyptian geese honked angrily to each other as they flapped across the dying green light of sunset. A sparrowhawk hovered above the rushes around the fishpond. Ruthi watched the hawk with brooding eyes. "Don't get worried. I taught mathematics in the army, remember? I can add up. What you have done always needed to be done. I take pride in what Yesnov is doing now. If I were a man I would choose the same work."

Jacob gave a small sigh as if he had reached a decision. "Everything we know about today is this. We have been challenged in the air by the Russians. We have been bombarded on three fronts simultaneously, which indicates a close coordination between Russian military advisers on the ground. We have suffered terrorist rocket attacks at Qiryat Shmona and Beit She'an . . . parcel-bombs in Haifa . . . grenades in Gaza." He ran mechanically down the list. "We see preparations for an amphibious attack across Suez by the Egyptians and therefore the bombardment of protective Russian missile-sites along the Canal must take priority. But today's massing of Syrian forces"—he glanced toward the Golan Heights looming over them—"could be a feint. It could be an attempt to draw off some of our strike aircraft."

"Or the closing of the wall around Israel?" the girl suggested.

"It's possible," Jacob said cautiously.

She watched his face. "Jacob, what is it you want from me?"

"A voice recording."

"And you think this will be enough to bring my brother out of hiding?"

"I think so." Again, Jacob rubbed his stubby bricklayer's arms. "Yesnov will be waiting. He will expect us to fetch him. He also knows that others before him have been tricked into delivering themselves into terrorist hands. An hour after sunset Major Zee will fly in, land without lights and if your brother fails to signal, your taped voice will be broadcast on the loud-hailers."

"It's dangerous for you," Ruthi said, turning to the major. "They've tricked helicopters into landing before this, too."

Zee lifted his shoulders. "It has to be done—"

"Because of the information Yesnov has."

"Careful, little one—" Jacob took her hand but she snatched it back.

"I'm not a child! I know the importance of what my brother may have seen. I know there's not a man in this country won't take any risk to bring back a flier. I know what they do to our pilots over there. But don't make excuses because this time there's more at stake than a pilot's body and mental health."

"I'm sorry," said Jacob. "One tries to be—to be kind, to be discreet."

"Then for the love of God stop being evasive. These new launchers mean the lives of all of us."

Doctor Golden had been studying the girl's face during the exchange. Now he said, "A portable one-man launcher is expensive, Ruthi. It is also difficult to operate. In theory, many Arabs equipped with many hundreds of launchers could become a problem—"

"A problem between sea-level and three hundred feet. I know that! And as fast as they try to build a wall around us, we must pull it down. Which is why I don't think it's enough to record my voice!"

Doctor Golden's shoulders sagged. He had seen this coming. "Not enough?" asked Jacob.

"No! It's bad enough landing in darkness in territory that we know is crawling with guerrillas. What happens when you start caterwauling?"

"It may not come to that," Major Zee interrupted.

"Oh yes it could," snapped Ruthi. "You've just made that very clear."

Doctor Golden lit a cigarette. In the gathering dusk, the glow of the match startled them. He said, "All right, little sister. What is it you want to suggest?"

"I'm not suggesting. I *must* go along with you."

Jacob exploded into a torrent of words. "Girls . . . never . . . not the place . . . in heaven's name . . ."

"Nevertheless," said Ruthi. "I'm going. There will be no lunatic broadcasting so that every bastard rattlesnake for miles around can strike you on the ground. There will be as soft a landing as possible, as near as we can to where Yesnov is hiding, and if he does not appear, I shall get out and look for him."

Jacob drew himself up. "You want me to speak in the name of the chief-of-staff—"

Ruthi patted his face. "You wear trousers and a shirt that hangs outside the belt like a good little kibbutznik. And in your good little sensible head you know perfectly well that I'm right. You may very well be a brilliant strategist, perhaps already a brigadier general in the making. But to me you are still Jacob. And the chief-of-staff is a former tank soldier who wears a tiny black beret to keep his head from getting wet and has a pretty wife called Tamar. And Tamar," she finished, "was once a corporal in the army with me."

"It's impossible," said Jacob. "Don't even mention it—"

"You think it worth putting the state in jeopardy for one girl?"

"I didn't say that."

"You said it's vital to the nation's security to get my brother—"

Doctor Golden shook his teddy-bear head and pressed his knuckles against his eyes as if they were buttons pinned into a head filled with sawdust. "Give up, Jacob. You can't fight a couple of thousand years of Talmudic argument and Jewish motherhood."

The girl, not waiting for any further response, ran back through the orchard, joined by her friend.

"I don't like it," Jacob muttered and turned with one of those sudden movements that betrayed the explosive energy that built up in times of crisis. He put his stubby hands on the fence rail and swung himself up, twisting to face the other two men, his short legs dangling. "You know what they do to prisoners. . . ."

"She'll be happier if she goes along," said Doctor Golden, resigned and realistic again. "She's more likely to die here of nervous exhaustion before morning."

"It's suicidal," Jacob persisted.

Major Zee gave him an ironic bow. "Thank you. It is an aspect you omitted to mention to *me*."

"Remember Hannah Szenej," the doctor said.

The major frowned but Jacob looked up, clasping and unclasping his work-knotted fingers. "Hannah?" His mouth tightened. Hannah Szenej had been one of the Jewish agents parachuted into Nazi Germany—at Ruthi's age, twenty-three. Caught and tortured by the Gestapo, her words to the tribunal that sentenced her to death were etched upon Jacob's mind for reasons which only the doctor knew, and then not entirely: "I volunteered to take arms against German Nazis because I have been taught to be free and proud of my Jewish origin by Palestine." She had gone to her execution knowing that when this vision of the homeland became the reality of Israel, the womenfolk would have reason to stand straight beside their men. And so it had come to pass, thought Jacob. In every unit of defense, the women fought alongside the men: with the tanks at El Quneitra, with the paratroopers in the Sinai, on the Jordan with the Golani Brigade. It was not a privilege but the right of every girl between eighteen and twenty to serve for twenty months. Equal rights, equal duties . . .

"Equal work," Doctor Golden was saying. "It's in the constitution, such as it is. Besides, Ruthi's still in the reserve."

In the reserve until her thirty-fourth year, Jacob reflected, mind still adrift. Ruthi . . . Hannah. He clenched his hands again, remembering Arab propaganda that "the Jews' army is a vast bordello where every soldier finds a girl beside him to satisfy his every lust." It was the girls who gave the armed forces their strength. It was Hannah who had foreseen the need for an army, had said in fact that it should be based upon the Prussian system but with a crucial difference: the Prussian system had militarized society, but here it must be the civilization of the army that took place. And had taken place. Because of girls like Ruthi. Girls whose sense of equality with men often mystified the stranger, for it was at one and the same time intimate and yet an effective barrier against unwarranted intimacies. By their very frankness, the girls made it impossible for a man to cross the bounds of good behavior, for their open manners put every man on trust.

Jacob jerked his mind back to present concerns. He had briefed Major Zee. There was no need to tell the doctor what to expect, which was the worst; nor what to do, which was the best with limited time and means. Jacob would remain here, plugged into the defense-communications network for the discussions that would proceed all night. He should have joined the High Command, or at the very least parked his compact figure in Hod's office. But somebody should be here to debrief Yesnov, to get as accurate a description of the new missile as possible. Here was the nearest piece of safe ground to where Yesnov had gone down. And if he were badly injured, each second would count.

It was not an easy decision Jacob was taking. His expertise had to be on tap. He was far too valuable a store of knowledge to lose on a rescue mission. Yet everything in his past dictated that he should act rather than wait. It was not just that his time in the defense forces had long ago taught him that nobody ever issued the command "Forward!" which did not exist in Israeli military regulations, the only possible order being "Follow me!" The need to act, to strike out, to struggle, these went back to his childhood and the spectacle of what happened to those in his family who thought that divine humility and meekness were the qualities of those who would inherit the earth. All the earth they'd inherited had been six feet down—and sometimes nothing more than whatever their ashes covered.

He looked up and saw Ruthi return, dressed in combat fatigues cut for desert operations and camouflaged for movement at night. For a moment in the twilight she could have been Hannah reborn. Perhaps she was.

He helped her into the Sikorski's cabin, already echoing the soft whine of a buried generator. His manner was courtly, as it always was when he bothered to think about it; as if he needed to compensate for the clumsiness that replaced the things he might have learned as a child. On ceremonial occasions he was always the most crisply and formally dressed, down to the black bow-tie that went with his IAF uniform. Ruthi knew this awkwardness in him: the awkwardness of a man who between the ages of ten and eighteen tried desperately to believe in the God of his fathers while he cheated and lied and labored through the Nazi slagheaps to stay alive, and then toiled in the desert and took on the tough disregard for bourgeois frills and pretensions that went with Marxism before limping back to a belief in his people's God.

She gave him a hug. "It will be all right, you'll see."

On his way through the leafy lanes around the kibbutz, breathing the heavy scent of jasmine, Jacob finished the prayer the Christian had taught him in a stone cell: "Where there is hatred, let me sow love; where there is injury, pardon; where there is doubt, faith; where there is despair, hope. . . ." The luminosity of the words banished melancholy and discouragement. They were the words of a good man, a man named Francis of Assisi, a saint to those of the Christian faith and a reminder—and dear God how badly Jacob needed to be reminded these days—that good men exist everywhere and must learn to recognize one another. He shook off the dark clouds gathering again around his mind. To have faith in man's essential goodness—was it possible?

Ruthi buckled herself into the seat, a Soviet Kalashnikov assault gun at her feet. She had watched Jacob's retreating back and she saw both humility there and a burden of sorrow. It was strange that this stunted man, made to feel old at forty-three in a land where the first six chiefs-of-staff were all in their thirties, should be a walking storehouse of vital knowledge. She was reminded of the Bedouins who sharpened their memories by the intonation of epic poems passed from generation to generation; and who thus had a ready-made network of communications, for the secret orders of guerrilla bands could be passed from mouth to mouth across the featureless sands from one end of Arabia to another. The strength of Bedouin poetry lay in its severe limitations; it could be passed only by word of mouth; there had never been a written form. Thus it provided a watertight security system. Written codes could be broken. Spoken lines, buried in ancient verse, were beyond capture and spread almost as swiftly as electronic pulses. Perhaps more swiftly. The Arabs, suspicious of strangers and unused to mechanical devices, would react trustingly when orders arrived by the nomad-telegraph.

Some of the fiercest Arab patriots had fought turn-of-the-century imperialists this way. The Mad Mullah used the *gabay* epic poems as a form of password. Fighters in the desert rejected a written language for the very reason that it might weaken Islamic law and reveal too much to a stranger. The man who carried secrets in his head was still the strongest proof against torture.

Which reminded her. She took a pack of sanitary towels from her knapsack and probed inside. Yes, the needle sealed in plastic was there. A needle with grooves near the point, to which clung a sticky substance called curare. She caught Doctor Golden's button-eyes watching her. Nobody, not even he, would guess where she had got the needle. She fumbled with the pack and the doctor turned away, suddenly embarrassed. Really, she thought, men are such dear sweet fools. Golden was already fretting about her. He would explode if he knew about the needle, which was faster-paced than cyanide.

Up front, Major Zee waited for the hour of takeoff. The luminous dials cast an eerie green glow on his impassive face. His hands moved restlessly for the hundredth time around the cockpit. There would be no radio gossip on this trip. No skipping at low altitude over the hills. He would claw vertically for height, knowing the risk of detection and the danger from missiles like telegraph poles, and then with fluttering rotorblades he would windmill down upon Hill PS-5. His navigation would be dead-reckoning, a fancy word in these conditions for guesswork. He glanced into the night sky. All the early evening stars had gone.

He whistled softly between his teeth. Ground mist and heavy overcast. Perhaps some rain. A pessimist would say the glass was half empty. He preferred to think it was half full.

"This is the night we must watch, the time of danger," he recited to himself. "This is the time of lying and deceit. The time for ferrets, for fear of any stranger . . ."

11

THE FLYING

GUERRILLAS

"They give us a lot of crap about the crews being overworked and tired," said the tall American leaning against the bar in Frederika's Pub, nursing a pre-dinner drink. "Jesus, I've seen those 'tired, overworked' bastards boozing it up with their chicks at Mandy's and that new discotheque under the Tirana at Herzlya. Overworked . . . bullshit!"

"They've been bombing round the clock." Another of the foreign correspondents balanced back on his stool. "They're overworked all right—"

The Frenchman among them slammed down his glass. "Nom de Dieu! I was with the RAF for three years. I flew with your American bomber squadrons in Korea . . . Half the time is spent sitting around waiting for weather to clear, waiting for generals to make up their minds, waiting for a stupid mechanic to get the dirt out of a carburetor filter."

"Look, old boy, let's face it. These people see spies everywhere." The London *Times*'s man loomed over them. "They lost a war in A.D. 132 and for eighteen centuries they were dispersed. That's a long time to be homeless and hated."

"Who the hell hates them?" demanded the American. "I get

goddam pissed off, hearing about the Diaspora and the ghettos and the holocaust. They've fought three wars in the space of a single generation and they've won every one of 'em."

"If another nation loses a war it loses its freedom," said a second American. "If this one lost a war, it'd cease to exist."

"Stop trying out your leads on me," groaned the first correspondent. "You new guys all sound the same. . . ."

The stranger S sat within earshot, finishing his beer. The press corps was fed up because the IAF guarded its secrets so well. S understood the frustration of the newsmen. He had just returned from Jerusalem, however, and he felt sorry for the airmen now being so vigorously cussed. Here in the Pub, surrounded by tourists and the gaiety of Tel Aviv, it was hard to believe that right now, all through the country, airbases were going on full alert while decisions were made that might change the Middle East picture again overnight.

All in all, S reflected, the air force had been astonishingly open. Right now, for instance, he had a fair idea of the crucial point it had reached. He knew the men who would contribute to the decision-making process, tired corporals working in darkened hangars as much as the young fliers in their underground ready-rooms.

"What are you reading?"

He glanced up. "Ilan! Join me in a drink?"

"I'll sit a minute. We have to leave in ten minutes for a base."

"Then have a drink—"

"Orange juice then."

S made room on the bench. He felt a surge of warmth for the youngster at his elbow. Ilan's English was not the most inspired. On long drives he had a disconcerting way of saying, "I think I will catch a little dream now" when he wanted to doze. He was at once eager to please and at the same time resistant to sudden changes of plan. The Little Lieutenant and Captain Ilan, both of them unwillingly pitchforked into the thankless job of escorting the stranger through the IAF security checks, had sometimes threatened to do a mischief to S's sanity. And yet he was goddam glad to see Ilan's boyish face right now. Ilan, who did mysterious jobs in between steering him around: Ilan, who looked at this moment like a crop-haired urchin in his jeans and faded shirt: Ilan was a relief and a joy after listening to the weary moaners at the bar.

The thought made S uncomfortable. It wasn't long ago that he'd done his own share of moaning. Specifically, he'd complained once that Captain Ilan was too bloody lazy to make an early-morning rendezvous on time. It was only by accident, much later, that he discovered the truth: Ilan was a specialist in electronics and had spent the night at a Sinai base dissecting some captured Russian equipment before driving back to Tel Aviv to meet S. When he found out, S asked Ilan why the hell he didn't fly to these emergency jobs. "I get air-sick" was the deadpan reply.

Ilan had picked up the book S was reading. It was open at a passage describing the author's mixed feelings about Israel's "atmosphere of secrecy and defiance that is often so distressing that it can lead one to imagine himself in a people's republic." *

"What," asked Ilan, "is a people's republic."

"Well, like Red China."

Ilan grimaced. "*We* are like a Communist state?"

"Not really. It's just that—you know, in China sometimes I myself used to get a feeling of claustrophobia. I guess *any* country that stands alone . . ."

"You were in Red China?"

S swallowed the last of his beer. "Several times."

Ilan's face never changed expression but the eyes hardened.

"Until," S added, "I was expelled."

The tension went out of the air. At the bar, the correspondents were arguing about "siege mentalities." Near the windows overlooking the Mediterranean, on the raised half of the Pub, a left-wing editor played chess against an off-duty squadron com-

---

* Jean Lartéguy, *The Walls of Israel* (New York: Evans-Lippincott, 1970).

mander who had two reasons for being there. He liked arguing politics. He was wearing a spinal brace. Around the chessplayers, evaluating the moves, lounged a couple of pretty actresses from the Bimot Theater and the producer of a film called *The Siege*. Here life bubbled up irrepressibly. On any evening you could count on finding writers, artists, soldiers arguing every political theory from John Stuart Mill to Marx; but arguing because of a firm Jewish hold upon the dimension of time, arguing on the basis of long memories and confident expectations for an indefinite future.

This was the paradox that kept every civilized value alive. Tonight the atmosphere should be doom-laden. Half the Israelis here must know about—indeed, would be contributing to—the difficult decisions being made. There were men here with little money to spend: colonels in mufti who came to enjoy the talk and who were not pressed into drinking; men who would be back tomorrow for another month under the relentless Egyptian guns.

Ilan interrupted his thoughts. "We should go."

They drove through streets overflowing with tourists: Hadassah tours, groups from the Midwest, American kids who flew here for a summer on the kibbutzim but worried if the water was safe to drink; dodging pedestrians skipping off the sidewalks and infuriating the drivers of awkwardly long buses; out beyond the neon lights going full blast on Dizengoff into the dark and narrow alleys and onto the single-lane wooden bridge that led to the base.

S was in a mellow mood. He realized he'd crossed an unseen borderline. He was on Ilan's side. The moaners in the Pub belonged to a different, indifferent world. There was something about this country that made the old heart leap, and one didn't have to be Jewish to feel it. Right now, under arc lights beside the Wailing Wall, there would be archaeologists patiently uncovering layer after layer of Jerusalem's past. The air later tonight would be filled with the music of Beethoven and Bach in the crowded auditorium graced by Pablo Casals and Otto Klemperer. The cultural contrast with the cross and petulant Arab world outside was far greater than that which marked off Byzantium from the threatening Turks.

He stopped the car behind a long line of stalled traffic.

Ilan said worriedly, "Your plane leaves in fifteen minutes."

"Where?"

"I can tell you now," said Ilan, as if S might have blurted out the secret to the Pub's customers. "You're Motti Hod's guest at the flying-school. It's a party for the graduating pilots. A wings' parade . . ."

"I was at the parade last week."

"This is the party," Ilan said firmly.

I wish you'd told me, thought S, feeling the first twinge of exasperation. I'm not dressed for any kind of a party and I'm certainly glad I didn't make any dinner appointments. So far as Ilan's concerned, breaking a social appointment would have been just too bad.

To soothe the sudden crawling of his nerves, S got out of the car. The traffic had backed up behind him now and there was no way to turn and take another route. He walked forward onto the wooden bridge. At the crest, a large truck confronted a small Fiat. The driver of the Fiat had left the wheel and was sitting on the bridge rail munching an apple. The driver of the truck hung out of his cab, alternately pleading and cursing. A crowd surrounded the apple-muncher, urging him to stand his ground in some cases and in others threatening him with instant disintegration.

"What to do with such a people?" asked a soldier who had been crossing the bridge on foot. He had stopped to address S in English. "Half of us want to go forward and the other half says, 'Back.' And so we go nowhere."

"What's the trouble?" inquired S with steely politeness.

"This one who stuffs himself with the fruit of Eden, he says he comes first to the middle of the bridge, therefore the truck driver must back off. The driver of the truck says he comes first to the middle of the bridge and anyway his truck is a lot bigger than a baby Fiat."

"Meanwhile," said S, "I am late to take a plane."

"Really?" said the soldier with fresh interest. "So are the men in the car back there."

S followed the direction of the soldier's tilted chin. He recognized a military staff car in the moonlight and a familiar figure climbing out. He gave the soldier *shalom* and walked back to the staff car.

"Hullo," said Elephant Moses. "A mess, eh?"

"A *damned* mess. I'm supposed to be taking off in a few minutes."

"Yes, I know," said Elephant Moses. "I'm your pilot."

S swung from his earlier euphoria to deepest gloom. "For God's sake, suppose this was a real emergency?"

Elephant Moses lifted his wide shoulders. "These things work out." S was suddenly reminded of flying with him in the Fouga-Magister, the calm voice ticking off the technical details of a nerve-shattering gut-wrenching reverse turn.

The colonel thrust forward to the point of confrontation. S watched him with dyspeptic fascination. How the hell could these people hope to survive? Here was a bridge wide enough to take only a single line of traffic. And on that bridge there stood two vehicles nose to nose. The stubbornness of their drivers meant that behind each vehicle there now stretched two crocodiles of cars. Even if one of the contending drivers did climb down, it was physically impossible for him to back up.

I feel, thought S, like a piece of sheet metal that's bent back and forth until it snaps. Several times a day I'm bent from admiration to exasperation and back again. It's as Jean Lartéguy said: Israel is discipline and disorder, perpetual argument and absolute obedience to orders, pride and self-doubt, ascetism and horseplay. It may be magnificent but it isn't war.

A sudden roar of laughter swept through the crowd around the apple-muncher. Men and women called to each other in the pale moonlight and began drifting back to their cars. Engines revved. Headlamps blinked. A spirit of anarchy seemed to seize the motorists at either end of the bridge where the road became indiscernible from the rough ground sloping down to the river. They swung their cars backward onto the river banks; and behind them, others throttled onto the broken pavement or reversed with a cheerful disregard for the two or three police cars which had appeared on the scene with an air of detached curiosity. Elephant Moses and the truck driver appeared to have buried the apple-muncher between their swarthy arms and S was faintly disappointed at this apparent resort to violence. It seemed out of character. Once again, he would have to revise all those ideas about Israelis being basically a thoughtful and good-natured people. Then the huddled men broke apart and S saw the apple-muncher toss the core into the shining river below, punch the truck driver lightly in the shoulder, shout some cheerful insult to Elephant Moses, and get back into his Fiat. Soon there was room for him to back off the bridge. Elephant Moses rejoined S and said, "Better get back to your car. See you at the crew-room in five minutes."

"But how . . . ?"

"The truck driver was my company commander when I was a rifleman in the '48 war," said Elephant Moses. "I told him to stop playing the fool. The strong should give way to the weak."

"And what did you tell the little man in the Fiat?"

"He was an Arab and kept calling on Allah to support him. I said he was worse than quarreling schoolboys who each say his dad is the bigger and stronger. He replied that his dad was Allah and certainly was bigger and stronger, and I told him, 'Aha, but my dad's Moses and he's chief of police.' He started to laugh and for good measure I said, 'Look, Moses wasn't all that hot. If he'd had any sense, when he came down from the mountain he'd have headed in the direction of Switzerland instead of this place.' That seemed to please him. 'Allah'd made a mistake too,' he said, and so we cleared the bridge."

One hour after sundown Major Zee engaged the Wright Cyclone piston-engine, heard the familiar creak and swish of the great rotor blades gathering speed above his head, and checked the tail rotor. His mechanic flashed the all-clear and scrambled aboard. Zee cringed slightly at the thought of the racket he must be making and was glad that his wife and children were at home instead of here in the kibbutz with her parents. The temptation to see his own mother had been strong but it was better that she knew nothing. He concentrated on lifting this 13,000 pounds of shuddering metal and wire through two miles of vertical height. His mother would never understand. . . .

Mosheko the mechanic listened to the note of the 1525-horsepower engine with the loving attention of a long-eared mother rabbit watching over her baby cottontails. He wore an old skull-tight helmet with long flaps that emphasized his rabbit-like expression and although he fussed around Ruthi, checking her lap-strap, his mind was busy on how to seduce the old Wright Cyclone into a little extra effort. To get the lift needed for vertical takeoff, the engine was geared to drive the rotor much more slowly than the propellor of a piston-driven airplane, the rotor itself being of much greater diameter. The rotor shaft created a tendency to turn the fuselage in the opposite direction. This torque was countered by the engine-driven tail rotor revolving in a vertical plane. When the helicopter moved forward, the advancing blade of the rotor met the airstream at a greater speed than the retreating blade. This meant that the advancing blade experienced the greater lift, and to equalize this lifting force over the whole rotor system each of the rotor-blade roots was hinged so that the blade could flap up or down according to the lift generated. The load applied to a rotor varied greatly so that the resultant oscillation could cause a violent rocking on the ground which would destroy the machine. To overcome this ground-resonance, another hinge at each blade root permitted a blade to lag behind or travel ahead according to the speed of the tip, thus dampening vibrations within the rotor assembly.

All of this Mosheko knew, and much more. Since the age of sixteen, when he had dithered between dropping out of school and searching for a trade, he had been drawn slowly into the world of flight. At the Haifa technical school he glimpsed something of the magic which was missing in his life at home. It was less the physical excitement of flying that attracted him than the mystery surrounding this. He thrived on the physical punishment of each day's hard routine because he came from a family that regarded work as a purifying experience—a family that perhaps unconsciously escaped into work from the harsh memories that made his father emotionally impotent and his mother terrified of expressing any love for her children. The mother was quite simply guarding herself against being hurt again by some brutal amputation from the people around her: she had been sent as a young girl to Palestine just before the British pre-1939 embargos on immigration and the rest of her own folk had been trapped in Latvia, where they vanished as if they had never existed. In the air force Mosheko discovered the comfort of family warmth which he had previously missed: the man commanding the technical institute seemed to have an infinite capacity for loving youngsters such as this one. In the classrooms, overcrowded as they were and lacking in the simplest refinements, Mosheko sat listening to what began to take the place of the fairy tales he had been denied (through no conscious omission) by his emotionally paralyzed mother. His need, his hunger, for tales of mystery and imagination were met by the romance of electronics and the beauty of mathematics. His toy soldiers were soldering irons and solenoids.

Mosheko, squatting in his rabbit-eared helmet, blinked gnomelike under the green bulb illuminating the interior of the S-58. When the green light went out, signaling the pilot's caution as they tilted forward at 10,000 feet to cross into enemy territory, there was almost no interruption in the flow of Mosheko's calculations. If he'd been in the back seat of a Phantom doing twice the speed of sound, his eyes would have blinked with just the same amount of concentration on some problem to do with jets. Now, proceeding at a stately pace of 80 miles an hour, he grappled with the question of how this particular machine might be made less vulnerable to attack. Since he'd worked on the Sikorskis, he'd become disenchanted with them. Right now, for instance, the damned machine was a sitting duck for an SA-II, and Mosheko rather resented the idea of being demolished by so crude a missile.

He'd been looking into the foreign technical journals when his imagination was gripped by the new computing devices that gave a tactical pilot a new freedom throughout the theater of operations. There was one, based on solid-state electronics, that sounded ideal for chopper sorties. For some months, these had been conducted at night and at low level. Tonight was exceptional because of the presence of Syrian ground troops and the need for surprise. But it was also an indication that tactics would have to change again. Mosheko recalled the description of a projected-map system: "Treetop flying leaves no room for error," said the handbook, "particularly in bad weather or at night. The tactical pilot needs an accurate position related to his immediate surroundings and to his waypoint. Hand-held or roller maps are not good enough today. The new system substitutes long-life film for tons of disposable maps. Slot the appropriate cassette of film into the system and the pilot has instant information at his disposal without the necessity for pre-flight paste-ups."

Mosheko crouched beside a window and watched a necklace of lights passing underneath: the last of the *nahal* colonies, astride the new boundaries of Jordan, Syria and Israel. *Nahals*, soldier-colonies, were formed out of groups of city youngsters who decided while still at school to become kibbutz-dwellers. When they reached military service they trained together, learned communal living on an established kibbutz, then separated to complete their combat duties (the men in paratroop units, where they became more than usually toughened). Then, veterans at twenty-one or so, they reunited to form pioneer villages in the danger zones.

The lights vanished abruptly, blacked out by cloud. When the ground became visible again, it looked to Mosheko like black velvet infected with ringworm. Here lay the enemy, their campfires burning carelessly and sometimes flaring in patches of fog.

If we hugged the ground, thought Mosheko, we'd escape detection and they wouldn't hear the noise of our approach until it was too late. But we'd have to be flat on the deck. This electronic system for displaying your position, with computers correcting your navigation, oughtn't to be difficult to design. We'd have fewer aborted missions. . . . If we invented the *nahal* system, there's nothing we can't invent.

An orange-yellow flame stuttered beneath the helicopter. Major Zee selected it from the arena of small Bedouin fires. He watched to see if it flashed across the horizon, turning into nothing more harmful than light reflected on the Perspex. Night flying played odd tricks. But the flame gathered speed.

Zee disengaged the engine and decreased the blade pitch of the rotor. The Sikorski dropped violently. He put her back into gear after losing a thousand feet and hurled forward, tilting the axis of the main rotor as far as it would go. Then he tilted back, the machine rearing up like a horse reined in, and slid sideways for as long as he could hold the clumsy fuselage at the necessarily sharp angle.

In the cabin, Ruthi gripped her seat and felt Doctor Golden's weight shift like a chunk of cargo torn loose from its lashings.

"*Tilim!*" The word for missiles was jerked from the mechanic's lips.

The air in the cabin was suddenly hot and stifling with the smell of high-octane fuel.

"If it's a missile," Golden muttered to himself, "no amount of evasive action's going to help."

They all felt the harsh bump of a distant explosion before the Sikorski began rocking violently.

Zee watched the glare die away. It couldn't have been an SA-II, which carried a quarter of a ton of TNT and would have destroyed the Sikorski, even exploding at a distance. It must have been a smaller missile, fired more or less blindly in the direction of his engine noise.

He glanced again at his watch. Yesnov would be expecting him. It was standard procedure known to all pilots. The rescue mission, if delayed, would be sent out at an agreed-upon period of time after sundown. Yesnov would have worked out his distance from the front line and a fairly accurate time for the rescue ship's arrival.

That time was now. Zee had flown the primary course given him by the Citadel, and he had worked out his position allowing for a southerly wind whose drift-effect he measured by the way he'd crabbed across the *nahal's* lights. It was all rough-and-ready reckoning but Major Zee had done it so often that he felt like an ancient mariner.

He studied the blackness below again. Someone down there had tried to blow him out of the sky. And down there was Yesnov.

It might be smart to cut the engine and put the rotor into autorotation, in effect transforming the helicopter into an autogyro in which the rotor acted as a windmilling brake. But he wasn't all that keen on the self-starting unit which his own men had improvised for these operations.

There was no sign of another launching. All was darkness directly below. He checked again that no lights were showing and began lowering the Sikorski into the abyss.

Then Mosheko was squeaking in his ear. "We've been hit. There's fuel everywhere."

Zee crouched over the dials. If they were losing fuel, it was scarcely perceptible. But the raw odor of gasoline stung his nostrils. He squelched the thought of all that 115-octane waiting to explode.

"It's the aft tank," said Mosheko, back again.

Aft? Well, that was the tank which one emptied first. Zee shrugged. "Make sure nobody's wearing studs in their boots. If there's a rupture in the fuel line, see what you can do to stuff it. And for God's sake don't let Golden move until we've landed." The smallest spark, a moment of friction between the doctor's steel-bottomed medical kit and the Sikorski's metal floor, and there'd be a doctor's lucrative practice for sale in Tel Aviv.

S, the stranger, stood in the wooden shack while Elephant Moses signed the log for the plane trip to the base.

The shack made a small pool of light in the darkened base.

The air was very warm and still.

Behind sliding glass windows, a girl bent over a tilted drawing-board. On the ledge beside her, the transistor radio played softly.

The mood transported S backward in time. He could see a crew-room beyond the squadron office where the girl adjutant worked out the next day's flying schedule. The boys sprawled in the easy chairs had their feet up and their noses buried in books and magazines. Their faces were marvelously innocent, like the faces in the dog-eared photographs that S had not brought out for many years until a few days before returning to Israel. Old photographs of another war in another place. He had studied the faces and wondered: Were we really so young? Few of them had survived to take on the used look of men surrendering to the petty thievery of civilian life. He had looked at the old photographs with black crosses imprinted on those cheerful faces, remembering how blithely he had struck off his friends, as if it were all a game, almost taking pride in the high percentage of losses, thinking then that it was worth losing a few years of life to hoard a precious second more of flying wing to wing. And then he'd put the faded pictures away again for a few more years.

Others were stamping into the shack now. A young woman, stylishly dressed, carrying a small beaded bag of the kind one associates with film stars on opening nights. A couple of pilots in dress uniform, neatly bow-tied. A gray-haired man in battle dress and an air-force beret tucked under his shoulder strap. Two girls, identical in appearance, looking as if they should be busy with their school homework.

The music from the radio was vaguely familiar. S, with little capacity for memorizing any tune more complicated than *Alouette,* said to Elephant Moses "Is that the Philharmonic?"

"Probably." The big colonel leaned through the window and called to the girl-adjutant. S saw her shake her head and her lips frame some words.

Elephant Moses withdrew his head. "No. It's a new Czech recording of Brahm's First."

S looked blank and the colonel added, "You thought you recognized it."

"Sort of."

"Sometimes it's called Beethoven's Tenth," said the colonel. He saw S look even blanker. "You see, Brahms pinched the theme of the finale from the last of Beethoven's symphonies and sometimes people get confused. . . . Well, let's go!"

The party shambled out into the darkness of the airfield. The music receded in the distance but S could hear it still as he climbed into the snub-nosed Cessna Skywagon. Others in the group were moving toward similar light planes pegged out in tidy rows. Presently the heavy Mediterranean air was shattered by the growl of engines. S relaxed in the copilot's seat and for some reason the verses written in another war returned to mind:

Sing, nightingale, let each successive note
Thrill higher; though you burst your throat
Pour out for them your liquid song
Who fly to different music. . . .

David Krohn, a former banker from Detroit, now manager of
the Israel Philharmonic, stood in the foyer of the Frederic R.
Mann auditorium with the phone to his ear.

"Yes. Of course. No trouble." He replaced the phone and
padded up the wide stairs.

Inside, tier upon tier of faces shone faintly in the glow from
the stage below. The orchestra had reached the marchlike opening of the last movement of Shostakovich's Fifth Symphony.
Krohn gave a small sigh of relief. The whole damned lot of
'em were in action, brass and all. He wasn't sure which he feared
most: an orchestra in which every musician was a first violinist
on the edge of a tantrum; or an audience that would kill him if
he dropped a pin in the pause between two movements.

After a great deal of ingenuity, he roused an usher from her
trancelike involvement in the sounds reverberating through the
great hall. Her expression changed from irritation to eager com-
pliance as he whispered in her ear.

A minute later, Mordechai Ben-Ari left the auditorium.
Founder-member of a kibbutz on the shores of Galilee, Ben-Ari
had become President of El Al Airlines in a period when air
piracy was at its worst. His bland face concealed his anxiety as
he went to Krohn's office to call back an unlisted phone number.

He almost laughed with relief when he heard Motti's robust
voice. No, no planes missing or hijacked or blown up. Just a
matter of general interest. Would he mind coming down to the
flying-school? Now? There would be a light plane waiting for
him.

Ben-Ari braced himself. His wife was accustomed to these
sudden exits; had been since the days when they directed the
traffic of immigrants out of Europe. She'd have to think up a

story to tell their guests. Funny how time changed things. Twenty-five years ago, Motti Hod was a cheeky young soldier "winning" Allied trucks, "organizing" Allied fuel, to shift all the young Jewish survivors out of the ruins of Hitler's empire. Mordechai Ben-Ari was the anonymous but powerful figure behind the scenes who later moved into aviation by a natural progression. His home in British-mandated Palestine was crying out for new settlers but the sea-routes were interrupted by Royal Navy patrol boats. Jews who had grown up in one form of concentration camp found themselves in another on the British-held island of Cyprus. So aircraft took the place of emigrant-ships and thus Ben-Ari embarked on his second career. A fugitive from the British in 1945, he had written his university exams while in hiding (his professor of psychology had traveled from Jerusalem to adjudicate, then was killed by Arab terrorists). He had become the underground-army commander for the whole East European area, negotiating with the Russians to extract ninety-eight thousand refugees, conducting the assembly of stolen military transports, organizing clandestine radios and passport factories. Then, in November 1948, as one of the first acts of the new State of Israel, the registration took place of the airline that was to graduate from the wholesale movement of refugees to the nonstop flights from New York of luxury jet transports.

Ben-Ari scribbled a note for his wife. She had been the underground-army girl who smuggled him through British posts to study and train secretly in Galilee. She, too, had known young Motti Hod by another name, for their villages adjoined each other. Now Motti ran the air force and Mordechai Ben-Ari ran the airline that was also Israel's umbilical cord.

Mordechai was a big man, heavy with years, but he was unlike any airline president that S had ever met. Now, as he skipped down the steps to the square outside, he might have been once again the student of psychology and statistics on a secret mission to Vienna. He was thinking, as it happened, that he'd never feel old so long as Israel continued to need an umbilical. Which, so far as he was concerned, was forever.

Motti Hod stood in a corner of the converted hangar. A desert wind blew outside but the sound and the cold would never penetrate this cheerful mob. There was the bandmaster in his dress blues, keeping his balance under the surging movements of the newly graduated pilots. Soon they would swing into the wild *hora* dance, lifting Motti onto their shoulders and working themselves into a free-for-all frenzy. Two sides of the hangar were lined with tables loaded with food and drinks. This was one of the few times when the crews let off steam. For these new pilots it marked the end of the most demanding twenty-months' training known to any air force. For the instructors it was a change from back-breaking routine: the fliers mixing air-exercises with three or four offensive sorties a day; the classroom instructors resting their feet before the new boys arrived to be pumped full of the theories of flight and navigation and engines and electronics when they weren't being jog-trotted through the midnight desert on survival games. For wives and sweethearts it was often the only glimpse they got of this invisible air force.

Invisible? The stranger S thought it so. Flying here with Elephant Moses, he had watched the moonlight dance on plastic sheets sheltering the hard-won fields of kitchen vegetables. Then the cultivation ran out. The plastic sheets that looked like shimmering lakes turned to a long and creamy shoreline. This was followed, as they turned inland, by the isolated and concentric circles of light marking the brave experiments to bring still more fertility to still more acres of desert. Down there lived the old lion Ben-Gurion among his bright red hollyhocks, alone in his wooden prefab, ascetic as ever, acidulous as always, wrestling with the Negev the way he once wrestled those who got in the way of his vision of Israel. "For him," Moshe Dayan had once written, "the colonization of the Negev is the supreme expression of a revitalized Israel, changing the wild desert into a source of life. . . . The antithesis, in his eyes, is the city of Tel Aviv and I have heard him murmur, as he walked through its crowded streets, the name of a place doomed because of its wickedness and excessive luxury." Perhaps the old man could hear the faint hum of planes slipping through the night to the bases buried under the desert he regarded with mystical awe. S could see the exhaust flames of the accompanying transports. He felt secure in the bubble of the Skywagon's cabin, listening to the steady rhythm of the motor and feeling the warmth of spirit from the panel's glow that a man gets in front of a good fire alone in the wilderness.

They landed beside a single line of widely spaced figures, and joined the lines of high-winged liaison aircraft tethered like wellbred horses in the stable of an outlying hangar. Small vehicles purred alongside. Voices murmured.

S was unprepared for the sudden explosion of light and energy inside the concrete cavern, reinforced against bomb-blast and louvered to catch the wind. He saw Motti Hod looking like a proud but shy father, creating his own small pool of authority by his mere presence which was not bolstered by a grand uniform and jingling medals. There, too, was Dan Tolkowsky looking very much the aristocrat: in 1953, when he took command of the air force, it had been a hodgepodge of preposterous old crates. Near him, tall where Tolkowsky was small, rumpled where the other was meticulously dressed, moved his successor Ezer Weizman who had taken the new air force fashioned by Tolkowsky's organizational genius and breathed into it a fieriness of spirit.

The seventeen-year-old twin girls who had flown here with S had been snatched into the whirlpool of dancers. Elephant Moses already had his arms linked with a ring of stamping young pilots. S recognized Czareko, who had once served in the Russian Air Force, and Aaron, whose encounter that morning with the Soviet spy-plane had started yet another minor crisis.

The mother of the twins came to talk with S. Perhaps she sensed that he felt a little lost in this tight-knit family atmosphere. She was wearing a coat against the chill air of the desert at night. She worried because S had not eaten and insisted upon filling him a plate from the buffet. They stood a small distance apart, shouting to each other above the hoots of the pilots and the oompah-pah of the band. At first S paid scant attention to her words, thinking she was being polite and motherly to a stranger. Yes, he said, he realized he was privileged to be standing at the heart of an air force which the Russians would give almost anything to see close up. What was different about it? Well, the contrasts. Like these banners and posters hanging from the roof, the work of the crewmen and the girls. Everywhere he looked, he saw this artistry. There hadn't been a squadron office which didn't have at least one talented artist to decorate air-regulations or illustrate safety warnings.

The woman said he should forgive her, but strangers were rare and one became self-isolated. Did he think they really had a chance?

S turned, not sure he'd heard the question.

"Do you think we can get through another year?"

S blinked. "Good lord, *yes.*" He glanced around, seeing the laughing faces, the huddle forming in one corner, the girls swirling under the floodlights, the veteran commanders and the older pilots being swung into boisterous groups of nineteen-year-olds busily inventing the daft games that young men play in war.

"I wish I understood why you say that," said the woman. She was dressed with fashionable taste but she seemed to huddle inside her coat for comfort. S had a sudden desire to put an arm around her and say, "Look, you're safe, all of you. You surely don't think the rest of the world will abandon you?" But he couldn't say it because he was not sure it was true.

The twins skipped out of the central throng of dancers and hauled their mother away, teasing her about the coat. One of the girls came back, her face alive with excitement. "You know that was the first time I had ever been in an airplane? I thought it would be like sitting in a bus."

"And what was it like?"

"Fantastic. Floating, like in those dreams where you try to escape the rotten things on earth." Her small face became serious. "Mother gets a bit weighed down at times. Is that good English?"

"Very good."

"Daddy says it's easy for us who were born here. When we hear the bad things that happened in Europe we say where was the Israeli Air Force? Some of the people at school honestly wonder. I try to understand what it must have been like where my mother was, and why they were defenseless. But it's hard to imagine. And then she worries about daddy."

"Which one is he?"

The girl pointed to one of the senior officers, a man S had met in the Citadel; gray-haired and handsome but hollow-eyed from the long days spent at a special kind of work that S knew was tremendously demanding. He heard the wife's question again: "Do you think we've got a chance?" It was infinitely more revealing than all the official bravado in the world.

At the other end of the country Jacob sat quietly reading in the kibbutz recreation room built deep under the canteen so that the entire commune could shelter there if necessary. Tonight it was empty. At Jacob's elbow was a telebrief phone and scrambling unit. He leafed through the papers delivered by courier, and stopped at one of the monitored reports from Cairo. *Al Ahram's* editor, Egypt's Minister of Guidance, was in Moscow with President Nasser. According to the minister, Nasser announced at the first session in the Kremlin that his soldiers had shot down two Israeli Phantoms and two Skyhawks that day. Communist Party leader Brezhnev glanced at the Soviet Defense Minister, who took the hint and told Nasser, "But, my friend, your men shot down more than four planes. Our technicians report that the number you brought down was six." Then the Russians unfolded a map of the Suez front and there were marks where the planes had been hit.

Jacob shook his head. The Egyptians were not only being humiliated, they boasted about it. Nothing could be more inviting to further Soviet intervention.

He turned to another report. The New China News Agency's dispatches from Peking described the departure of a new ambassador to Cairo. Now that *was* interesting. His predecessor, Huang Hua, had tried to clear up the mess of 1966 when President Nasser acted on reports that his Moslem ally in Indonesia, President Sukarno, had been nearly deposed by Red China's agents. Huang Hua had been in trouble himself later: accused of financing Maoists in Egypt's schools and letting Red Guards from his embassy try to kidnap a defector. Was it possible that Peking was changing tactics?

Jacob lit a cigarette. A change in direction, yes, because Mao stuck to his doctrine that world revolution zigged and zagged. Whatever the Chinese were cooking in Cairo, their real interest was in organizing and arming the Maoist-type guerrillas just over the borders.

The phone rang. "No," said Jacob. "It's too early yet."

He could hear the *hora* and the thump of a band in the background. "Sounds like a good party."

"Everyone's here except you," said the familiar hoarse voice. There was a pause. "It looks as if they're moving into Phase Three."

"Ah!"

"Try not to sound pleased."

"Worry about your own decibels," grunted Jacob, and replaced the phone. It was typical of Ezer to be fretting about a missing pilot when the lousy railroad and manic motorists were supposed to be his chief preoccupations.

Phase Three, eh? He stared at the floor. Phase One had been

the shipment to Egypt of Soviet SA-IIIs along with Russian crews. Phase Two came with the MiG-21s piloted on operational missions by Russians, and deployed around the interior of Egypt to block IAF strategy of deep-penetration raids to take the pressure off Israeli troops on the Canal. Now came Phase Three after the SA-IIs were moved secretly and at night to within eleven miles of the west bank of the Canal. This changed the IAF's concept of the 32nd meridian, the north-south line some 20 miles inside Egypt and west of the Canal which provided a kind of buffer zone. Within that zone, Egyptian military forces had to expect to be attacked so long as their guns continued the steady bombardment of Israeli lines.

Political considerations had made it necessary to avoid direct conflict with Russian-flown warplanes. But then two Phantoms were destroyed almost simultaneously by missiles, and this didn't square with the SA-II's record in North Vietnam, where the kill-rate against United States aircraft was less than one hit per thousand launchings.

Motti Hod called it "the Russian fist in the Egyptian glove" and would begin the steady hammering of missile-sites, straining the IAF's resources still further. If Russian technicians got in the way, that was too bad. He must prevent Phase Four: an Egyptian assault across the Canal under cover of Russian-flown MiGs and bombers, supported by Russian missiles in which Russian officers made sure "the button is not pushed before or after it should be," to quote Haim Bar-Lev. The chief-of-staff had been in Golda's Kitchen when Mrs. Meir said, "We're facing a struggle more critical than any we have ever had to face before."

Some of the pilots were slipping away now from the party to catch four hours' sleep before the first of the predawn missions.

Elephant Moses, avoiding the stranger's eye, said, "Motti will fly you back."

S knew better than to question any change in plan. He knew about the Phase Three flap. Nobody seemed to be hitting the panic button. But you could never tell. He glanced again at the small knots of older men standing by the littered tables. Between them they represented all the hopes and frustrations, the fears and the bloodshed, of an air force that adapted as swiftly and casually to each new threat as an outfit of partisans in the mountains of Montenegro or guerrillas in the jungles of Asia. If man was still superior to machine, then these men surely must win.

"*Ma ihieh hassof?*" the woman in the coat had asked. "What will be the end?"

It might have sounded pretentious, thought the stranger as he walked over to join Motti Hod, but he wished now that he'd voiced his answer. The end would be a triumph of human spirit over the mindless machines walling Israel in. Otherwise there was no hope for any of us.

12

A PHOENIX

FROM THE DEATH CAMPS

Mordechai "Motti" Hod was one man who would always beat the machine.

The way S recorded their first long conversation was eerie. Motti's day had few fixed points. At dawn he sat on his veranda digesting military and intelligence reports. These pretty much decided his future movements. He could be in Bar-Lev's bunker for breakfast on the Canal, and circling the lush valley of the Jordan to supervise a strike while his staff in the Citadel stalled a ten-o'clock coffee-break visitor. He tried to keep his appointments but there was always, metaphorically speaking, this switchboard in his head that was an integral part of the country's nervous system. His quicksilver nature had its impish side. The RAF told a story that, true or not, was a peculiarly British tribute to the man. One of their snottier vice-marshals had condescended to fly with the IAF during a visit from Cyprus. Motti strapped him into a two-seat jet and whizzed him over a golden city of domes and minarets. The English dignitary, who regarded Israel's defenders as a rag-tag-bobble mob anyway, grunted a brief appreciation of the vista. "Fine place, Jerusalem. But why are they shooting at us?" "Because it's Damascus," Motti is said to have answered.

Waiting for Motti to pop into the Citadel office, S was recording Elephant Moses' early life. The burly colonel had described
how physically fit inmates of the Nazi death-camps were put to
work. Because he was then just sixteen, Elephant Moses had
lived in a concentration-camp workers' blockhouse.

"We were in the charge of criminals—thieves, murderers—
who would be normally in a jail," Elephant Moses said. "These
'block-masters' exercised the discipline. They beat us for any
reason. There were hundreds of us crammed in a single block
and someone was always in trouble. If you had diarrhea and
made a mess before you got into a latrine outside, that was pun-
ishable by death. I saw block-masters execute boys who could
not bring themselves to wash in the open air at temperatures
below zero. How did they execute? One way was for the boy
to lie on his back with a piece of wood across his throat and a
blockmaster standing on each end of the wood, see-sawing. . . ."

At this point S was jerked into Motti's presence. There was
no time to change cassettes. He was left therefore with a piece
of tape that went like this:

Elephant Moses: ". . . so from fourteen to sixteen, I lived in
in terror of this casual execution. . . ." The voice is introspec-
tive, troubled, and in vivid contrast to the way Elephant Moses
sounds when flying.

Motti Hod follows immediately: "I was fifteen—I was fourteen
when I trained as a soldier—fifteen when the Second World War
started. I was uneasy hearing what they were doing to my people in Europe. I lived on the kibbutz, Degania. At the south
tip of what you call the Sea of Galilee. My father was born here
and my grandfather too. Actually you know, I'm the first sabra
to command the air force who trained entirely as a pilot in our
own air force."

The voice now is strong, staccato, sure, full of life and opti-
mism, bubbling with humor. No black memories here.

S found Motti Hod a mixture of shyness and pride. "The
Russians are concentrating all their attention on us," he said as

early as February 1970. "The war goes into a new phase. For the first time since World War Two, the superpowers will test all their latest equipment against each other."

"Is it the Spanish Civil War again?" asked S.

"Not at all. We don't take foreign volunteers, and we have no hinterland. Nor is it like Vietnam with ourselves in the position of unarmed peasants united by some simplified ideology, their faith hammered flat and leaving no room for a real culture. This war is unique. It is becoming an electric war—an electronic war revolving around the deployment of new weapon-systems. There will be big aerial battles. . . ."

Motti talked in machine-gun bursts. He was a muscled wildcat, relaxed one moment and then triggered into violent action by something he'd seen on the air-defense console behind his desk. Women found him handsome. His dark hair was thinning. He had a neatly trimmed mustache and neat taut-skinned features. S never saw him without a wry grin on his face. Even on ceremonial occasions he seemed, though ramrod stiff, to be chuckling to himself at the brief but unavoidable display of spit-and-polish. Yet S also knew that Motti was unforgiving in the way he chewed out anyone in the air who endangered life or risked losing a machine for frivolous or stupid reasons.

He could be soft-hearted too. Once, in a melee near Cairo, a fighter-pilot overlooked a MiG sneaking away from the battle. Motti noted this, watching on the consoles of the computerized air-defense command and control system. By the time the pilot returned to his desert base, Motti was already waiting.

"He gave me such hell," said the pilot later, "I thought for sure I was going to lose my wings. Then he said—and after that all was forgiven *on both sides*—'You sat there reading a book, boy, while Brigitte Bardot walked past you stark naked.'"

Once, after aerobatics in the Israeli-built version of the Fouga-Magister, S had said, "It's the smoothest plane to fly—"

"Too smooth," Motti replied. "Pilots should learn on aircraft with a few built-in vices."

Another time, S asked if the air force—by attracting the ponderous weight of Russian hostility—had not been *too* successful.

"That," said Motti, "is like saying a woman can be too beautiful."

He had a tremendous curiosity about things outside his own experience and something in common with Ben-Gurion in his appetite for books. Like Ben-Gurion, who was a corporal in the British Army in the First World War, Motti became one in the second. Ben-Gurion devoured everything that came his way, speaking many languages and learning new ones (such as Spanish in order to read Cervantes). Ben-Gurion piled his shelves with every textbook on the art of war from Clausewitz to Napoleon. Ben-Gurion had labored on the land and so had Motti. If Motti's studies were becalmed, it was because he was forced to cope with tactical problems that Ben-Gurion never dreamed about. The air chief kept his flying gear in the anteroom to his Citadel office along with souvenirs from those parts of Africa and Asia where his pilots had helped build independent air forces. He was apt to interrogate the stranger rather than talk about himself. Then one day, with Elephant Moses' fearful recollections still ringing in his ears, S managed to question Motti about his own contrasting youth.

"I was raised in the shadow of war," said Motti Hod. "You know, it created a sense of uneasiness in myself that here the world is turning round, turning upside down around us, and here we sit in a very quiet and beautiful corner and it went against my nature. I'm a person that when I feel I should do something about something and it's within my way of thinking and—and, well, my judgment—I normally do it. So this is what forced me to leave the kibbutz and enroll in the army. At that time of course it was the British army."

"Did life on a kibbutz prepare a youngster for military service?" asked S.

"We're making an investigation now to see why so many

pilots come from the kibbutz. It is not so easy to tell. Perhaps communal living makes it easier for a boy to fit into the army at an early stage and gives him a start. Where I come from, Degania, this is known as the mother of our cooperative settlements. It was the first in the Jordan Valley. The Syrians tried to destroy it in the 1948 war. Long before that, when I was perhaps ten or eleven, I had my first experience of seeing planes. There was an RAF squadron nearby, of Gloster Gladiator biplanes like the three defending Malta later—what were they called? Hope, Faith, and Charity.

"This is the first time I think I was close to an airplane. Then the flying boats would land near the kibbutz on their way from London to India. I would watch how they landed, how they taxied, how they took off. The third time I saw airplanes, the Haganah* opened a flying club. This was 1936, '37, '38, I don't remember. You know we had a lot of problems at the time. The Jewish population was small and scattered and you had to go through Arab territories so communication was difficult. Our solution was to start flying clubs that were really serving the Haganah, for liaison between settlements."

S asked, "Wasn't that an eerie kind of prescience?"

"Using planes? It was logical. When you think of our history, the only real way for us to go is up. And of course the British were always a fair-play people and the sport of flying was very legal and so was gliding. It was difficult for me at fourteen to train as a soldier but the kibbutz of course is the ideal place for underground training. Then when I was old enough I joined the Jewish Brigade of the British Army. The big war was almost over."

S: Where did you get your formal military training?

HOD: Geneva.

S: *Geneva?*

---

* Forbidden any military organization to defend themselves by the British, the Jewish Palestinians formed an army of Resistance (Haganah) which had to train in secret.

Hod: This is where I had my elementary training after going through Haganah training here. But of course we were not supposed to expose it when we got to the British Army. We pretended to start all over again. That's why they, the British, thought of us Palestinian Jews as very good soldiers. It was interesting to see how experienced British instructors picked out the experienced boys in the mob. After a week or so, section commanders had to be appointed and the British sergeant would go down the line and say, "You, you, and you." It was always exactly the boys who were already half-trained by the Haganah.

S: So you really started as an infantryman?

Hod: And then I was a driver. I was posted to 178 Company, Royal Armored Corps, for what they called GD—General Duties. And with this company I went to Italy and then Germany and all over Europe. I started looking for Jews. We were all looking. We had our own organization under cover, inside the British Army, and some of us were full-time rescuing people for emigration to Israel. We used army vehicles, army stores. It was a big operation and everything was short—food and fuel were the most precious things at that time. You know, just simple benzene for cars. And here we had to move thousands. Well, the organization between American and British troops was not as tight as it should have been. After a war, everything is chaos. We drew petrol, benzene, for an entire RAC company for one whole month—a nonexistent RAC company—from an American depot which we knew never made its accounts up until the end of the month. And we got trucks and clothing from the quartermasters by driving into depots to deliver these things back to stores. We would drive in one side of a depot, get a signature for delivery of a truck, say, and then drive out the other end. So the army thought it had the trucks back, and we had trucks that had ceased officially to exist. I worked for this illegal-immigration outfit for two years until 1947.

S: Was the present chief of El Al Airlines with you?

Hod: Ben-Ari? You mean El Al's president? No, he was in

Vienna. We had branches in Italy, France, Germany, Austria, and even in Czechoslovakia for some time. I was in the Italian bunch. We were looking for new ways to transport people, which is how Ben-Ari got into aviation, by the way. We made connections with a couple of American pilots who flew charter-Dakotas and they agreed to try and fly a charter from Rome to Tel Aviv. Well, they would show this route on their flight-plan when they filed it in Rome but actually they would land at a prepared field in the south of Italy, pick up a lot of kids, and then land the kids somewhere on a deserted airfield in Palestine before arriving empty in Tel Aviv.

We organized forty-five kids. I had to stand in the field with a torch—a flashlamp. The boys stood in corners of the field with lights. The Dakota landed and we loaded the kids on board. Immediately the police heard in the village and they thought —well, you know—they thought it was a crash, the Dakota circling at night and then the engine stopping. Well, the Dakota succeeded in taking off just in time for the police to miss them.

There was a woman who was head of the organization. She and I were the ones who got caught. I was pretending to be her driver and we had the car on the road with the wheel off, jacked up. The police got hold of it. They saw something peculiar about a car with a Milan plate, a rich Italian signora, and a refugee driver. It didn't make sense to them. We were suspected of smuggling arms to the partisans, to Tito's men, in Yugoslavia. At the time the Italians and the Yugoslavs were arguing about that northern part of Italy—Trieste. So they were a bit worried about us and kept us in prison for ten days. Interrogating us. And in those ten days I decided flying had a future in it. This is actually how I got to fly. What is it Doctor Johnson said? "When a man knows he is going to be hanged in a fortnight, it concentrates his mind wonderfully."

S: This is off the point, but I've noticed how often pilots— airmen—like yourself, how often everyone quotes from foreign, especially English literature.

HOD: We had to learn English in the British-mandate period. And people read a lot, especially on the kibbutz where, don't forget, there is a strong ideological motive and communal activities of a cultural kind. And then we never had television until lately. . . .

S: When were you demobilized officially from the British Army?

HOD: Officially, I was called for demobilization at the end of '46 and instead of me going back to Palestine to get discharged, the discharge was here but someone else took it.

S: How's that again?

HOD: Someone else, a refugee, no papers, not allowed to go to Palestine because of the British ban, he took my papers and became me and came here as me.

S: Who are—I mean, who *were* you? At that time?

HOD: I—er—I took the name Gersham Rosengard and used it for two, three years. I took, I just simply took his refugee papers and on this paper I worked myself for the next few years and I ended up with an identity card and an American permit and driving license and I used the same name to join our underground flying club in Milan.

S: So you could in fact create a person?

HOD: I could create a person, actually.

S: But who were you in the army, what were you called?

HOD: Originally I was—my family name was Fein. My grandparents were from Russia or that part of Rumania that was Russia.

S: Did you ever *meet* the man whose name you took?

HOD: Rosengard? I'd never met him. I still don't know him. These things were all organized. I was then only twenty-one so the whole thing must be taken in the context of a very young man who left home when it was under British rule and came back three years later flying a Spitfire. And this young man lands in a place which is not called Palestine any more, it's Israel.

One of the things I will never forget in my life was standing in Tel Aviv after so long. I landed the Spitfire after a long flight from—well, it was Central Europe and you know what it's like, flying a Spit, all by yourself, hour after hour.

All I had was what I wore. I looked a displaced person. Not a piece of paper on me, no identification. I got to Tel Aviv about eight o'clock in the evening. Air-force headquarters then was in a small hotel in Allenby Square. I stood in the Square for about an hour and I kept thinking to myself these are Israeli soldiers and Israeli policemen and Israeli taxi-drivers. I just kept watching them, my own people, doing ordinary jobs that all my life other people were always doing. Everyone was shabby and everything was poor but—well, they were Israelis.

Motti, the first pilot of the Haganah to complete his formal training, had graduated on Course Minus-Two. Officially, there was no air force. In fact, everyone was confident that some day it would come into existence. So the still-secret flying courses were numbered backward, as in a countdown. And Motti's was Minus-Two. He mentioned this casually one day to the stranger. "And this," he added, "is my twenty-first birthday as a pilot." The words came out, plain and untarnished as the man himself.

He had gone from the "flying club" in Rome to help ferry fighters from Czechoslovakia. (There is a well-attested story that as a student on his first solo, he dived on the Vatican and was arrested on landing). It was a dangerous period. The United Nations had voted for partition of Palestine, recognizing the right to the Jews' right to national independence in November 1947. The "air force" consisted of two British Tiger Moths, three or four battered light planes whose exact identity to this day is hard to establish, and several British Auster four-seaters whose numbers were concealed from the British authorities by the simple device of giving two aircraft the same registration and never letting them both be seen at the same time. There were thirteen Palestinian Jews who had served with the RAF, eleven Haganah mechanics, two Palestine Jews who were amateur pilots, nine foreign Jewish pilots, and two Catholic volunteer pilots.

Against this, Egypt had lined up a force of some substance: 40 fighters (mostly Spitfires); 40 light bombers (mostly Dakotas with bomb racks); 20 transports; 15 reconnaissance planes. Syria had 15 Harvards with bomb racks under the wings. The citizens of Tel Aviv were resigned to Egyptian raiders flying overhead until the first of the war—surplus fighters intercepted and shot one down. There are many Israelis, including Naomi, who remember the tremendous sense of relief they felt when the threat of surprise bombing was so dramatically removed.

In the same month as the United Nations partition vote, an Israeli bus was ambushed and passengers were killed. This attack marked the beginning of the Arab wars, which escalated to the unbelievable and certainly unforeseen dimensions of 1970. Other attacks followed. On Motti's kibbutz at Degania, as at other settlements, the value of aircraft was recognized without much opportunity to put this awareness into practice. Aircraft were based at two British-controlled airfields and were needed to link the Jewish settlements, which were often surrounded by hostile Arab villages. The fighting had also cut off the settlements from the cities. It was decided to concentrate all aircraft on Tel Aviv and a businessman from Tiberias was asked to intercede with the British Department of Civil Aviation. The man was Jacob Brin, now one of the country's most successful businessmen.

("I was asked by a very young man one day if I would get into the open cockpit of a Tiger Moth," Jacob Brin was later to tell S. "The biplane looked very old and unsteady but we flew from Galilee to Jerusalem, where I persuaded the British to let us use the airfield. My pilot asked me what I thought of the trip. I said it was most comfortable. He said 'Would you mind telling that to my CO? I've only got twelve hours' experience as a pilot.'" When Jacob Brin recounted this to S, his daughter had just completed her service in the IAF and one of his supermarkets had been bombed by an Arab terrorist who was later caught. "The air force is a lot bigger and the war is much more violent but on the whole these past twenty-three years have seen an improvement," said Jacob Brin.)

The first light squadron of what began as the Haganah Air Service was thus created. It had only one squadron and the pilots wanted to elect a squadron-leader once a month in the best kibbutz tradition.

By May 1948 there was Arab bombing of Tel Aviv and other centers. A metal plaque records what happened at Motti Hod's kibbutz in consequence of its being cut off: "Degania bore the brunt of the Syrian attack. . . . Syrian troops sought to destroy it and open the route to Galilee and the Valley of Jezreel. The turning point came on the 18th May 1948. The battle raged three full days following the fall of nearby Semakh. Syrian tanks tried to overrun the settlement and one penetrated the perimeter. But they were halted by members of the kibbutz equipped with small arms and Molotov cocktails."

S visited Degania to piece together the air-chief's background and also because of its unique place in kibbutz history. There was a rusting Syrian tank in a grove near the plaque. The settlement was hot and dusty, and the banana plantations were dotted with tall watchtowers. It had that unfinished look of a busy and expanding kibbutz (the word in Hebrew simply means "group") and Degania was the first. Settlers on a Jewish National Fund farm on the banks of the Jordan offered to take it over. The place was then called Um Jouni. It was Hebraicized to "Degania" which means cornflower, although sometimes it is interpreted as wheat. All this happened in 1909 and by 1920 the number of kibbutzim had grown to forty, with a total membership of six hundred and fifty, whose experiment in communal living was not automatically supported by Zionist leaders. These, in that period, favored the *moshav* form of small holders' cooperatives.

Many of the founder-members of Degania left for the moshav settlements. But the rise of Nazism in Germany helped to put the kibbutz system into the limelight. A kibbutz needed less investment than a moshav. The Second World War brought to the Middle East allied armies which provided big markets for agricultural produce and also stimulated the development of light industry for replacement parts in the war machine. Refugees from Europe filtered into the kibbutzim. At the same time, keeping pace with the rise in Nazism and feeding on German propaganda of the time, the Arabs in the 1930s and 1940s had become so openly hostile that the concentrated nature of the kibbutz made defense easier. By 1948 there were a hundred and forty-nine settlements and fifty-four thousand kibbutzniks, representing almost half of all who lived on the land.

S found in Degania a wry sense of humor and the anti-hero attitude that typified sabras from farming settlements. Nobody was ready to pay the air force any more tribute than they would have shown to other fighting services. If Motti Hod was proud of the kibbutznik record in the IAF, fine and good. Perhaps there was something about kibbutz life that accounted for the distinction with which their boys flew. Perhaps not.

The Haganah's squadron grew out of the kibbutz system of self-defense, and this established a traditional respect for the quality of farm-boy fighter pilots. In the early days, however, the improvisations that worked on the ground sometimes made the hair of foreign volunteers stand on end. The first operational squadrons in 1948 had to show its strength. Amateur armorers built a 110-pound bomb known eventually as the Pushkin. It looked like an enormous egg and was armed with a delayed-action fuse. The "bomb-chuckers" had to pull a wire to arm the bomb. "How do you drop it?" the designer was asked by the pilots. "You push it," he explained in English. "Push—push—push!" So the pilots called it the Pushkin.

Airlines were created by the Jewish Agency abroad so that planes could be purchased despite Western embargoes. Curtiss

46s could be bought from United States junk heaps for $5000 apiece but the problem was getting them out of the United States. Beaufighters could be bought in England for even less money but the British were determined to stop arms from reaching the Jews in Palestine. Fliers, Jewish or not, were volunteering all over the world to help the new state into being: but funds were low and there was little to fly.

The surplus war planes from the United States were smuggled, with some losses, by way of airlines whose names were less inspired than their exotic purposes. Ben-Gurion had said, "You can't hide a plane in a basement. We have to try and buy them where we can, hold them until the British leave, and then somehow fly them here." One device was Service Airways, Inc., with headquarters on West Fifty-seventh Street in Manhattan. The daughter of a wealthy rancher in California, Eleanor Rudnick, had a private airfield where volunteers trained. The name of the agency purchasing airborne supplies was Yakum Purkan from the ancient Aramaic prayer *"Yakum purkan min shemaya"* meaning "salvation from the skies." Teddy Kollek,* by 1970 the mayor of reunited Jerusalem, moved into New York's Hotel Fourteen, which was a cover for buying arms after the United States government embargoed weapons to the Middle East (although $37-million worth had been sold legally and officially to the Arabs). Nearby, in Panama, the resurrected United States warplanes, some with engines and machine guns scavenged from a naval air station in Hawaii by the imaginatively labeled Universal Airplane Salvage Company, became a national airline invented for the sole purpose of making one scheduled

---

* Kollek, who came from the kibbutz where Major Zee parked his rescue-helicopter before overflying the Golan Heights, displayed a characteristic Israeli view when he told S, "Jerusalem paradoxically ceased to be a Jewish city on the day of conquest [in 1967]. A city holy to Christians and Moslems too, it became multi-ethnic. There's very good Arab leadership and we've got to make the two groups complement each other like English-Canadians and French-Canadians who fight a bit although mostly respecting each other's separate ways, and live together in Montreal. It's better than the melting-pot concept in some American cities."

flight with the entire fleet and crews to Tel Aviv. At the time, it took ninety hours to fly from New York to Tel Aviv, almost ten times as long as the nonstop commercial route of today, pioneered by the entirely respectable state-owned airline, El Al.

Back in those less formal days, the Beaufighters were assembled in England for a film glorifying the achievements of New Zealand pilots in the RAF. The script called for the Beaufighters to take off in two pairs. This they did, while cameras rolled, but the planes kept going and stopped only once to refuel at a secret base in Corsica before scraping into Tel Aviv too.

Motti Hod was under the orders of Pinchas Kozlonsky, to become better know later as Israel's highly respectable Finance Minister Pinchas Sapir. The center of his organization in 1947–1948 was Geneva. From there went instructions for Motti Hod and other raw pilots to move to Prague, where the Czech government was already attuned to the original Russian policy of backing the newborn state of Israel to hurt the West. The Czechs had contracted to sell ten Me-109s and would later add a number of Spitfires. An airbase was made available at Zatec: an old German field code-named Zebra. Through it passed, in great secrecy, some of the warplanes needed in Israel. But by mid-1948 pressure was put on the Czech government by Washington, which had discovered Zebra's role in the ferrying of United States surplus warplanes. The balance of air-power now showed Israel with two Spitfires, three B-17s, three Beaufighters, fifteen Me-109s and a number of "sports" planes. Against these were ranged thirty-five Egyptian Spitfires, nine Sterling heavy-bombers, five Iraqi Furies, and ten Syrian Harvards plus other machines already noted. The pool of Spitfires in Czechoslovakia was urgently needed and there was imminent danger of the Czechs yielding to United States demands to plug the leak. Nevertheless six Czech Spitfires were adapted to fly fourteen hundred miles, the distance between a secret intermediary base and Tel Aviv, and more than twice the longest distance any

Spitfire had been hitherto known to fly. The intermediary base was in Yugoslavia.

Motti Hod got a little practice on the Czech Spitfires, which were very tricky to handle by comparison with the Italian sports-club planes he had only just learned to fly. Motti himself being too modest to describe what happened himself, the rest of his story was pieced together by S from other sources. A DC-4 was to lead the Spitfires from Czechoslovakia to the refueling base in Yugoslavia and thence over the ultralong leg to Israel. The DC-4 brought fifty cases of oranges from Israel to Prague in the hope of placating Czech officials, who had already demanded several hundred thousand dollars in "extra payments," possibly as a delaying tactic while the government decided how to react to pressures from the big powers. Permission to take off on the arduous flight was finally given in the middle of one of Europe's worst blizzards. At dawn on December 18, 1948, the first six Spitfires were pushed out of the hangar into a light snowstorm. Among the pilots, only Motti, known then to the others as Fein, was an Israeli born and bred. The clandestine radio in Yugoslavia reported the weather there was clear between storms. The six Spits left in close formation. There was an agonizing wait at the Zebra base for news of their safe arrival in Yugoslavia and then four of the Spits appeared back overhead and landed. They had run into blizzards and two smashed into mountains.

Motti tried again next day, this time in the company of eleven Spits. In Yugoslavia they were delayed for three days. On December 22, ten of them arrived in Israel. And Motti was home.

By such means a force of seventy combat planes with about a hundred pilots and two thousand ground crew was in being by the end of 1948. "The fact that the State of Israel exists today," wrote Ben-Gurion who was then both Premier and Defense Minister, "is due in great part to the Israeli Air Force. We would surely not have been able to repel the Arab invasion without air superiority."

The terrible expense of maintaining air superiority nevertheless caused difficulties. Israel's leaders felt they could get more for their slender means if they concentrated on ground weapons. The first air commanders were men with no knowledge of air warfare. It was nonetheless an expert in armored operations, General Haim Laskov, who recognized when he was appointed in 1951 that air forces were not managed with the flexibility and last-minute improvisations that characterized the army. Laskov began the work of molding the air force into a disciplined body and he was responsible for sending the first Israeli pilots to England for training on Meteor twin-jet fighters. Until this period, the watchtower-and-stockade philosophy, the idealism of the settlers, and the soldier-citizen concept had become acceptable to a people who by nature and religious background shrank from violence. If it was necessary to fight, then one fought as a citizen; a concept that was gladly endorsed by the British son of a Christian minister, Orde Wingate,* who created the "midnight battalions," the first Haganah regular units, under cover of training the Jewish auxiliary police. That was just prior to the Second World War but the influence lingered in fighting units such as the paratroopers. Wingate taught his Jewish squads to use captured weapons, to break their sleeping patterns in order to catch rest when it was feasible, to manage with a minimum of equipment, and to complete a mission even if it was left to the lowliest private to take command.

The unavoidable clash between army leaders and the modern air strategists came in 1953 when the ex-RAF fighter pilot Dan Tolkowsky took over the air force. He seemed dandified where the army chief-of-staff, Moshe Dayan, was boisterous. He was formal where Dayan could not bear formality. The spirit of the kibbutz did not manifest itself in Tolkowsky, whose English

* Wingate died in 1944 while commanding "Chindit" commandos behind Japanese lines in Burma. His strong pro-Zionist sentiments made him unpopular among the pro-Arab elements in Britain but he is honored in Israel with a physical training institute named after him, and by the fact that elite fighting men stick pretty closely to the commando tactics he taught.

background and knowledge of the RAF had made him incapable of accepting that an air force could be run like a desert armored corps with commando outriders. Furthermore, Tolkowsky saw the false economy of patching a motley collection of old aircraft. His theories were many and imaginative, but they also sounded costly to a government groaning over the bills for defense. "But he broke the hymen," one of his deputies told S. "We ceased to be virginal in a new world of avionics."

In this period Motti Hod distinguished himself as a fighter pilot with the sabra's way of attacking a problem as if a solution always existed and was always attainable. He would have been tagged an ace if Israel went in for that sort of thing, at a time when all fighting units wanted to be led by Israeli-born sabras for fairly obvious reasons: a pride in their new nation, a wish to disprove Arab propaganda about foreign mercenaries, and a desire to develop a uniquely Israeli philosophy of defense that was in tune with Jewish tradition and did not betray the legions of Jews put violently to death. The kibbutzim were the spawning ground for the ascetic, disciplined, and yet self-restrained fighters who reflected these needs. The technology of modern air warfare had to be adjusted to the quintessential character of the kibbutznik, who had an absolute *need* to preserve his individuality within a communal society. The Israeli soldier was trained to question every detail of a planned patrol or ambush but how was this spirit to be reconciled with the dehumanizing sophistication of aerial weapons?

An old man in Motti Hod's kibbutz had said to S, "Our kibbutzniks make up four per cent of the total population and twenty-five per cent of the victims." No one could explain why a large proportion of kibbutzniks chose to fight in the most hazardous conditions as frogmen, heliborne commandos, paratroops, and airmen. Yet it seemed to S that the spirit of the kibbutz was far more widely spread throughout the community, including the cities, than most Israelis fully realized. Motti Hod had spoken of an investigation relating life in the kibbutz to the high quality of kibbutznik pilots, and the stranger carried this a step further by staying both in the cities and on settlements to test his own impression that the communal spirit impregnated the whole nation. One kibbutz where S spent some time was the one where Jacob waited at the end of Day X.

About twenty miles east of where Jacob waited, Major Zee groped toward a landing as delicate as a descent on the moon. The great difference was that behind Major Zee there were no armies of technicians, no banks of computers, no multimillion-dollar space brains to work out trajectories and alternatives. There was only Zee's skill without an audience to applaud if he succeeded. There was Zee's manual control and there was no alternative once the shrill buzzer sounded.

The alarm, triggered electronically when the ground came within a certain distance, was loud enough to be heard above the motor, startling Ruthi, who reached automatically for the Kalashnikov assault gun. Doctor Golden gave her a reassuring squeeze of the arm and then clipped himself to a long nylon rope so that he could reach the open door, where Mosheko was already hanging out like a monkey on a leash.

Zee switched on the descent light. He had used it once briefly while still above treetop level to check that he was clear of high-tension wires and other hazards. There was no way to prevent landing in a minefield, however, and his mouth was already dry. He used the descent light again now to maneuver between white boulders on a ledge high on the lee of the hill which was the main feature of PS-5. He doused the light as soon as he could and the beam was still dying when he bumped down. He killed the engine. It was risky but in two thousand hours of piloting helicopters, he had developed a sixth sense. He had picked up wounded soldiers behind Arab lines so often, and he had been so frequently misled by well-meaning crewmen warning of ambuscades or promising him that the way was clear, that he relied on his own judgment. Some day, he was sure, it would let him down. He had no delusions of infallibility. Right now a prickling at the back of his neck simply told him that if he showed lights or continued making a racket, he would draw mortar or rocket fire.

For a time there was no sound but the swish of the rotor blades and the soft drip of oil. Then the machine settled its bones.

Mosheko dropped onto the soft earth first. He carried the standard Uzi submachine gun and held it in front as he pitched forward, flat on his stomach. Ruthi followed, and her body spreadeagled beside the mechanic, her arms stretched ahead with the Soviet assault gun held crosswise between her two hands. Golden was next, and then Zee. The four figures were now spread along the left flank of the Sikorski in such a way that they covered the maximum area of ground and remained within reach of each other. They had all known nights like this: the three men had been trained to "pick over" the desert; to make a smokeless fire, to find water in certain kinds of plant, to weave fiber blankets against the sharp desert cold in the predawn hours, to travel great distances between dusk and dawn. Ruthi's training had been less arduous but she had learned a great deal in a *nahal* soldier-colony. There was no need for talk.

The sounds of the desert at night began to be heard above the dying creak of the Sikorski. A shooting star blazed across the sky so vividly that Ruthi could imagine she heard it sizzle. Major Zee glanced up, unsure if a falling star in this clear sky was a good omen. He was grateful to find the hill clear of the mist in the valley but he had counted on a continuation of the low overcast to provide cover later. He carried a pistol, and a knife strapped to his leg. He reached forward with his free hand, testing the ground. It was hard packed and arid.

A flare zoomed out of the valley, moving in a great upward arc and then halting. The blaze of light grew fiercer and the flare began its painfully slow descent on the end of an unseen parachute. Silhouetted against the glare, the Sikorski loomed like a prehistoric monster. Zee touched Ruthi, who tapped Mosheko's outstretched arm, who shifted his foot against that of Doctor Golden. Then the major wriggled to the extremity of the shadow cast by the helicopter in the flare's light. The others followed. Each was tethered by nylon cords to spring-loaded reels inside the Sikorski. Each cord provided a range of 600 feet with an extending auxiliary line by which written messages could be wound back by anyone at the end of these spiderlike threads.

By the time darkness returned Major Zee had a sense of the terrain lying immediately ahead. He saluted the enemy for favors received although God knew the next rocket, instead of illuminating the landscape for him, might tear the helicopter apart. If that happened, it was likely to be more luck than judgment. He had placed the Sikorski in a position just below the hill's crest. From any distance it resembled an umbrella tree growing on a shelf below an outcrop of rock.

Another flare came curling out of fog that lay like a drift at the mouth of the valley. A third burst on the other side of the hill. The enemy was restless and foxed.

The flares were going up at regular intervals now, casting an almost continuous light. Zee worked his way down the shallow slope, thinking wryly and inconsequentially of the last diplomatic conversation he'd overheard in Herzlya when a foreign military-attaché's wife deplored the folly of officers leading their men into action. Foreigners had no conception of the conditions in which most of the fighting took place, nor could they get it through their thick skulls that rank in this country was a mark of competence and not privilege. "Thirty per cent of their casualties are officers," the woman had howled, as if this couldn't be remedied by the next sergeant, or corporal or private in the line.

He brought his party up against a vertical wall of rock at the eastern extremity of the ledge. If the Sikorski's fuel tanks exploded, through some unlucky hit, they were reasonably safe. They had arms and compasses and they could try to make their way independently back to their own lines if need be, although it was a way of escape that in the past had ended in catastrophe. The lower slopes of the hill fell away at a gentle angle, dotted with dry-looking shrubs and dark depressions. If Yesnov were here, he should be signaling by this time. Always supposing he was alive and conscious. And always supposing he was not afraid of a trap. The Syrians had a number of Soviet Mil Mi-2 helicopters which had been used before to catch unsuspecting fugitives.

There was a third possibility. Ruthi knew it even if the others avoided any mention of it. Yesnov could be already in Arab or Russian hands. They might use him for bait.

A rifle shot echoed through the hills. It was answered by an irregular fusillade. A machine gun stuttered. The horizon was lit by a red glow. Under cover of the noise Zee said, "Spread out. You, Mosheko, take the extremity of the ledge. Ruthi—"

"*Ken!*" She knew what to do. She waited for an interval of darkness and then ran, half-crouching, over the lip of the ledge and into the nearest depression in the ground falling away below. Golden held the cord clipped to her belt, feeling the nylon slip between his fingers.

The random rifle fire continued. Jackals began to howl in the wadi far below. Zee thought of Ruthi and her brother. The jackals seemed to be in one spot and he had a sudden vision of them tearing at Yesnov's body. He loathed them as biblical symbols of desolation. *Ubi solitudinem faciunt, pacem appellant.* His knowledge of Arabic was better than his Latin but he could still remember his staff-college studies and the bitter truth that in war "they make a solitude and call it peace." The firing stopped, the last of the flares went out, and there was nothing now but the wail of the pack.

Doctor Golden felt three sharp tugs on the line before it went slack. He tossed a stone in Zee's direction.

"*Wait.*" The major's warning was little more than a hiss on the wind.

The jackals slipped along the foot of the hill. Their howling was a long-drawn *Oooooh-awe* on an ascending scale. Somewhere in the cry of the banshees was another, human sound.

The three men went over the ridge together, holding a wide formation. Golden felt his way down the line to where the girl had taken cover.

"There's a man down there," she said softly. "But it's not my brother."

It has to be, thought Golden. This was the hill. Here was the place where widely spaced radio-stations had fixed their bearings as the site of Yesnov's crash landing.

"Listen," said the girl. She whistled in imitation of the sandgrouse: two long and one short, followed by a sharp *quit-quit-quit*.

It was the signal they had used as children in the kibbutz: a signal that Yesnov might recognize.

There was no response.

Over to the right, Ruthi heard the faint click of a rifle-bolt. She lay very still, cuddling the Kalashnikov.

The moon, invisible to them because it was rising behind the hill at their backs, began to flood the valley with its pale light. The contours of a twisted olive-tree changed, and a shadow broke free. The liberated shadow took a form of its own. A tall figure shattered the shape of the shadow and became a man in robes. The man called out *"Salaam,"* which among Arabs is the word for peace just as *"Shalom"* is among Israelis.

Mosheko was halfway to his feet when Yesnov shouted a warning in Hebrew from the wadi.

13

MAN AGAINST

MISSILE

Another man who would always beat the machine was Colonel Aaron. He had come to the flying-school bar mitzvah*, like other squadron commanders, to discuss the day's events and the Cabinet's reactions. He was joshing the air-chief when a girl called him into the kitchen behind the buffet tables. He took the oddly shaped phone from its cradle beside a giant dishwasher.

"*Ken?*"

Jacob's voice was brisk. His words, as always, went straight to the point. He was at the other end of the country. In the background, Colonel Aaron could hear the song of nightingales. He could also detect a subtlety of tone that told him a lot more. Jacob, waiting out the crisis on a kibbutz, was worried.

Inside the converted hangar, someone was telling S how Aaron had become a colonel.

"It was a party after graduation, like this," Aaron's friend shouted above the noise of the band. "Motti was handing out certificates—you know we don't get medals, just a bit of paper

---

* When a boy reaches his thirteenth birthday he is admitted formally into the Jewish community as an adult, and this ceremony is called a *bar mitzvah.* The IAF adopted the phrase, quite unofficially, to describe the moment when a boy gets his wings.

for knocking down a MiG. Aaron was still a major and Motti had been reading names out and must have been getting tired. He's such a stickler for discipline on formal occasions that when he called out *Colonel* Aaron's name a great roar went up. Aaron took the certificate and then grabbed the mike. Motti said, 'Hey, you can't do this.' But Aaron wrestled it away and said to the entire air force, 'You heard him—I've been promoted.' Well, it's the kind of spirit Motti admires even if he pretends he doesn't. He shrugged and said, 'Okay, boys, he's a colonel.'"

S watched Aaron struggle through the mob near the kitchen door, work his way over to Motti Hod, who nodded, and then slip into the cool night air outside. It was impressive to a stranger to see how the other pilots instinctively stood aside. The decorated hangar was in a state of apparent pandemonium. Faces glistened under the fierce lights. In any other air force, at least in the stranger's experience which was fairly extensive, this was the psychological moment when boyish high spirits broke loose and things were said, done, and broken, resulting in a flurry of apologies next day and stern reproofs from above. Yet something about Aaron's manner, which had been the most boyish of all before he went into the field-kitchen, communicated sudden sobriety.

One of the stand-by vehicles, with a girl at the wheel, whisked Colonel Aaron across the sprawling desert base. Oddly angular shapes loomed up and rushed away again. They raced through a small forest of young trees freshly transplanted, past artificial dunes like giant sarcophagi, between rows of army tents glistening with moisture under the moon. The car squealed to a stop beside Aaron's Phantom. The young QRA pilot was already descending. "I'm sorry," Aaron said hastily. "No problem. I understand," said the younger boy. Another car burned rubber as it skidded into the lee of giant blast-shields supported by sand. Aaron's "radar head," Talik, the same Flight Officer who had vectored him onto the spy-plane earlier, jumped out looking owlish in the hooded lamps of the ground crew. Having skipped the graduation party to study (he was busy on a Ph.D. from the university at Jerusalem) Talik was still adjusting the inside of his curly black head to the operational requirements of what he took to be a night interception. *That* notion was quickly dismissed by the appearance on a trolley of equipment, which he recognized as an ECM noisemaker used for disrupting the guidance systems of Russian missiles.

Aaron checked around the aircraft. It was one of the new breed of abnormally "dense" machines that caused maintenance headaches because damage to one item inside the aircraft's skin often meant taking apart several other devices that might in turn become unserviceable in the process of being dismantled and reassembled. This jungle of wires and plumbing lay, during flight, within centimeters of rapidly changing temperatures outside; and it included fuel, hydraulic, high-pressure air, and electrical lines. There were, for instance, three hydraulic systems alone. The utility system powered landing gear, flaps, inflight refueling probe, and other normal extensions and retractions. The remaining two systems duplicated each other and provided the power for flight controls. The Phantom's pumps and inverters were electrically powered for the most part, and had each a back-up source of power too. Flaps and landing gear could be blown down in an emergency by the high-pressure air system that opened and closed the cockpit canopy.

Aaron sometimes wished he were not as familiar with the details of his aircraft as he was. Abroad, he had been astonished at the superficial knowledge displayed by many pilots of their craft: the attitude was often one of so-long-as-I-know-what-to-do-in-emergency-why-worry? It was all part of the irony of life here that a Phantom was so precious, so hard to get, so necessary to keep airborne, that everyone wanted to tear it apart and see how it ticked. Here, the need to make a Phantom do the work of six Skyhawks was acute; the need to make one Phantom perform the tasks normally allotted to six Phantoms was taken as routine. And yet, Aaron thought with a mental shrug, the Japanese Self-

Defense Agency had just announced it was making one hundred and four Phantoms under license. *One hundred and four!* Just the figure made him salivate with envy.

He climbed into the cockpit. The trouble with knowing so much was that you also knew how much could go wrong. He was glad these were Israeli mechanics down there in the under-wing glow. He wouldn't have trusted anyone else.

Five minutes later his Phantom sucked up its gear while it was still rumbling less than a hundred feet off the runway.

S felt the vibrations of an express train under his feet and guessed it was Aaron. He wished him luck. He wished too that he was a little less of a stranger and might ask where Aaron had gone. Uphill, that was certain. The Phantom climbed faster than it came down. This odd inversion of Newton's law was most evident at night. Going up, the pilot rapped the burners and kept the nose high. Coming down, he had to fly on instruments and watch that his speed of descent stayed below the point where his own impetus would otherwise cause him to "sink" as he flattened out from his dive. A jet was inclined to keep losing height after it had completed any high-speed descent, so that it could be pointing straight and level at 300 feet and still sink into the deck.

When S first met Colonel Aaron, they were both passengers on a beat-up Dakota. It was the spring of 1970 and already the Dak must have been twenty-five years old. Aaron wore blue denim dungarees and a discolored sweat-shirt. S mistook him for a mechanic who was acting as a cabin steward for the occasion. The Dakota was transporting the wives and children of IAF crews to a private flying display. There were two or three young women who might have been IAF personnel in mufti, or girl friends; and a few IAF officers in uniform. They had assembled in the usual offhand way at the base near Tel Aviv. There was an American in the party who said he was the guest of a major who wore his blue battle dress as if it were a riding master's hacking jacket, with a multicolored scarf knotted around his neck and a beret tucked into a trouser pocket.

Before they boarded the Dakota, the major said chattily to S that he'd flown RAF Mosquitoes. He wore a tremendous RAF-type handlebar mustache and S saw him suddenly in his true context. The major was the ghost of all those odd young men who dressed according to taste in the Desert Air Force of the 1940–1945 war. He had a scar that covered one side of his face and was clearly a result of burns.

These preflight gatherings always struck S as having some of the mystery of a secret society. Nobody seemed to take a lead. Outsiders simply followed a move in the general direction of some unappointed aircraft. Frequently, S had no idea where they were going or when or how they would ever come back.

The group shambled out after the customary period of waiting in a shack, where strangers eyed each other somewhat nervously. The ex-Mosquito pilot seemed, however, to enjoy using on his American guest his fluent and idiomatic English. It was an echo of another era too, sprinkled with phrases long out of fashion. He talked all the way past sundry planes, around each of which the uninitiate passengers would cluster for a moment until a general movement swept them on, indicating that this Skywagon or this Arava was not for them.

Aaron, in his dungarees and suede shoes, hoisted the children into the Dak and placed a discreet but not unappreciative hand under the elbows of the ladies, who took hold of a rope with one hand and lifted their skirts with the other and thus accomplished the six-foot climb into the battered hull.

The American, a businessman from New Jersey who was immigrating to Israel, sat next to S on the bench seat that ran the length of the aircraft. The bench on the opposite side filled up. "I guess this is used for dropping paratroops," said the American from New Jersey. "It was certainly never intended to take people up *and* bring them all down again."

He smiled up at the ex-Mosquito pilot, who had been telling them about a certain Wing Commander Jackie Darwin* who was dancing with his wife in the Café de Paris in London the night it was bombed. "She was killed in his arms," said the major, twisting his mustache. "Poor chap never recovered. Went bonkers. Flew Hurricanes like a madman, kept his full hunting kit in his tent in the desert—boots, breeches, and pink coat. Darwin and his pilots used to hunt desert foxes when they weren't flying. They did this in jeeps and Darwin was all dolled up in hunting gear when they got a 'Scramble!' He was still wearing hunting pink when he crashed in no man's land and the Eleventh Hussars picked him up. 'Jolly good show,' said the Hussars' CO. 'First time I've seen an air-force wallah properly dressed!' "

Still chuckling over his memories, the scarred major went forward into the Dak's cockpit. The American from New Jersey peered down the aisle. "My God," he said to S. "Is *he* our pilot?"

Shortly after that, Aaron climbed the sloping floor of the cabin and disappeared inside the cockpit too. Noises emerged. One engine burst into life. There was a pause. Then Aaron walked back down the aisle and pushed the rear door open against the slipstream. The mustache of the major appeared in the opening to the flight-deck; he put two fingers in his mouth, and a shrill whistle pierced the fuselage.

"All out," said Aaron, in Hebrew and then in English. There was a dazed and remarkably casual exodus, women and children first.

Outside, a truck drove up. Aaron took a coil of rope and a kitchen-type ladder from the back. He climbed the ladder and tied one end of the rope to a propeller blade. It seemed to S that Aaron then wound the rope a couple of times around the propeller shaft but while he was watching, a colonel came up and said,

* Wing Commander J. Darwin, RAF, was a regular officer who had served on the North-West Frontier of India and took command of the 244 Wing, composed of two squadrons of Spitfires and two squadrons of Hurricanes in 1942.

"Please stand back, with the others," the others having been herded to a safe distance.

Three colonels and two majors in full uniform braced themselves along the rope while Aaron, still in the stranger's eyes a mechanic, gave the order to pull. Like a tug-o'war team, the colonels and majors pulled obediently while a large handlebar mustache could be seen tilting like an artificial-horizon inside the cockpit. S never discovered how the trick was done but suddenly the malfunctioning engine emitted a puff of black smoke, coughed, and joined its roar to that of its twin. Simultaneously, to the applause of the passengers, the three colonels and two majors fell over backward. "That," said the stunned businessman from New Jersey, "must be what they mean when they talk about flying by the seat of your pants."

There was a similar turmoil after they landed at a desert base. Two rattletrap buses were drawn up, and everyone filed aboard, recognizing by this time that the ex-Mosquito pilot must be their leader since he had flown them here. This, it turned out, was not necessarily so. Wetting his fingers to adjust the tips of his mustache to the proper angle, he seemed to have withdrawn from any further responsibility. A couple of air-force girls argued with the drivers about the directions they should take, and this discussion extended to embrace almost all the passengers. After a false start or two, the buses trundled behind hangars and around embankments, sometimes doubling back under the urgings of various young ladies, and taking as long to reach their destination as the flight itself. It was during this period that S discovered yet again the misleading nature of the IAF. Aaron, who had tucked the girls and the babies into their seats, who pulled up ladders and fastened doors and served coffee in flight, had been the winner of a top award * while going through the RAF's experimental test-pilot's school; had bagged enemy aircraft at reg-

* The nature of the trophy cannot be disclosed without identifying Aaron's official name.

ular intervals since 1956; and was simply bumming a ride now after a short leave.

The chaos of the morning ended sharp at eleven. The Dakota's passengers were delivered finally to an area marked by a large tea tent of the kind one used to see at durbars, princely levees, in India.

There was an improvised grandstand which S mounted along with a few hundred others who had arrived presumably by equally uncertain and circuitous routes. By what he hoped were skillful questions, the stranger established that everyone else was related to IAF airmen, or had been invited as personal guests. The occasion, in fact, was the very antithesis of the grand parade and the pomp and circumstance which accompanies the routine display of military prowess. Admittedly, there was a military band. It consisted, however, of twenty or so young ladies.

At eleven a.m. sharp, a dozen jets screamed out of the sun and climbed vertically before bursting apart in the maneuver known as the Prince-of-Wales' feathers. A taciturn voice over the loudspeakers explained what was happening and called in each formation of aircraft that followed. They came in at all angles, in every attitude. They were aircraft of every type. Helicopters danced grotesquely to the band's waltzes and sidled away in time to make room for supersonic jets. To S, with some experience of the difficulty in moving objects of different speeds through the triple-dimension of the sky, it was a superb bit of split-second showmanship made all the more impressive because it was entirely a family affair.

At eleven fifteen it was all over.

At eleven sixteen the aerobatic team flew straight down the runway that extended forward from where the spectators sat with their heads still ringing. The jets touched down, a dozen together like onions on a string, and shot down the runway with nose-lights blazing, slowing down a hundred yards from the grandstand and stopping a few feet from the tea tent.

Before the jets had finished whining, children scrambled

across the tarmac to greet fathers and brothers. As Aaron said conversationally, and rather proudly, to S, "It all turns to shit pretty quick, doesn't it!"

The canopies swung upward and back and the pilots in bright orange coveralls swung onto the wings. The ladies' band tootled and thumped its resolute way through the kind of music to which generals inspect regiments, adding a kindly rhythm to the gymnastics of small boys and little girls fingering a passage up the slippery surfaces of papa's airplane. The older and wiser visitors had already repaired to the tent to escape the harsh sun, there to imbibe orange juice or bite into apples and cake. Somewhere S heard a familiar voice say "Bang-on" and "Wizard." There was a glimpse of a colonel with a patch of concrete dust decorating his rear. Beside a bus, an argument was already starting about when to leave and where to go.

When Yesnov had ejected early on Day X, he went through the sequence of escape-and-survival in a mild state of shock induced by the sudden switch from swift forward flight to the sinking, sickening swing of a thistle naked on the wind. He was aware of burying his chute, cocking his pistol, bundling his helmet and harness, and running to one of the caves that riddled the hillside.

He was betrayed by an old Bedouin. She had been sitting motionless as a boulder and seemingly no more perceptive. By late afternoon she had directed the *fedayeen* to where he lay.

He was spreadeagled at the mouth of the cave. The ground sloped away, scarred by rocks. The noise of battle rolled across the plains from where the cannons of both sides were still engaged. He supposed the guerrillas who had brought him down were searching in the wrong direction, for he had seldom seen so barren a wilderness. The brief dogfights of the day had flashed overhead. He guessed the rescue mission had been postponed until after sunset. He had all the confidence of a young man who knows his prime minister will be as intimately aware of his plight as his own squadron mates. So he lay comfortably in the shade and watched a hawk patrol an invisible crest of rising air. By following the movements of the hawk he could trace the contours of the thermals. He worked out a theory that the heat from the sun beating into the arid basin below had combined with a prevailing southerly breeze to create a standing wave of warm air which curled along the face of the hill and provided a permanent source of lift for the hawk. This was borne out by the hawk's stiffly bowed wings and the delicacy with which it had only to tilt its tail to twist back upon itself. He watched the hawk with envy, trying to penetrate the aerodynamic secrets that permitted it to float tirelessly at the same precise height along the same exact path, back and forth, only the head cocked while the eyes glittered and searched the ground below.

A stone rolled into a cleft. Yesnov covered the pistol with his hand. He hoped, in his slightly dazed way, that he might get a chance at one of the hyenas. He had been forced to eat hyena before; indeed, had lived off it for several days, after hanging and boiling and finally spicing the meat. He dismissed the thought. One did not shoot in broad daylight at scavengers in enemy territory. He took a tighter grip on his thoughts. He could see the crunched bones and the droppings and wondered if the pack was lying up, just as he was, mangy and exhausted. Another and larger stone rolled down and then there was silence.

He continued to stare down into the shimmering bowl. He had gone on archaeological "digs" in this kind of country, climbing like a goat along the razorbacks above the Dead Sea. That was how he'd started flying, come to think of it. Yigael Yadin, the former chief-of-staff, had been in charge of a summer's digging to which Yesnov went as a student. General Yadin's father was Professor E. L. Sukenik, who had brought the Dead Sea Scrolls to light. The boy was fascinated by the story of the Scrolls. He read all he could lay his hands on about them. He had even done some research in Jerusalem. There he was permitted to see a copy of Professor Sukenik's diary covering the period when the Scrolls were recovered. The diary covered the War of Independence too. There was an entry about the death of his other son, Yadin's brother, for December 31, 1948, that impressed the boy: "An historic year . . . A painful year—Matti died."

Matti had been one of Israel's first fighter pilots. Along with Hod and Ezer Weizman, he'd fought in the first air battles. Something about all this caught the boy's imagination. He was not religious but he had a deep respect for the right of human beings to live and let live. To defend his own people in the air seemed an honorable ambition. He looked more closely at Yadin, who had been a general, who was chief of operations in the year his brother was shot down, and he saw that Yadin was also an Arabic scholar who had once recited ancient Arabic verse to King Abdullah of Jordan. It seemed that one could combine soldiering with scholarship. To become a scholar, however, one needed opportunities in a country where the universities were besieged by the young. Yesnov found that basic IAF training would prepare him for university; that his flying pay would cover his later expenses; and that he would get a deep satisfaction from following in the footsteps of a fighter pilot who died in the year that his father dropped among the scholars of the world a major bombshell.

He was startled out of this reverie by the shrill *cheee-tii cheee-ti* of a small honey guide flying out of a wadi. The white tail-feathers flashed in the slanting rays of the sun. He had heard stories that the honey guide would lead men to other things than honey.

The hawk wheeled and stooped onto the smaller bird. It flattened out of the dive behind the honey guide, which came zigzagging up the slope toward Yesnov's cave. The hunter was a Levant sparrowhawk with bold bars of color across the chest and tail. It reached one foot forward, and the two birds turned in front of the cave so that Yesnov saw the talons like crooked fingers of an old man's yellow hand clutching the empty air. The honey guide screeched and jerked sideways. It had an ability to change direction fast. It had, thought Yesnov, an advantage over the hawk in the same way that a slow old jet could outmaneuver a supersonic MiG. Stick close to the ground, he told the tiny fugitive: keep your turns sharp.

He was totally engrossed in the battle. If only the honey guide had not panicked. But here it was, fluttering above a gray block of stone. The hawk stretched forth a second foot. Its wings changed their configuration and now formed a graceful curve like the half-moon of a fingernail. The tail came down, feathers spread to break the flow of air and convert it into the force that enabled the hawk to bend back its head in which the eyes appeared like fierce spots of gold. The talons raked the spine of the honey guide and tangled in the tail. The two birds merged a few feet from Yesnov, on his level, but still some distance from the sloping ground directly beneath them. He saw the hawk pull itself up the back of the honey guide, one foot following the other until the smaller bird staggered, its wings no longer beating the air. A shadow crossed the sun and when it passed, the honey-guide's wings seemed as broken and useless as a crumpled kite. It struggled under the talons and its sudden loss of flying efficiency brought the hawk tumbling with it. They crashed together.

A bony hand knocked the pistol from Yesnov's side. A knee pinned him back. Another hand forced back his chin. At the same moment, a dozen figures rose out of the rubble around the cave. A bare foot stamped hard on the pistol before he could make a grab for it. He felt powerful bodies on his back. He remembered in a brief flash of self-condemnation that many of the caves in a hillside were connected. He should have crawled further back into this one, instead of assuming that it ended at the first narrow bend in the tunnel. It was too late now. He was pinioned as effectively as the honey guide straining upward against the hawk standing on its back. The honey guide fell limp and the hawk, curved like a claw, turned its head so that the fierce eyes seemed to fix unblinkingly on Yesnov.

By nightfall, the operation to recover Yesnov was in full swing. Aaron had brought the Phantom over the Syrian border at the height most convenient for any newly installed Russian missile site. With Talik, his "radar-head," he was playing a double role. They were to draw the fire of SA-II missiles now suspected to be in the area, and thus possibly distract attention from Major Zee and the rescue-helicopter now perched on Hill PS-5. They were also to destroy any site they might locate.

The Phantom's ECM device was the product of workshops that had once long ago served as a school for the RAF. Desert warriors of an earlier war would have recoiled from the prospect of aerial warfare in which machine seemed to fight machine. This would have been the nature of the present conflict if the IAF did not wrench it back into the area of personal combat. The ECM noise-maker in Aaron's plane contained jammers that radiated electromagnetic waves in the same frequencies used by the enemy's radar guiding the missiles. When Aaron switched on the ECM, this radiation of "noise" disturbed the missile's system and left it heading blindly into space.

The enemy radar devices had been examined by Israeli experts. Whenever a new system was uncovered, a commando unit would attempt to steal it by helicopter. In this way, the IAF kept ahead of each new development. But lately there had been evidence that enemy missiles were operating on more sophisticated systems. In essence, a missile radar operator acquired his target and then tracked it on his scope. The missile was launched and a terminal-guidance radar would navigate it onto the target aircraft.

Tonight, despite the seemingly mechanical nature of this kind of combat, Aaron was pitting his wits against the machine. The early suspicion of new missiles in the Syrian zone, which began with the curious way Yesnov's Skyhawk had been brought down, had hardened as reports came in from ground patrols. It now seemed likely that two developments had altered the odds on the northeastern front.

Guerrillas appeared to be in possession of the new one-man mobile missile launchers, which were aimed and fired like a gun.

New missiles for SA-II units might be going into operation. The new missiles were thought to be tuned to new frequency ranges, in which case the ECM device should be enough to misdirect them.

Aaron and Talik loitered around PS-5. The beauty of the Phantom was that it could stay on station just as long at five hundred feet as it could at thirty-five thousand feet. This did not mean it could travel the same distance at low altitude, but this was not the point. Endurance was what counted on-station. And they were there to goad the enemy to launch his missiles. If a launch came from the sophisticated sites, Aaron and his FO would be warned of any radar frequency-switch. The trick then would be to shift the Phantom's jamming frequency fast enough to avoid destruction.

It was a dangerous game. There were many reasons for playing it.

Jacob had heard the Phantom passing overhead. It was a bond with Major Zee's rescue party, forced to keep radio silence, and with Yesnov if he was still alive.

He sat in the silent room under the kibbutz dining hall, continuing in his mind the debate which obsessed them all; the debate that exploded again in Golda's Kitchen that afternoon; trying to disentangle his thoughts from earlier memories that crowded in upon him at times like this.

He checked his watch again. We live by the clock, he thought. I spend my time counting the seconds. Ever since that first strike in 1967 we've seen our lives chopped into the minute quantities that are inscribed upon a watch. Grandfather spent his time bent over other people's watches, sitting inside the ghetto, refusing to listen to the warning noises outside.

He jerked back his head and lit another cigarette. Most of the members of the kibbutz would be going to bed. Their working day started at five. He fought back a selfish impulse to call a friend for a game of chess.

Back-timing was the secret of success in night operations like this. When Yesnov crashed, he knew that if nothing had happened by nightfall it was necessary to wait the period of time stipulated for that day. In counting the hours, however, he back-timed from sunset.

In the same way, Major Zee's departure with the rescue-helicopter was noted by Jacob and all those involved in the mission as 1200 hours, irrespective of the actual time, Greenwich Mean or any other. Everyone back-timed from 1200 down to 00:00. A series of actions took place in series. At 11:00, if the rescue-helicopter had not returned, patrols and the nearby *nahal* soldier-colonists were put on a Green Alert, which scarcely added to their routine frontier responsibilities. At 10:30 they went onto Yellow Alert and the routine patrols would extend their activities. One or two patrols might be designated to probe deeper into Syrian territory. At 10:00 everyone went onto Red Alert. At this stage, a number of options were open depending upon the circumstances of the case. Tonight, it was more than a question of rescuing a lost pilot—vital as that was. In the interval between 1200 and 10:00, Jacob had worked out a further course of action and had consulted with the Citadel and with his bosses, including army, air, and intelligence chiefs. Until 10:00, it had been in the cards that Yesnov would be recovered and could tell them exactly what he'd seen of the missiles both when he himself was hit and later, while hiding on the ground.

There was still hope. Two hours was not such a long time for a delicate mission like this one.

A boot grated in the doorway. Other footsteps sounded on the concrete stairs leading out of the underground restroom.

"Excuse me, comrade." It was the mother of Yesnov and Ruthi. She was younger than the wrinkled face and thin body indicated. Still, she's old enough to know better than to call me "Comrade," thought Jacob. It's a habit. No harm in it. Being a comrade had cost her everything, back in what she regarded even yet as the old country.

A man's voice said, "We just wanted to ask, before sleep. Will Ruthi be back tonight? It's a question of rearranging the work schedule, that's all."

"She'll be late," Jacob said gruffly. "Midnight, perhaps."

"Midnight—dawn. Come, mama," murmured the man. "He's talking Jewish time. An hour behind everyone else."

Jacob listened to the tired tread of their retreating feet. Let them keep their innocence another Jewish hour.

14

THE VERTICAL FRONTIER

The time to strike was always in the minds of two men who also, and paradoxically, would always beat the machine—paradoxically, because they had tuned the air-force machine to a very fine pitch in order that when it struck in 1967 it did so with a maximum of precision and a minimum of wasted time. Now, while the whole of Israel chewed on the question of another lightning attack, these two men watched the dying embers of the flying-school festivities.

Ezer Weizman had flown down in his Spitfire. He bore one of the most celebrated names in Israel's history—that of Chaim Weizmann. But Ezer, deliberately spelling his name differently, would dismiss him with the sharpness of a third-generation sabra: "There are many Weizmanns and Chaim exercised the least influence over me, because he lived overseas. . . ."

Dan Tolkowsky was an entirely different breed of cat. Like Ezer he was a former RAF fighter pilot. But where Ezer was flamboyant, Dan was a stickler for the formalities. The combination had worked very well. When Dan Tolkowsky took command of the IAF it needed a few sandbags of discipline to weigh down its buoyancy. When Ezer Weizman took over, the IAF needed the kind of pride that made him unashamed to proclaim Israel's defiance of anyone hostile: "Our guard is always up—to an altitude of forty thousand feet and more if necessary."

The funny thing was that Tolkowsky, who left an impression on S of prim good manners, had been jailed as an alleged Communist in Greece after World War II through the connivance of the British Secret Service, which (according to his friend Colonel Benjamin Kagan) was trying to prevent ex-Flight Lieutenant Tolkowsky from smuggling aircraft into Palestine. The charge, of course, was quickly exposed as a delaying tactic. Five years later he was General Tolkowsky.

Ezer Weizman, on the other hand, had told S that it was just as well someone as meticulous as Tolkowsky had taken the IAF in hand. Yet it was Ezer who wrote what must be surely one of the most startling and prophetic documents in the history of air warfare. In August 1962, when Egypt tested its first ground-to-ground missile, Ezer wrote of the strange new world of combat that lay ahead. His words show the same prescience that Dr. Weizmann had shown in World War I by bringing chemistry to the aid of Britain's war effort.

To protect itself from Egyptian missiles [wrote Ezer Weizman in 1962, when he was a thirty-seven-year-old General test-flying Israel's first jets] Israel must improve and reinforce its air force without letup. The missile, which constitutes a deterrent to war, demands astronomical investments that threaten to lead a small country to the brink of bankruptcy. Israel needs a long-term deterrent that can guarantee victory . . . the most modern and best-equipped air force in this whole region. The primary task of that force consists of demolishing the enemy's air power. Once this task is accomplished, when the skies of Israel have been made inviolable, the air force can devote itself to the second task of lending assistance to the ground forces. The first task is the function of several factors, of which the most important is surprise.

The first country to launch a surprise attack stands the

chance of achieving air supremacy and thus of gaining victory. Egypt not only possesses missiles that enable it right now to launch a surprise attack and to wreak serious damage on civilian and military bases; it also has at its disposal three formations of bombers, eight of fighters, and three of transport. In other words, Egypt possesses about 100 MiG-19s and 50 MiG-21s.* Sooner or later these planes will be armed with air-to-air missiles. It is probable that they will also be equipped in the near future with air-to-ground missiles. Egypt will, furthermore, receive ground-to-air missiles. . . .

Under these conditions, the Israeli Air Force will have to fight for hours and perhaps days to gain aerial supremacy. Meanwhile the rear will be uncovered and will necessarily serve as a target for ground-to-ground missiles and enemy bombs.

But another factor must be taken into consideration, a factor known as "absorption capacity"; that is, a country's capacity to sustain aerial bombings. The fact is that Egypt's absorptive capacity is greater than Israel's. To grasp this, it suffices to compare the extent of Egyptian territory with that of Israel. Egypt has infinitely more opportunities to disperse its military and civil bases throughout the whole of its territory. In the case in which the enemy has air superiority, we must at all costs keep that superiority from being prolonged for more than a day to a day and a half.*

The idea of not obtaining air superiority until after the first phase [of an Arab attack] during which our strategic

---

* The reader will note the consistent accuracy of official Israeli analyses of Arab strength and future intentions.
* Eight years later Defense Minister Moshe Dayan talked to graduating pilots: "Battles in the skies over Kutamiya and Salhiya are no holiday gifts. But better the battle for our future be fought there than at the fences of Nahal Oz and with the blood of children of Qiryat Shimona." He was referring (July 16, 1970) to a new Egyptian airbase at Kutamiya, halfway between Cairo and the port of Suez. Salhiya was another base about twenty miles west of the Canal. Both stood on the northern and southern rim of concentrations of SA-IIs and SA-IIIs. Both accommodated Russian-piloted MiG-21s, which could cover a surprise cross-Canal assault and challenge Israelis maintaining the relentless bombing of the same area in order to prevent a surprise attack.

points will have been devastated—this idea is absolutely inadmissible and unrealistic. We are consequently forced to provide ourselves with a thorough antiaircraft defense, not only aircraft that possess what is needed to paralyze the enemy planes on the ground or shoot them down in combat but also a protection system including the most up-to-date antiaircraft weapons. Only an effective protective system can create an impenetrable defense curtain against enemy aircraft, which will approach from the four quarters of the compass.

The third factor, also decisive, consists of the number of missions our aircraft will be able to complete within a given time in comparison with the number of enemy missions in the same period. Put another way, this means the number of effective combat sorties that each of our planes will be able to execute. That number is a function of the quality of the planes, their quantity, their speed, the number and location of our airbases, the level of upkeep of the aircraft, and the competence of our pilots. The Israeli air force is quantitatively inferior to the Egyptian air force. It can permit itself to remain so if it is nevertheless capable of accomplishing at least as many missions as the enemy. If not, I doubt that we can obtain air superiority.

The integration of strength is the final factor on which the outcome of the battle depends. We need a plane capable of penetrating Egyptian antiaircraft defenses, carrying out bombing raids in spite of radar and avoiding hits by ground-to-air and air-to-air missiles. It is a question, in other words, of a plane that is fast but also capable of carrying bombs. From now on it is inconceivable for us to use outmoded bombers. . . . We cannot allow ourselves to maintain three distinct air forces, one for tactical support, another for combat, and a third for bombing raids.

Here, in a nutshell, was the IAF's doctrine. If it seemed astonishingly farsighted, it was also a logical progression from the early days when flying-club machines were often the sole link between Jewish settlements. "If you will it," wrote Theodor

Herzl, the father of modern Zionism, "it is no dream." The faith of Israel's *Mayflower* generation was reflected in something Dr. Weizmann was reputed to have said, "I don't say a Zionist has to be insane, but it helps." Ezer once said to the stranger S, "This is a mad outfit, this air force. Mad keen. Mad as hatters to take on the Soviets. Mad as the Few in the Battle of Britain. Mad in a way that counts."

Ezer, tall and gangling, curly-haired, disrespectful of stuffed shirts, seemed to S to be determined to project an image of the gung-ho fighter pilots whose squadrons used to operate with half their supporting men and equipment, so that one half of a squadron moved to another base and prepared to receive aircraft; the planes carrying out missions and then landing with the advance party; the whole nomadic existence being a permanent game of leapfrog. Yet beneath the panache was a passionate intelligence.

An English scholar, who knew how Ezer's cousin Michael died testing new scientific equipment for the RAF, recalls how he presented himself to Ezer when he still occupied the air-chief's office. The scholar, a little in awe of a general, drew himself up straight as a ramrod and made a careful little speech by way of preface. Ezer, in open-neck shirt (few ever saw him with a tie), waved the visitor to a chair with the cheerful greeting, "For God's sake put your bloody feet up and relax."

The scholar had come to report what had been previously the secret circumstances of Michael's death. The boy was the eldest son of Dr. Chaim Weizmann. "In the February of 1942 the boy was killed in action and the blow crushed Weizmann," wrote Christopher Sykes, an Orientalist who served in Britain's Special Air Services. "Dr. Weizmann still had some great and brilliant services to render to the Zionist cause but after the death of this young man in the RAF he was never quite the same again." Now, many years later, Ezer heard that the boy was testing a new antisubmarine-detection device over the Bay of Biscay. At the time, U-boats were playing havoc in the Allied shipping lanes.

Michael Weizmann was forced down into the sea at the very moment the German battle-cruisers *Scharnhorst* and *Gneisenau* were making a break through the English Channel. There were no Allied aircraft to spare for air-sea rescue and the boy died a solitary death in his life raft.

Ezer listened patiently to this account and thanked his visitor politely. He seemed, said the visitor later, remarkably stoic about the whole thing. But an Israeli dignitary recalls catching Ezer in his house one day gripped by emotion because he had come across a letter written by his grandfather, Dr. Krishevsky, who in 1900 was in Cairo. The paragraph that moved him read: "The Basle program (which makes it imperative that a Jewish State be established) is Holy—Holy—Holy. . . ."

Like Motti Hod, he had pioneered on a kibbutz before he was old enough to fight in World War II, and like Motti he was admitted into the British Army in Palestine as a truck driver. But Ezer managed to talk his way into the RAF flying-school in Rhodesia.

The intimacy of Isaeli life was again apparent to S when he discovered that one of Ezer's predecessors as IAF commander was Haim Laskov, who used to make him run up and down Mount Carmel when he was one of the sixteen-year-olds training in the underground Jewish resistance army.

"We had this military experience in the underground," Ezer told S in one of their more formal conversations which the stranger taped. "This made us a little different. Nevertheless, the most interesting thing to me in the last twenty-five years is that Israel shares the distinction with other small countries of being small. Nigeria perhaps is the exception. But most new countries are small and so there are certain characteristics which we have in common when trying to exist as distinct entities.

"If we perform well, if we survive—as we shall—Israel establishes the possibility for small nations to go their own independent way within the general framework of world citizenship. Now this is very important. It's all very well to talk about great international communities and superpowers with supranational authority, but you see, in the world ahead, it's individuality that will have to count if we are really concerned with human values. And this means leaving room for small communities to develop their own cultures. This can't happen unless the two or three big powers are obliged to stop imposing *their* ideologies (innocently or with calculation) upon us. Power blocs obliterate the individual. Diversity, peaceful coexistence of small and big communities, this is where the future lies.

"Now, with the air force, we've had to put this idea into practice. In an age of sophisticated weapons we try to make the man in the cockpit count above everything.

"You see, lack of experience is an advantage to a small nation. We came suddenly into maturity and nationhood. The first problem is how to protect your own identity? Basically—how to organize an army, how to organize an air force, tactics, command system, organization—all this had to be learned by us from scratch. One of the things that typifies this situation is that you have to ask for help from outside.

"Even before we came to statehood, two of our present enemies were receiving this tuition from professionals in the art of warfare. Syria was highly influenced by the French, Egypt by the British. But at that time, learning from a big brother meant living under his thumb. We had to learn from others without becoming their slaves, and I think if there's any value to what we are doing now, it is that we show others the way to resist absorption.

"So, what have we done? We had to know more than simply how a squadron has to be organized, how a wing is formed. The basic question is how to squeeze the maximum from your men in times of crisis. This means understanding the soul, the inward thinking, the behavior and the environment of the men. One of the greatest problems for those of us serving in the RAF was food.

"Food! Really! It seems a small thing but it's vital. I went through agonies trying to swallow a diet that was probably good for a Yorkshireman but was repulsive to us!

"Human beings today are freethinkers and so you don't have the square-headed soldier who gets his sixpence a day and he's kicked in the ass by the sergeant and he's happy that he gets his mug of beer and then takes his rifle and goes off to fight somewhere. Today you can't command or lead men unless you are part of their lives and this is why a small nation today, if it's got a good educational system, no longer meekly follows some larger power. Then, you learn to do a hell of a lot more with a hell of a lot less in manpower.

"You also define your defense problems. It's hard for anyone who comes from a large power to shrink himself into our small concerns. Relatively small. Our air force is relatively small but it's still the best tactical air force I know anywhere. One reason *is* its smallness. When an airman of any rank gets an idea, it jumps right up the way to headquarters and right out to the Air Officer commanding and he catches it within a day or two. Now what happens say in Vietnam? A squadron has to wait for a new proposal to work its way all around the Pentagon and then the idea probably gets lost in the files—well, I won't elaborate on *that!* Now we had to fight the '48 war with foreign friends—from the USA, Canada, Britain, South Africa. . . . Out of twenty-five fighter pilots, only three of us were Israelis."

S said, "To break away for a moment, what exactly did happen to you, personally, during that period?"

WEIZMAN: It was the last day of the War of Independence, the 7th of January 1949 and we flew patrols in sections of two. We'd jumped some Egyptian Fiat fighters in the morning and the Egyptian armies had got within a few miles of Tel Aviv. There was a lot of confusion and I'd got a Spitfire and I was getting itchy because reports were coming from a number of Jewish settlements of aerial bombing. What upset me was that the RAF kept encroaching into our airspace and seemed to be giving support to the Arabs by surveying our own activities. I picked up the phone and said to headquarters, 'Look, I want to show any bastard who tries to kill us that we *do* have planes and we *can* fly. . . .

With the Red Alert now ten minutes old, Jacob took a call from the Citadel.

It was Captain Naomi with a summary of the night's tactical situation. Her voice was cold and official until she finished reading the routine digest. Then she said, "Will you be gone long?"

"You know more than I do," said Jacob.

She remained silent.

"Only let there be peace," said Jacob.

She repeated the words which had become part of the communications lingo, the routine sign-off. And yet not so routine.

In the Citadel she put away files, turned off the radio and sat quietly for a moment staring into space.

For some reason the memories of a certain period in her childhood came crowding back. Perhaps it was because Jacob was sitting through this crisis in a kibbutz. She remembered vividly the first aerial victory by Jewish planes. She was a small girl then at a place called Ben Shemen. It lay outside Tel Aviv with a large Arab community between, and frequently her widowed mother was unable to visit Ben Shemen because of terrorist attacks along the bus route.

The first aerial battle she had witnessed was the one in which Ezer Weizman helped to shoot down RAF intruders and later took on Arab warplanes. It happened to be the moment when Naomi had decided that somehow she would learn to fly some day. Ben Shemen was a children's village combined with a local kibbutz and Naomi was there because a Lithuanian director of orphanages, Dr. Siegfried Lehmann, decided in 1927 to continue his work with distressed children in what was then Palestine. He took children from broken and unhappy homes and gave them formal schooling combined with work on the farm. By 1948 there were four hundred children farming one hundred and twenty-five acres of land, with a large amount of livestock, which the children themselves managed. Its badge was an ear of corn encircled by an olive branch, because among the Lithuanian doctor's endeavors was the cultivation of good relations with the neighboring Arabs.

S had taken Naomi back to this experimental village, after he learned from Ezer Weizman a little more about her background. She had never before gone back, she said. Not since she went into the army and then took her training as a pilot. Her late husband had been a kibbutznik and even he had never succeeded in taking her back there. When he was killed she became too burdened with staff work, she said, to take the time.

She said a great deal in justification of never returning there, and when S finally persuaded her to go, they had to stop on the way for beer and sausages at an imitation English pub called The Golden Star, which seemed to be filled with airline crews from the nearby international airport.

S was struck at once by Ben Shemen's emotional atmosphere, which was warm and friendly. They had warned nobody that they were coming. They found half the students in airy but very simply built classrooms with mud-and-wattle walls. The other students were busy on the land. Some were tending goats and rabbits. There was a small zoo with a particularly fine specimen of peacock which rustled its radiant tail feathers for them. A tiny girl sat on a high stool in the middle of a field of kitchen vegetables which seemed to be bursting out of the soil under their plastic and ventilated canopies. The little girl was doing her homework and guarding the vegetables. "Whom against?" asked S, and Captain Naomi gave one of her infrequent smiles and said, "Other little girls, I expect. Unless things have changed since I sat on that same stool."

Naomi, who seemed so composed in uniform at her desk in the

Citadel, remained self-collected until they stopped in the principal's office for a chat. The principal came from Iraq and translated Arab poetry and literature of other kinds in his spare time. He was explaining the psychology behind Ben Shemen when S suddenly saw that Naomi was looking strained. She sat as gracefully as ever, translating the principal's Hebrew in the same noncommittal tones she had used in speaking to S about the gift of Jaffa oranges in the days when he had called her "a shy kid."

The principal said the reason for keeping so many animals was that children from broken homes needed some way to express the love that otherwise found no outlet. "They frequently make quite large sacrifices," he said. "Like spending their free time with their rabbits, cleaning out hutches, and giving part of their meals to the livestock."

"That's right!" burst out Naomi. "I remember I used to get up early and go first to the animals, and sometimes I'd miss meals. . . ."

The principal removed his glasses. "You were here?"

"Of course," said the one-time copilot of a paratrooper's Dakota, and for the first time S saw some sign of emotion in her face.

"And you never came to revisit us?"

She shook her head.

"Then we must have failed somewhere," said the principal, equally distressed. "You can't just donate your love to something as large and amorphous as an air force."

It was a peculiarly shrewd shot in the dark.

Jacob shot out of his seat at 09:08 on the back-timing.

"Forty-one, this is Eight." It was Major Zee on the rescue-helicopter's transmitter. "You read me? Over."

"Eight here. Loud and clear. Over."

"This is Forty-one. We've recovered our Mutual Friend alive and kicking. Over."

Jacob frowned. The signal was far from clear. Zee was keeping his transmissions so brief that he must be still on the ground. "Hullo Eight. You need help? Over." "This is Eight. Affirmative. Is that one of ours overhead? Over." Jacob paused. Then he said, "Hullo Eight. Possibly. Repeat. Possibly. Call back in five minutes. Meanwhile keep blacked out and maintain silence. Over."

"Roger," said Eight and there was no time for Jacob or Zee to add the customary let-there-be-peace.

Within the five minutes, Jacob had put the jigsaw together. He had learned through Aaron in the Phantom that sporadic small-arms' fire could be seen around Hill PS-5. In the absence of other signs of activity, Aaron had started to circle the hill at low altitude to keep down what he guessed to be bands of marauders.

Jacob glanced at the sweep-hand of his watch. Precisely at the end of five minutes Major Zee was back on the air. Again the exchanges were curt. A lot nonetheless could be conveyed by indirection. Yesnov, injured by rifle-fire, had been on a fishing expedition. The catch was a big one. But there was trouble. . . .

The transmission stopped.

Jacob called the Citadel. Yes, the conversations had been monitored and were labeled top-priority.

He got Naomi still lingering at her desk. "We'll have to move fast. . . ." His voice was tense with anxiety and the orders came mechanically one after another.

"I've got that," she said, preparing herself for the sleepless hours ahead. After he'd gone, while the signalsmen located Special Services, she sat with her hands in her lap and stared dully at the floor. O Jacob, Jacob. Carrying the whole air force on your back isn't the answer.

15

A CRACK

IN THE WALL

Like all IAF pilots, Yesnov had been trained both as a commando and paratrooper. When he was captured earlier in the day, he had started at once to look for ways of escape. By nightfall an entirely different prospect had opened up.

He had been taken to the foot of Hill PS-5 by disciplined Syrian troops. A man leaning against a BTR-40 Russian armored-personnel carrier had introduced himself as Grechko, asked if he was hurt, offered him food and drink. He spoke English with a Russian accent but wore khaki drills without insignia. His manner was authoritative. His pale features were pock-marked and shaded by a cloth Maoist-type cap. He leaned a bare arm against the vehicle, cursed in Russian when the metal scorched his skin, and then jerked his head for Yesnov to follow him into the shade of a thorn tree.

"You will recognize, doubtless, I am Russian?"

Yesnov shrugged. He was not prepared to betray his own knowledge of the Russian language. Captured pilots who were received with civility could always count upon a trap being laid.

"Sit and rest," said the Russian. He turned and walked to where a Syrian captain waited by a bivouac.

It was an open invitation for Yesnov to run. But why? If they wanted to shoot him, no excuses were needed. The only witnesses were the soldiers now squatting between light vehicles too far away for Yesnov to identify. Long shining barrels stuck out of the backs of the vehicles. One of the men shouldered a similar weapon. Was this the new missile that had shot him down?

He stretched out in the shade. His pistol and knife had been taken from him, and his boots removed. The soldiers beside the vehicles were, he supposed, missilemen and therefore obliged to obey the Russian who was presumably not only their instructor but also the controller of all this hardware.

The Russian returned with the Syrian. "This is Captain Nayef. He has some questions."

Yesnov made no effort to get up. "Tell him I have nothing to say."

The Russian translated in Arabic. The captain's expression never changed but his voice grew angrier.

Yesnov listened, staring at the ground and drawing circles in the brittle earth. His own Arabic was good—better, perhaps, than the Russian's. He was intrigued and then puzzled by the Russian's attitude as the argument developed. Captain Nayef was claiming the right to interrogate the prisoner. The Russian recommended patience and at first his manner was courteous; but the tone sharpened, the circumlocutory phrases began to vanish, and at the end of five minutes the Russian was stating in bald terms that if Captain Nayef would just stick to his own job, he, Grechko, would attend to the affair of the Israeli pilot. Finally the Syrian withdrew, concealing any anger he might have felt.

"Barbarians," said the Russian, dropping beside Yesnov.

Yesnov pillowed his head on his arms and closed his eyes. The Russian said nothing more.

Beside the personnel-carrier, Captain Nayef was giving orders. Groups of *fedayeen* converged on the bivouac. The missilemen huddled together. A dramatic figure in combat fatigues and headdress mounted one of the smaller vehicles and began a speech.

Yesnov opened one eye and studied the Russian. Away in the distance the speechmaker was saying, "Long live the solidarity of all sections of the resistance against the external and internal attempts to liquidate the Central Committee."

"Central Committee my backside," said the Russian. "That savage over there believes the Central Committee runs the Arab revolutionary groups."

Yesnov watched him curiously. The Presidium of the Central Committee in Amman had been reportedly taken over by Maoist Chinese advisers. Here in Syria, the revolutionaries were sponsored by the ruling Baath party, which called itself socialist and took gold from the sheikhs, took direction from Peking, and took Russia for a ride. Was it this that was biting Grechko?

"There will be a rescue mission arriving for you here tonight," said the Russian. "All right, don't answer. We know your procedures." He paused for long seconds. "If I help you escape, will you take me with you?"

Yesnov made no attempt to move. "Why?" His question was little more than a whisper.

"Sit up and pretend to cooperate," said Grechko, drawing the gun at his belt.

Yesnov sat up. "You want to defect?"

"I don't like the word."

"Explain yourself then."

Off in the distance the Presidium's speechmaker was saying, "From Vietnam to Palestine! One struggle! One fight!" Overhead whined high-flying jets, their silver wings almost invisible against the fierce milky-white sky. The Syrian captain and two junior officers sat beyond earshot, under a fly-sheet extending from the rear of the personnel-carrier, watching. Heavy guns rumbled in the distance. The late-afternoon heat turned the landscape into a shimmering haze, blurring Yesnov's mind so that the Russian's words seemed to conjure up a mirage. The more Grechko talked, the less Yesnov liked the sound of it.

Suddenly the Russian broke off. "You find this hard to believe?"

"Perhaps."

"Put yourself in my position."

Yesnov tried, as the words came tumbling out. When Grechko was a young captain at the siege of Stalingrad, he was proud to be part of what was then called the Red Army of Peasants and Workers. So what in the name of thunder, he asked Yesnov now, was he doing here with cut-throats who took money from the oil-sodden conservatives of Arabia? What kind of a peasant army was this which could be seduced by the new emperor of China and wooed by King Hussein when he said, "We are all *fedayeen*"? Grechko spoke of his sister and her family, thick-headed bureaucrats no doubt, but nonetheless important enough to shop in Section 200 of the GUM department store in Moscow—and still obliged, for all that, to live in a rickety apartment house where the plumbing was years behind the times. Guns before butter, yes, for his own people. But not the several hundreds of millions of dollars in hard currency which was the price Russia paid to give military support to these whirling dervishes who called themselves Communists and yet took millions of dollars a year from King Faisal of Arabia. Communists? Was that the word for the two fairy princes from Kuwait who pretended to be revolutionaries?

This outburst from Grechko was too eloquent for Yesnov. He listened and grunted sympathetically, and from time to time shaped words to maintain the impression of a successful interrogation. But his thoughts moved in another direction. Whatever this Russian had in mind, it was *not* a genuine defection. Or was it?

The wilderness on the edge of the Golan subdued a man. Grechko had come from the world's biggest missile range in Kazakhstan, at Sary-Shagan. It lacked charm, certainly. It was far from Moscow's military clubs. But at least there were foot-hills and distant mountains and cultivated land, and a rhythm of slopes and mounds suggesting the shapes of gods and nymphs and recumbent shepherds. Grechko was a colonel with several engineering degrees, but he was also a man with cultivated tastes. That, at any rate, was the impression he was now trying to create. He laid out his technical qualifications with skill, implying that Israel would gain considerably from acquiring such a defector.

"Why this sudden—conversion?" demanded Yesnov. He pictured Grechko enjoying the small comforts supplied by Russia's Strategic Missile Force: the hunting lodges, the ski resorts, officers' quarters with swimming pools; even Kazakhstan couldn't seem so bad. Were a few months here sufficiently awful to produce this dramatic shift in loyalties? Here, among sun-bleached ridges and dry slopes sprinkled with black figures like mouse-droppings on a loaf of stale bread? Here, in a stark land where for months Grechko had little to do but think?

Grechko had come, he claimed, with an unconsciously romantic image of Arabia. He had found libraries in Damascus where, pretending to improve his knowledge, he had learned other things. He had learned that the early Jewish settlers were ideologists; and from this knowledge he progressed to other matters. Science and technology were subjects he understood; and these were the weapons with which Israel tackled her problems. His disenchantment with Arab myths was counterbalanced by his fascination with men such as Chaim Weizmann, who could save a nation by finding a vegetable substitute for TNT. The last bit of poetry had died that morning when his two Russian colleagues were struck down by the bug that caused a certain painful loosening of the bowels. And this, said Grechko, had given him the thing he needed most: opportunity.

"Let all guns point to the Zionist-imperialists!" intoned the Presidium's speechmaker, and the Russian winced.

Yesnov massaged a bruised knee. Was it only twelve hours

ago that he was rushing from leave at the kibbutz that now seemed a million miles away? Already the sun was swelling like the yolk of a broken egg into the layers of twilight mist.

Nayef approached. "The Jew is talking," said the Russian in Arabic.

The Syrian captain nodded. "He will cooperate?"

"No doubt. There will be a rescue-helicopter, count on it. Disperse your men. It will be here by midnight or later."

The Russian betrayed a familiarity with procedure that deepened the pilot's suspicion. It might be true that the Russian wanted to be taken back to Israel as a defector, in which case, all this chatter was an elaborate deception. Or perhaps, to the Syrian, the deception consisted simply in luring the rescue-helicopter into a trap.

By the time Major Zee began to lower the helicopter onto Hill PS-5 that night, the captured pilot had weighed all the dangers. He saw the Syrian captain move up the escarpment. He knew the guerrillas were in radio contact with an Al Fatah movable base, because he had heard their distant transmitter. It seemed certain, as Captain Nayef rose and declared himself to the crew of the helicopter, that the Syrian was thinking purely in terms of an ambush.

It was at this point that Yesnov shouted his warning in Hebrew, fully expecting the Russian to put a bullet into his head. Instead, Grechko threw him to the ground and pushed a fist in his mouth, snarling to the nearby *fedayeen* "Scatter yourselves! I'll take care of this one."

Above them, a rapid-fire gun chattered. Nayef, the Syrian, cried out and fell.

Talik, in the back seat of Aaron's Phantom as it circled Hill PS-5 at 09:08 hours on the back-timing, early in the evening of Day X, was not a computer. He felt very strongly about this, having read an American admiral's opinion that the Phantom 2 "introduced the future of air combat into a contemporary environment wherein for the first time missiles, electronics, and supersonic performance were the order of the day; and the eyeball, optical gunsight, and machine gun were relegated into place as back-up systems."

The boy in the back seat was not even a back-up system. He took a dim view of anyone who thought he was. When he first met the stranger, for instance, he rebelled against being introduced merely as the Flight Officer. Talik held a B.Sc. in chemistry and physics and he was continuing his postgraduate studies in his native Jerusalem. For all this, as combat-flier and student, he got the equivalent of $57.50 a week in the United States plus the cost of the taxi whenever he was recalled from his weekends of study to range the Middle East skies as a radar-head. He knew this function was regarded elsewhere as difficult and dangerous. Nevertheless he did not see his head as a computer taking data from a television tube and converting it into information or orders to his skipper.

He checked his own cockpit again and glanced outside. They were loafing along in wide and deliberately eccentric circles at heights between 500 and 5000 feet, dragging their coat, taunting the unseen enemy to come up and fight. A few fires burned in the solitude below, their pinpricks vanishing abruptly whenever shreds of cloud interrupted his vision. The horizon glowed fitfully and he could imagine the rumble of the guns. He turned back to the radarscope. Switching from the witches' brew outside to the subtle interior glimmer of instruments was breaking the rules—not his rules, the rules of other air forces. Eyes took time to adjust to changing densities of needlepoint lights. Precious time. Sixty seconds were all you got from the start of a single head-on air-to-air intercept to the awful moment when the enemy exploded. If he didn't explode it was because you had lost a second of time and thereby lost the battle and your life.

Talik broke other people's rules, not those of the IAF. His cockpit was simplified because Israel could not afford the tremendous cost of equipment that was too sophisticated for day-to-day operations in the restricted theater of the Middle East war. Therefore, although he was trained to handle the full range of Phantom gadgetry, he was not required to work with his head buried in the machinery. Furthermore, Talik was in peak physical condition. He had the reactions of the paratrooper and since boyhood he had made forced marches in the pitch black of night. In paratroop exercises, he had been taught to suck the fullest nourishment out of four hours of sleep. Normally, a Phantom Flight Officer handled systems of navigation, communication, inflight coordination, and weaponry. He conducted the radar-search and acquisition of targets. He could take over the manual control of weapons when the automatic functioning was either disabled or deliberately confused by enemy electronic interference.

Tonight, however, Talik's job was to respond with his own native wit and experience to any new form of missile attack. He knew Colonel Aaron was so familiar with the terrain below that radar was an aid, not a necessity. If MiGs came up, Aaron needed no artificial guidance to help him bend the Phantom round to a good launch position while he listened for the buzz from the heat-seeking missile head that would tell him he could pull the trigger.

Talik was free to concentrate on the whole bag of tricks with which he must engage any enemy who played with the new toys of death in the valleys now echoing to the scream of the Phantom's engines.

The noise drowned all but the most intimate sounds in the wadi. Yesnov could see the glowing exhaust rings of the Phantom as it swung past.

Grechko said, "Run ahead of me. Quick. Go now."

Yesnov scrambled to his feet. The guerrillas had moved into positions along the foot of the hill. Nayef the Syrian had vanished. If the Russian meant to shoot him in the back and claim later that he had tried to escape . . . Well, it was hardly worse than the prospect of the rescue-mission's being ambushed. He began to claw his way out of the dried riverbed, the rubber-ridged soles of his flying boots gripping the slope. With each second he expected to feel the thump of a bullet. He slid over a ridge and found the fissure which cracked open one side of the hill and must bring him to the ledge where the IAF Sikorsky waited.

Halfway there he stumbled over the body of the Syrian captain. While the Phantom was moving back to a position this side of the hill where its jets thundered like wagon wheels on a wooden bridge, Yesnov knelt and ran his hand lightly over the captain. He felt the warm stickiness of blood but the man was alive. He straightened up, and the Russian collided with him. It was incredible but the fool seemed to be following him like a faithful dog.

He faced Grechko. It *had* to be a trap.

The Russian pushed his gun into Yesnov's hands. "Run!"

The Phantom's engines were fading again. Yesnov checked the gun. It was loaded.

He called out to the unseen rescuers above, using his code-name.

A scatter of rifle fire far away told him the *fedayeen* were uncoordinated and confused.

The voice of his sister came down to him. His heart stopped. Then it truly had been Ruthi using the signal of their childhood, that wild whistling complaint of the sandgrouse. She seemed very close. He felt like a climber hauling himself up the last few feet of a steep rock-face, moving steadily toward the ledge. Behind him the moonlight pierced the scudding clouds and again spread across the valley. He reached into the void and touched her hand.

Jacob got the fuller report at 08:45 on the back-timer. The Sikorsky was still grounded. No matter. But the mechanic Mosheko was badly hurt by a stray bullet. Yesnov was safe and had brought in a Soviet missileman who wished to defect. The Russian, in token of his good faith, proposed they should take possession of certain equipment including the new blowpipe missile-launchers left in the wadi. There was also a regular Syrian army officer, trained in the Soviet Union. He, too, was seriously injured.

Jacob's first impulse was to tell them to get Yesnov out. The Russian defector was a prize, but a questionable one. History was full of the stories of false turncoats used to deceive and confuse. This would have been Jacob's advice: forget the booty; gamble no more; get back while you can. But others had heard the exchange and would be evaluating the information. Jacob bent his head in patience.

The defector was interesting. A Russian who came over was likely to be a disenchanted political officer who had discovered that the Kremlin was strengthening its archenemy, China, by putting arms into the hands of Maoist guerrillas. Russian technical experts, on the other hand, could not have cared less. They were absorbed in the science of war and the rare opportunity to test new weapons in the cockpit of Israel. For one of these to defect was significant, and probably a trick. Thus Jacob rationalized his own inclinations. There was a point beyond which he did not believe in gambling the lives of fliers. In his mind they were "his" fliers, not in any possessive sense, although each of them was to him an individual. Those who were dead would always haunt his dreams, and there was a limit to the number of ghosts that any one man could sustain.

The decision, however, was out of his hands. Captain Naomi

relayed the information. A Piper Cub from the flying-school was on its way now to pick Jacob up.

"Excuse me again." The old man had come down the cement steps so quietly that he took Jacob by surprise.

"What is it?"

"My son is safe?"

Jacob stared into the seamed face of the father of Yesnov and Ruthi. He should have known that an old kibbutznik like this one would be somehow informed, and was entitled to be.

"Your son is safe. And Ruthi, both."

The old man nodded.

"Did your wife know it was your son?"

"No," said the old man. "She—she's been sick. Certain things are not always plain to her if you catch my meaning, comrade."

Comrade. Long after the old man had gone again, the word echoed. The founders of this kibbutz had come from East Europe with the deliberate intention of creating a Jewish working class. They were part of the only intentionally downward-mobile movement in the entire history of immigration. Their leaders saw that Jewish social life had been distorted by the Diaspora. Almost all Jews had been pushed into the ranks of the middle class in Europe, and many of those who came to build the foundations of Israel were turning their backs on bourgeois backgrounds. The old man had been a *halutz* of this kind, seeking personal and communal redemption by working as a laborer on the land. Hence the strong influence in a kibbutz where Marx, Engels, Lenin, and Trotsky all had their audiences and even a few lingering devotees.

The irony was profound. Jacob himself remembered arriving in this land after practicing kibbutz-type living in a camp in Italy. The years of boyhood had withered in the dark barns of death. When the allied armies came swollen with victory, his own sense of personal worth had shriveled still more and his spirit lay in chains. For him, therefore, the first impact of the Jewish settlements had been astonishing. His soul, thirsting for ideas and hope, revived in the communal washrooms on the day he'd overheard an argument between two farmworkers. It concerned one laborer's interpretation of Oliver Cromwell as a seventeenth-century English strategist whose political links led directly to Marxist concepts. The other man regarded Cromwell's revolution as a reflection of the vested interests of anti-Catholic landlords. The two farmers had stomped back into the fields, still debating away.

The father of Yesnov and Ruthi might have been one of those men. What Jacob knew for sure was that the old man had twice commanded reservists holding the bridge at B'not Ya'ako, the ancient passage over the River Jordan below a fortress of the Crusaders. And twice the old man had helped to throw back the spearheads of Arab onslaughts.

The irony was profound because the old man and many like him were such idealists. They believed in a pragmatic approach to the dream that so regularly failed Communist intellectuals. He was opposed, like his brothers, to the creation of white colonial-style societies. Instead, he had preached self-reliance and the need to perform one's own labor (*avoda atzmit*). He had resisted, with his brothers, the exploitation of cheap Arab labor by the early Jewish landlords. Yet they were identified by their enemies with the white colonists left behind by the departing imperialists in Africa and Asia. They had taken the spirit of the Marxist revolutionaries and cast aside the structure that required thought-control. For this they were denounced by Moscow and Peking as enemies of the people.

Making his way in a kibbutz truck to the airstrip, Jacob might well have recalled his exchange with the stranger. S had asked if people here suffered from a persecution complex which distorted their view of the world. Jacob replied, "Did it ever occur to you that a man may have a persecution complex for the very good reason that he *is* persecuted?"

At 08:03 on the back-timing, at that period after midnight in Tel Aviv when the crowds thin along the waterfront, a fixed-wing aircraft touched down lightly on the Galilean shore. The pilot was an *ab initio* instructor. His Piper Cub was used to weed out those cadets who seemed least likely to make good fliers. The system was ruthless because the IAF could not waste time. A fledgling got ten flights. At the end, he was either a potential pilot or he washed out. (*Hadacha,* to get one's wings, means in the IAF the opposite of normal usage in the United States. An Israeli cadet who "gets his wings" has failed; is, in effect, dead and on his way to another world). The plane that eliminated these unfortunates, the sturdy Piper Cub, bristled with plugs and external racks so that it could be quickly converted to a combat role with electronic gear and light weapons. The pilot himself doubled as a fighter-bomber and flew both the Skyhawk and the Super-Mystère B2, known in the IAF as *Sinbad* from the acronym SMBEDE. He had started his air-force career as an electrician, he once told S, and liked the routine of his present job. "I'm like a businessman," he had said beside the squadron tents in the desert. "I kiss my family good-by and go to work five minutes from here. It's more convenient, actually, than being a New York commuter because I can always slip home to fix something or play with the kids at lunch."

He waited now for Jacob to cross the strip. "You know Aaron is in direct contact?"

"So it seems." Jacob leaned into the cockpit. "You know who the downed pilot is?"

"Of course."

"His father's here. Mind if we take him?" The question was a courtesy. The response could be nothing but a formal affirmative.

Jacob jogged back to the truck. The rescue-helicopter would overfly the kibbutz now. He didn't want the old man to wait, as he knew he would, in that tomb.

He was reading there and raised his head slowly at Jacob's entry. "Ach, you caught me. . . ."

"They won't be landing here."

"Not even Ruthi?"

"An urgency has entered the situation. I have a seat for you in the aircraft."

The old man unhooked wire-rimmed spectacles and placed them on the book open in his lap. "I can wait here. It's better. For my wife. For the work tomorrow."

Across the room a corporal was packing away the telecom. There was no point, thought Jacob, in pressing the old man. He asked, wanting simply to convey a sense of comradeship, "What are you reading?"

"A contemporary account of an event that was both melodramatic and historically important. Have you thought"—the old man stared up at Jacob with sudden force—"does it not seem important that there is no such thing as definitive history and therefore that sometimes an author must attempt to explain events through a single pair of eyes? The fraudulence of the god's-eye view becomes plainer with the years. We live in an age of vast movements that tear the hearts of men." He tapped the bone of a finger against the open pages. "We know, in a way that our ancestors never could, how many lies are told, how much deceit and tomfoolery enters into diplomacy and war."

Jacob sank onto the arm of a chair, anxious to leave, yet curiously moved.

"We live in times of great emotion."

"Exactly," the old man said. "Right here we live at the center of a great emotional storm. I find myself drawn increasingly to those writers who do not pretend to know everything, who declare their emotions so that we have some way to measure what they tell us. You know, it's much easier to write a scholarly work and abdicate all responsibility for making a judgment."

Jacob stirred. He had important work to do. But the old man had more than that. He had a son and a daughter in danger. In the kind of danger from which there had never been any respite. He deserved a few more minutes.

"I take it," said Jacob, "you're reading about our country."

"In a way, perhaps. It is a reconstruction of the way Stalin hunted Trotsky halfway round the world. When the Russians wish to dispose of an enemy they are remarkably meticulous."

"*Trotsky!*"

"Yes. Is that so odd?"

"Trotsky was a failure."

"He was alive. He offered an alternative to men who, through blind idealism, became the victims of dictatorship. So the Russians set a dozen traps for him and in the end the most skillful of their assassins destroyed him in the heart of the Americas where it seemed nothing could be safer."

"Don't carry the analogy too far."

"I won't, comrade, I won't indeed. I am perfectly sure the Russians felt compelled to destroy Trotsky because his political ideas were dangerous competition, and not because he was a Jew."

16

PHANTOM AMONG

THE *TILIM*

News of the Russian's defection followed hard on the heels of the guesswork surrounding the Security Committee's meeting earlier that day. The word spread by some mysterious grapevine across the land until it stopped at the Canal some two hundred and fifty miles away. It would have been difficult for the word to travel further without running out of Israeli-held territory. Eighty yards further on, across a fetid stretch of dirty Suez water, stood the Egyptian guns. When one was knocked down, two popped up in its place like a multiplication of monsters in some horror movie. Inside the sunken multistoried bunkers, men white as cheese played backgammon or cleaned weapons. The Bar-Lev Line was not a place for sun-bathing.

A group of men with blackened faces, preparing to go out on night patrol, questioned one of the eavesdroppers who (by ingenious misuse of equipment and misapplication of skill) had intercepted certain messages.

"How many prisoners?" "It's not clear. The chopper's still on the ground." "Is it disabled?" "Why don't we dispatch commandos?" "What's this new missile?"

It had been another day of artillery salvos. Each barrage sent tremors through the cramped forts but scarcely shook the lattice of steel, ripped from the old trans-Sinai railroad, supporting layers of timbers and concrete topped with sand. Those who lived under the artificial lights, eating from disposable plastic mess-gear, sleeping on foam rubber, called themselves "moles." The war itself shrank to a battle of endurance along one of the hottest front lines in history. Here Nasser had broken the 1967 ceasefire and here suspicions were deepest about promises of peace. The Bar-Lev Line was a tripwire. Most able-bodied young men had either served in it, or over it, and felt entitled to debate each move of the politicians and commanders.

About a hundred and twenty-five miles eastward, the paratroop general of Southern Command, Ariel Sharon, kept his headquarters at the place where Abraham once watered his flock, Beersheba, crossroads of camel traders and some twenty miles from the Middle East's largest nuclear-research center.

In this same general area was a base with an underground room that duplicated the primary operations center. It resembled a large operating theater. Instead of medical students, senior officers looked through sealed glass onto the aircraft plot around which moved girls equipped with surgically neat telebriefs. The plot was spread horizontally on what was known as the Table, and overlaid a map. From the newly developed ski slopes of Mount Hermon down to the Red Sea, every airman and aircraft was accounted for upon this map or its neighboring electronic consoles. From Baghdad in the east to Russian bases in Libya far to the west, the tracks of Israel's enemies were pursued. The map and the information chattering out of machines or splashing across radarscopes was enough to rattle the toughest old warrior. Here, condensed and laid out with precision, was the total picture of a land under siege. Dotted lines traced the spoor of Russian warships from the East Mediterranean to the Red Sea. Curving lights followed the progress of

Russian transports flying from East Europe to Cairo. For a general such as Ariel Sharon, grandfather of the paratroopers, it must have looked like a nightmare expansion of the situation when he led Unit 101 in commando raids against the surrounding Arabs nearly twenty years earlier: "Against the unknown and against the foe," as he was fond of quoting from the Hebrew text, "from sea to sea and mountain to mountain."

The crisis at PS-5, where Major Zee's helicopter now awaited instructions, came when many of the air commanders were still in the desert. There was always a base handy, such as this one, where everything known to the central War Room was repeated faithfully. The commanders trooped down the concrete steps and filed along the sound-proofed balcony of this duplicate hub of the web. Above their heads, voices spoke with the tinny rattle of ghosts at an electronic séance. The voices came out of the right. The men on the balcony were themselves soft-spoken or silent. Their arrival made one think of a warship's bridge to which the admiral has transferred his flag.

A nuclear physicist, taking advantage of the midnight surge in available power, was working with the tandem-accelerator at the Weizmann Institute at Rehovot near the wine-cellars established eighty-three years earlier by Baron Rothschild. Wine was not the physicist's tipple. He could have used a stiff drink, however, when he came away from the phone. He had been shooting beams of nuclear particles at target atoms, jolting the atomic nuclei to test the reactions. He was known for his work in the field, helping to comprehend the nucleus of the atom and why it behaves as it does. He visualized the atomic nucleus as being composed of particles arranged like the skins of an onion. It was difficult to tear his mind away from such matters to the analysis of destructive weapons. But he shut down the lab and then called his wife. Yes, he needed the car. No, he couldn't say why. Yes, it meant a long drive—into the Negev. No, he wasn't being called up for reserve duty or anything as alarming as that. . . . How the hell did she know about the Russian?

In matters of this kind, there were routine actions to be taken. Mrs. Meir might be called out of bed, for instance. If machines or men had to be dispatched, there were procedures to follow. For long-range plans, a Battle Order would be submitted to the chief-of-staff, who might request approval from the Defense Minister or the Cabinet. In such a case, the Operations Staff worked out details down to the smallest responsibilities of the lowliest servicemen and -women. Drivers in the air force, for example, were girls who would be provided with pick-up times for crews. Clerks in Intelligence would gather files and update the information on targets. When there was time for a Battle Order, there was also time for the squadrons to carry out air reconnaissance and make assessments on the kind of opposition they could expect from enemy aircraft, missiles, and ack-ack guns.

Tonight Major Zee was on his own. The rescue mission on Hill PS-5, if it went well, would deliver information on which the operational planners might have to act. It happened, however, that the Security Committee that day had drawn up a new set of contingency plans based upon the possibility that Israel might be walled in as a result of the latest Russian and Arab moves. These were the kind of plans which are standard safety measures today in most parts of a world where modern weapons have made the pre-emptive strike an acceptable defensive concept. Events were pushing Israel very close to squeezing the trigger. Hence the sudden atmosphere of tension. Men who had lived all their lives on the brink, and who discussed the possibility of Israel's liquidation with cold objectivity, were drawn together by the sheer drama of a situation they could only attempt to visualize.

To be sure, the facts in their possession were already surprisingly varied. A tentative identification had been made of Grechko. The Russian, according to the file at headquarters, had recently interrupted his service in Syria to seek contacts with yet another revolutionary movement among the sultanates in the Persian Gulf vacated by Britain. There he'd been rebuffed by the Peking-led Popular Front for the Liberation of the Occupied Arab Gulf. It was not clear why he should have strayed out of his role as a leading tactician in the use of missiles but many Russians now in the Middle East were openly worried by Red China's large-scale intervention.

The missile for which Grechko seemed to be responsible could be, it was thought, of considerable significance. With an unlimited number of Arabs to draw upon, Russian instructors could distribute the one-man launchers like pea shooters to children. If one accepted the view that the IAF's air offensive was the sole reason for making Arab leaders such as Nasser think again, then the wholesale sprouting of new missile-launchers could be the final act before Israel went over the brink. On the other hand, the early capture of the new model might give defense-research scientists time to devise countermeasures.

To a stranger, the scene was bound to be reminiscent of that other night of June 4–5, 1967, when time ran out and the air strike was launched that left Israel naked in the skies. General Hod listed the reasons for that lightning victory: "We lived with the plan, slept and ate the plan. We kept tight operational control—the ability to absorb and integrate any new information into existing plans, and the ability to pass new information to pilots already in the air."

His own quick-wittedness saved Ezer Weizman, who, though chief of operations in the 1967 war, nevertheless took to the air for the heliborne descent upon the Egyptian garrison at Sharm el-Sheikh. The commando-type operation was Moshe Dayan's proposal. Halfway there, Motti Hod warned Ezer's slow-moving convoy of helicopters that enemy fighters were overhead. Ezer led the helicopters to shelter at the foot of Moses' Mountain (Jebel Musa), where they took cover like a gaggle of geese until the danger passed. Later, Ezer Weizman radioed Motti Hod to tell Moshe Dayan that everything was okay; Sharm el-Sheikh was in their hands. "I can't do that because Moshe is at the Western [Wailing] Wall," Motti called back, which was how the chief of operations got the news that an objective had been captured that represented the dreams and prayers of countless generations. Then Motti phoned Ezer's wife, Reuma: "I'm calling to give you regards from your husband and your brother-in-law. They are both fine. Your husband is at Sharm el-Sheikh and your brother-in-law is at the Western Wall." Which was how the wife of the chief of operations discovered that her men were safe and the most important military goals had been reached.

This flexibility was accompanied by the dash and verve of what the French would call a *corps élite*. And yet there has always been an underlying modesty. A French reporter, remarking on this, noted a single exception when Motti Hod said: "Dayan came with me in a helicopter and asked what I wanted for my aviators. I showed him Mount Hermon and said 'That mountain so they can go skiing.' 'It's yours,' said Dayan. By radio I ordered commandos to be landed below the 9,232-foot peak by helicopter and now we ski on Mount Hermon."

This intimacy between the fighting forces had become more evident in moments of crisis. The army was still the senior service. It had learned by Day X however to exploit the IAF's elasticity. There was on the one hand a talent for planning a raid comparable to the Dam-Busters' attack in World War II by the RAF against the Möhne and Eder dams when crews had to be hand-picked and trained over and over again in simulated conditions while scientists devised a new kind of bomb for this one mission. Yet side by side with this meticulous concentration upon detail went a readiness to put aside formality and if necessary to rearrange or abandon a major operation. The stranger had seen cases where a voice on the radio, calling for help, was promptly recognized by a pilot or an infantry officer, who would then feed into his existing mission an adjustment to cover the emergency. Reasons of security prevent any specific description, but a senior IAF commander had told S, "Look, discipline is very tight once we scramble. But there's a mutual trust between men in the field and men at headquarters, and squadrons have a lot of leeway. Their commanders may be overridden for broader political or strategic reasons. Tactical decisions are usually made at squadron level and where a complicated operation is concerned, pilots are selected on the basis of their records and their ability to make on-the-spot judgments. It takes a special kind of man to fly according to orders that fit him like a pressure suit, and yet to improvise if the conditions suddenly change."

Major Zee was in this special category.

So was Colonel Aaron, piloting the Phantom guarding the rescue-mission.

But what about his FO, the radar-head Talik?

In that place where the central control room was duplicated with great precision, a senior officer just back from jousting in a sky full of missiles over Egypt was able to recall a matter concerning Talik that brought smiles of approval.

Talik had once been almost expelled from the Institute of Technology in Haifa for cracking the code of the public-telephone system and sharing the secret with other students, who caused a major flutter in the finance department by making free calls to all parts of the world.

Talik had been blamed for the publication of a do-it-yourself sheet that disclosed three ways to cheat the pay-phones, using (a) stout wire, (b) strong thread and a piece of cellotape, (c) an IBM punch-card. More advanced students could call Helsinki or Shanghai by ingenious manipulation of a six-hundred-Ohm electrical resistance.

Obviously the young inventor's talents had been misapplied.

Like the safecracker who becomes a valued spy in wartime, Talik's swift advance in the resistance movement of an inventive air force was guaranteed.

The machine that challenged his ingenuity and met his needs was the Phantom F-4E. Sitting in the back seat, in direct contact now with Major Zee's grounded helicopter, Talik was happier than a Chinese-puzzle-maker. Imprinted on his mind were the notes he had paraphrased from Ezer Weizmans' sermons of the past decade: We need a machine capable of tactical support for troops, *and* combat in the air, *and* bombing, *and* escort duties on combined ops, *and* if necessary willing to stand on its head. One machine: because we cannot afford a variety of fancy planes for different fancy roles. We need one plane able to penetrate Arab defenses despite the newest radar and missile systems to guarantee us air superiority. It has to be a machine that places full power back where it belongs, in the hands of the man in the cockpit.

The machine in the hands of Talik and Colonel Aaron had been stripped and simplified. It was ugly and graceless. Its redesigned radome gave it a bulbous nose, heavy and predatory. It was a mass of technical compromises forced upon it by the seemingly impossible demands of naval carrier forces. The Phantom emerged from all those restrictions which in the past made naval aircraft inferior to land-based planes. It required good stability for the low speeds needed to drop onto a ship's deck—and this alone was a contradiction of supersonic combat design. Its cathedral tail was angled *downward* because of hangar limitations and also because of the tremendous gyroscopic forces that shove a jet sideways if it tries a rolling motion at 1500 miles an hour.

Talik thought there was an odd similarity in the *effect* of the demands first imposed by the United States Navy, and later by

Ezer Weizman—the limits on naval aircraft were imposed by problems of tight stowage space, the absence of surrounding space where planes in trouble could land, and restrictions in the numbers of aircraft. Where a carrier was surrounded entirely by unaccommodating seas, Israel was surrounded by hate-infested territories and a sea where Phantoms could never land. A carrier had room for only so many jets. Israel was limited by embargos and money.

Talik had worked it out, for instance, that the price of the hundred extra Skyhawks and twenty-five more Phantoms, which Israel still desperately wanted was $250 million or the equivalent of all contributions from the United States Jewish community in one entire year.

At 08:00 on the back-timing, Talik expected a *go/no-go* from the control cell that had now taken over the Phantom's mission. Colonel Aaron had been working out tactics with Major Zee below, but the control cell had overriding powers. Dead on the hour Aaron got a *go/go* with an unexplained order that he first zoom to Flight Level 150 (15,000 feet). At this height the Phantom flew into cloud, which, by the light of the full moon, seemed to be a newly developed thunderstorm. Rain streamed over the canopies, there was turbulence and lightning, and suddenly every part of the Phantom was bathed in the dancing blue light of St. Elmo's fire.

"Corona discharge," Aaron said matter-of-factly from the front seat.

The eerie light played like flaming brandy on *crêpes suzette*. Talik had never seen anything so full of evil portent. They were sitting on tanks of highly combustible fuel. He knew the fire was a harmless display of electrical discharges but still he bent closer to check all the instruments in his cockpit. The thought of being flambéed was not an agreeable one.

They broke out of the storm into air so clear that Talik could see the oil rigs burning on the east flank of the Gulf of Suez. The order came to descend directly to FL 10, a thousand feet above the crashed Skyhawk. Speed, rate of descent, patter of movements were fed to them and then the control cell politely withdrew. The rest was for the Phantom crew and Major Zee on the ground to work out between them.

Zee's voice on the other channel was crisp and clear. He had two injured men and wanted to recover the Russian missile-launchers within very narrow time limits. Would the Phantom hang around at low level to keep the guerrillas scattered? And watch out for the new mobile missile-launchers.

Aaron acknowledged the message. His sudden climb and descent would give the enemy confusing signals. He knew what to expect if missiles were operating in the area. He had once described to S what it was like flying through a sky full of *tilim*. "They're fired in clusters. Each missile is like an enemy jet but faster—up to 2,500 miles an hour. You pick the one that looks most dangerous and dodge it first. You don't have time for self-congratulation. You're already outthinking the second, then the third. By day, you're warned by a burst of smoke on the ground. At night, the flame is dirty yellow. The missiles chase you as if they had brains, but some are less stupid than others. Two minutes of evasion takes two years off your life."

He spoke reassuringly to Talik, whose breathing had become noisy. Aaron knew his whiz-kid reputation. He had also seen the Phase Two flying-school report. Phase Two was the four-month training period when those cadets who survived the Piper Cub selection stage were pushed to the limit of physical endurance. In this time they saw nothing of a cockpit but went through field exercises that tested their guts and their capacity to think fast and aggressively under severe strain. Talik had come out top of his class, and already he was being watched as a potential leader. He had that rare combination of strong nerves, superb physique, and a genuine curiosity about life in general. He had thrust his way through technical school, and by sheer persistence won the esteem and the cooperation of the professors in Jerusalem. He had the kind of background that seems to exist nowhere else in the word: both his parents had taken university degrees in the 1940s while on missions for the underground armies. Unless Aaron was mistaken, the boy had the stuff to go all the way to the top in the tradition of the soldier-scholar. And he had the quick wit that made his excellence forgivable.

A lot depended on Talik this night. The Phantom had taken off with a curious mixture of weapons. It was not equipped with certain refinements, and thus imposed a greater responsibility on the crew. For instance, the automatic pilot was not in use (in a May 1970 record-breaking nonstop flight from London to Singapore, one Phantom RAF pilot used automatic control for twelve out of the fourteen hours in the air, but such occasions never arose in the IAF's theater of war). The plane was cleared for continuous flight up to fifteen hours but this required in-air refueling and was not practicable. It could carry the Sparrow III missile but if the pilot miscalculated or the radar-head had guidance troubles, the missile might "go stupid" or even refuse to launch: therefore Sparrows were out. Both Aaron and the back-seat boy were happiest with simple weapons of great variety, and in an emergency the boy might have to choose.

Aaron had caught him one day stripping and reassembling the guns in the IAF armory. They had talked about aerial gunfighting and Talik had become lost in his own eccentric history of the development of the machine gun. He'd gone back to the fourteenth century, when repeating-action guns fired like machine guns after the gunner waved a light across the touch-holes of several barrels mounted together. A repeater built in 1718, Talik had reported in tones of wonder, was said to have fired round bullets at Christians and square-sectioned bullets at the infidel Turks. And the ultimate machine gun was the one now in IAF service: the GE Vulcan 30-mm linkless feed firing 6000 rounds a minute.

Talik knew the Phantom inside out. He looked upon it as an ugly beast with beautiful assets. It lugged twice the Skyhawk's load and performed very much more work. It accomplished in a day of strikes what might take hundreds of infantrymen several weeks to carry out with conventional artillery. It hauled 13 tons of fuel and arms in addition to its own 15-ton weight at Mach 2+, more than 1520 miles an hour, and it took a lot of punishment. In the early days it had been known to land with chunks missing as if a giant bird had bitten prehistoric teeth into the wings and tail. This was because parts of the wing and tail were made of sandwiched aluminum stuffed with plastic foam and glue: until improvements were made in the bonding, bits of the sandwich broke off in high-speed maneuvers.

The first fifty Phantoms began to trickle into the IAF early in 1969 as a result of President de Gaulle's freeze on the sale of the fifty Mirage M5Js. One Phantom was capable of performing the work of a squadron of Mirages, but the cost was equally impressive. The bill for the first batch of Phantoms, including spares, weapons, support-equipment and the training of ground crews and one hundred and twenty pilots at a USAF base in California amounted to an estimated $272 million. The United States government put a ban on news of the sale but by the time the last of the fifty were arriving in 1970, it was no longer a secret, although still a political hot potato.*

Warplanes always had been political hot potatoes in Israel's experience, and Talik felt, like most airmen, a pressing need to become independent of outside suppliers. The Phantom was a long way from the two-hundred-mile-range Spitfire flown by Ezer Weizman, and yet every step of the way to air superiority had been dogged by crises abroad. The air force between 1958 and 1967 had been forced to standardize on French weapons: their first fighter-bomber was Marcel Dassault's Ouragans, followed by Mystère 4As, Super-Mystères, and Mirage 3CJ multi-

* These figures were published in a 1969 edition of *Flying Review*. It reported that Israel was denied certain equipment with a capacity to deliver nuclear weapons because of "the widely acknowledged possession by Israel of an atomic warhead production capability."

mission fighters. An all-weather multimission attack bomber, the Vautour 2A, the training Fouga-Magister jets, helicopters, radar, and electronic equipment all came from France. Nonetheless, although Frenchmen have emphasized with enormous national pride the victory of their planes in the 1967 war, the truth is that the foreign ministry, the Quai d'Orsay, opposed the sale of French-built jets from the year 1961, when Israel already saw an urgent need to match the MiG-21s being delivered to her enemies. The Quai, whose diplomats, like the Arabists in other foreign services, coldly balanced the small value of Israeli resources against Arab oil, stopped the delivery of the Mirage 3s. An interministerial meeting attended by Premier Pompidou and Foreign Minister Couve de Murville was dominated by General de Gaulle, who, at the last moment, released six squadrons of twelve Mirage 3s in time to tip the scales in the Six-Day War. The price on the Matra missiles that went with the Mirage 3 was outrageous even by the standards of international arms sales: one missile and its associated equipment cost $50,000, and as General Weizman said at the time, "To hell with burning several thousand dollars each time you have a near-miss." So the IAF armed with 30-mm guns the Mach 2.5 Mirage 3s, which the manufacturer claimed were too fast for dogfighting. In fact, all but one enemy plane destroyed in aerial combat in 1967 was downed by cannonfire.

Colonel Aaron had flown Mirage 3s. He had spent a great deal of time with Serge, the son of Marcel Dassault, whose French factories benefited tremendously from the IAF's demonstration of Mirage superiority. Aaron had seen the Mirage improved out of all recognition. He could dot the i's and cross the t's of General Weizman's statement to S that "we virtually remade the Mirage into the outstanding combat plane that became a worldwide best seller." The Mystères, too, were retailored. Marcel Dassault designed them to last for 900 combat hours. In the IAF many had logged 3000 hours by 1970. Mirage operational missions were raised to twelve a day: a fantastic performance, commented the American magazine *Aviation Week,* noting that "the 140 to 150 first-wave attack planes on June 5, 1967, did the work of 300 to 600 warplanes." The turnaround times to rearm and refuel, for Mirages in NATO's West European squadrons, had been pegged at twenty minutes, whereas IAF pilots and groundcrews got the interval down to seven minutes by ingenious use of manpower. One of Colonel Aaron's squadron pilots reported a turnaround time of less than five minutes between two sorties. The 1967 war therefore established the reputation of Marcel Dassault, which was already very high. His 8550 skilled French aircraft builders handled orders worth, for the Mirage alone, $2 million each and happily produced them for Israel's new enemies: one $200-million order went to Libya.

The sense of betrayal when the French government stopped delivery of fifty Mirages to Israel, although they had been ordered already, cut especially deep because Marcel Dassault was born a Jew. He had converted to Catholicism and although he had the right to speak out against the decision as a member of the Gaullist Party in the National Assembly, all he would say was, "The French Government makes the policy of France."

The pain of betrayal was something you learned to live with, like physical pain. But it left you wary and unyielding. It left you, Mosheko was thinking through a fog of pain, unyielding and probably unattractive to strangers. It was the hard shell that a person grew as protection against treachery.

He lay inside the hull of the helicopter, his knees drawn up to his chin to stem the bleeding from the rip in his belly, watching the Russian. It went against all reason, it outraged his pride as a mechanic trained to fight, as well as any infantryman, that he should be suddenly reduced to the helplessness of a baby. Curled up in the fetal position, he resented both himself and the Russian. A defector? That, too, went against all reason.

Grechko sat under the green light. The mutter of radio voices emerged from the pilot's cabin above. On the oily metal floor, Doctor Golden worked on the Syrian captain, Nayef, helped by the girl.

Grechko looked first at the Syrian and then at the little mechanic curled up in lonely agony. The Russian's big hands dangled between his knees and the weight of his body seemed to push out his stomach. His back curved forward and his head bent back, leaving three thick folds of flesh in the neck. His eyes were black currants under such a foliage of eyebrows that the crisp hairs formed a continuous hedge of brambles out of which he peered like a frantic sow. He had removed the Mao cap and his thick red hair sprang up around a small patch of bald greenish-yellow skull. He could not understand why the Jews were doctoring the dying Syrian when one of their own kind was wounded. The hedgerow above his eyes became a zigzag. He decided the Jews wanted to prolong the Syrian's life in order to interrogate him.

Mosheko the mechanic studied the Russian. Why would such a man defect? It must be a trick. There was the Phantom circling overhead again. In the arithmetic of war, was a Russian colonel and the possibility of capturing a new weapon worth risking a Phantom? Not really. Not in this air force.

Mosheko would have liked to express his doubts but his mind kept sinking into a vortex of pain.

Major Zee came down from the cockpit. "We'll have to take the chance," he said to nobody in particular.

Leaning on the doorway, his feet on the ground outside, Yesnov said, "Let's get it over with then."

Zee jerked his head in the Russian's direction. "He'd better come with us." He crouched in front of Grechko. "How many?"

Yesnov repeated the question in Russian.

"How many *what?*" demanded the Russian.

"How many men to carry the equipment? How *much* equipment? Is it all in one location?"

"You speak Russian," said Grechko accusingly.

"Of course I speak Russian," Yesnov replied. "My mother's family were four hundred years living near Tiflis. Until one day they discovered they were not Russians after all. They were Jews. No rights as citizens. No land. The cemetery where generations lay buried—even that, it seemed, was a larcenous occupation of territory. Because we were Jews."

The Russian slumped deeper into the bench-type seat. "You spoke no Russian back there." He sounded resentful, as if this disclosure changed everything.

"I was your prisoner *back there*. You think I was also an idiot?"

The Russian shook his head slowly, staring down at the Syrian, whose torn body had been dragged up the slope by the girl and Mosheko. The mechanic had been shot in the stomach by a wild burst of machine-gun fire from across the gulch. The machine gun had been silenced either by the sudden reappearance of the Phantom preceded by a thunderous sonic boom, or by the grenade hurled in that direction by the doctor. Nevertheless the explosions had rattled the Russian's head, perhaps breaking the trance in which he had moved from the idea of defection to the move itself. He said, "There is a battery of twelve missile fire-units and a first-line repair wagon. Each fire-unit is complete in itself. The launcher is of the blowpipe design. Tracking systems vary and there is an independent power supply. Carrier . . ." He lifted one of the hands hanging like a huge paw, counting off the items with fingers like small Somali bananas; counting them off in an Oriental fashion, fingers and thumb outspread and bending a digit as he called out an item.

"Are the units in a cluster?" asked Yesnov, trying to keep his voice steady. "Who guards them now?"

The Russian lifted his head and their eyes met. He said, "You were there. You saw." He seemed suddenly sly and secretly pleased, as if he had tricked Yesnov.

"I saw very little."

Doctor Golden was working under a small high-intensity beam which cast a narrow circle of light over the Syrian's split groin. He looked up. "This man is going to die if we stay here long."

Ruthi said nothing but the line of her jaw tightened. She glanced across at Mosheko. "I think he needs more morphine." As she said this, a nerve twitched in the corner of her mouth.

"No," the mechanic said, raising his head, his voice suddenly clear and firm.

The Russian swiveled his eyes between the two men. There was the Syrian in a litter with his entire inside lying beside him in purple coils, hands twitching vaguely over the gap where his intestines had been. Across the oil-black greasy floor, in another litter, Mosheko's body streaked with blood and sweat. The Russian shook himself. "Bring a map."

"Get the charts," Yesnov translated.

The Russian bent over the detailed map of the PS-5 grid. "Two clusters. Here and here." His right forefinger was cut short at the second knuckle and he used it to stab the thick paper, prodding as if the foreshortened finger were a blunt instrument with which he could bludgeon his late allies. "Finally, here, one fire-unit unguarded." The crinkled stub of the finger thrust into the wadi.

Yesnov glanced up. "There were three Syrians under that one's command," he said in Hebrew, lifting his chin in the direction of the dying captain. "The rest ran off, frightened."

"You realize what this is?" demanded Mosheko, crouched like a baby in his litter. His face was contorted with the effort of speech again, and the need to disguise the pain. He wanted no more morphine. If ever they were to lift out of here, the Sikorsky's self-starter needed to be nursed. He would like a clear head for that. He swallowed. "It's a trick to destroy ourselves and our friends up there."

They were all conscious again of the steady growl of the Phantom's jets.

"I'll worry about that," Major Zee cut in abruptly. He jerked his head at Doctor Golden, who followed him into the forward cabin.

"Mosheko . . . ?"

"Bleeding internally. I'm afraid to move him." Golden shrugged. "The Syrian is more badly hurt. If I neglect him for Mosheko he could die while my back is turned. If I give him priority, Mosheko could end up a permanent invalid—or worse."

There in the faint luminosity of the flight-deck the two men stood locked in the familiar dilemma. What does one do, when lack of time forces a choice between two badly injured men of whom one is the enemy and possibly dying too? Each time this situation arose, the IAF crewrooms were swept by the same debate.

"What chance does Mosheko have?"

Doctor Golden said without hesitation, "A good chance. But better if he's put in the hands of the specialists at Jerusalem."

Zee rubbed the back of his stubbled jaw. "The poor child."

The doctor backed out of the cramped cabin. The helicopter pilot's hand paused over the radio switch. He hated himself for the brutality of the next question, and his voice hardened. "How long can he stay conscious? I need him."

"Without more morphine, as long as you like." The teddy-bear face loomed in the doorway. "Unless the pain kills him."

"Estimated time, twenty minutes," Talik repeated mechanically. He marked the coordinates on the grid beside his knee. As soon as Major Zee was off the air, he said to the Phantom's pilot, "We could plant a gouger in each cluster. It would divert them, take pressure off Zee if all he needs is twenty minutes." His pencil skimmed across a pad strapped to his other thigh. "If all goes smoothly, they could lift off within thirty minutes."

Colonel Aaron settled back in the plastic front seat, weighing the odds. The loss of a Phantom and two expensively trained crewmen was a large price. The Russians were playing one-sided chess. They could afford to sacrifice all the pieces in the world, including a senior Russian missileman. "This so-called defector," Zee had reported on the radio, "could be a decoy. These are the positions he gives for the two main clusters of missile fire-units, but—"

But. The temptation to go down and knock them out was hard to resist. It meant getting into their range. If the new missiles were just moving into the Syrian theater, the Russians would want to boost morale with a quick victory. If the self-proclaimed defector spoke the truth, the two clusters made up the bulk of a battery of twelve. The twelfth was the one which Zee proposed to recover from the wadi at PS-5. On the other hand, the Russian could be telling just half the truth, the other half being that the remaining launchers were lying in wait for the Phantom.

Another voice cut into his thoughts. The forward control-cell again, chipping in with new information. The voice was that of the piece-of-cake Mirage pilot, the Confectioner. Good. The Confectioner would have been patching his own firsthand knowledge of this region with the back-room analysts. Neither the Confectioner nor Colonel Aaron needed to use call signs. They knew each other's voices as well as they knew the voices of their own wives. The wives, in fact, jointly ran a nursery school. It created an extra measure of mutual confidence. No matter how concerned a man might be about the life of a comrade, he became a shade more cautious about the husband of the girl next door.

"We have neutral feelings about Ringmaster," said the Confectioner, using pseudonyms. "He's probably a tour conductor but watch for yellow. Go for Griselda." There followed a series of equally meaningless sentences ending with the phrase that meant "You have command."

Aaron ran through the mixed load of weapons he carried. The Confectioner had told him that the Russian defector was not known by Intelligence to have links with Soviet political or psychological warfare departments; he was clean but not positively above suspicion. Aaron should continue to work with Major Zee, but it would be useful if he could provoke a salvo of the more sophisticated missiles, to confirm their presence and also to get data on their electronics. These were missiles with which they were all familiar and against which the Phantom was equipped to react. The new blowpipe fire-units had now been analyzed. The missiles had impact fusing instead of the usual proximity fuses and they were based on a command-line-of-sight system. They were designed specifically for low-level work to fill the gap between the ground and 300 feet. It was immensely important that Major Zee be given every opportunity to bring one back. Aaron should take whatever action he thought necessary.

So the ball was back in his own court. Aaron grinned. The decision was his, but now he had facts on which to go, as well as the tacit understanding that headquarters were just as puzzled as he himself. He listened while the Confectioner reeled off updated figures: time into the Red Alert, estimated fuel-flow if the Phantom continued to cruise at maximum continuous power, margins of permissible speeds in the event of emergency maneuvers, and a revised flight plan.

"Give me the first coordinate," he told Talik the moment the Confectioner shut down.

He repeated the figures and checked his own chart. The cluster of missile fire-units here would be some two miles from where Major Zee was already working his way down to the wadi below PS-5. "We'll plant a gouger," he said, and in the back seat Talik indulged in a split-second of self-congratulation. It had been his idea to bring the concrete-gougers along.

Colonel Aaron brought the Phantom round onto a steady course, allowing the speed to decay from six hundred and fifty to five hundred and fifty miles an hour and shedding the few feet of height needed to level out at 330 feet. This was coming dangerously close to the new blowpipe-type missiles whose assembled strike-units he hoped to knock out. But to get the maximum benefit from the concrete-gouger, he was required to fly at this level.

They came up on the invisible target nice and steady. Talik had time to fix their exact position on the radar and arm the gouger. The ground below them was a broad valley at some height above sea-level and it was impossible to use the standard barometric-pressure altimeters. Instead he made a precise check electronically, meanwhile watching signals for any report of missile activity below.

At 07:20 on the back-timing, Talik released the first of the six gougers, each weighing about 1200 pounds (a maximum bomb load for the Phantom was 24 × 500-pound bombs). The weapon fell away and began to operate in its designed sequence.

Aaron pulled away in a climbing turn. The gouger was designed to tear chunks out of runways. Ordinary bombs made craters but seldom prevented a determined air force from continuing to operate. The gouger, on the other hand, inflicted a far more disabling amount of damage at greater depth.

If the Russian defector had been telling the truth, Aaron had just laid an egg which should have spectacular consequences.

At 07:17 a display of pyrotechnics lit up the valley. At 07:12 on the back-timing countdown, more explosions rocked the ground as the Phantom pulled away from the second cluster. Colonel Aaron was still climbing when he saw the first of the orange-yellow flames from conventional *tilim* rising to greet him. He felt the familiar tightening of stomach muscles and heard Talik in the back call out a warning. They had hit something down there—*and* provoked the Syrians or their Russian masters into revealing the presence of SA-IIs or -IIIs.

Aaron watched the sputtering flame. An old hand at this game, he waited as long as he dared before taking violent evasive action. If one had the nerve to delay, the missile's brain got stuck in a groove; became hung-up on the idea that one was flying steadily in a certain direction. Aaron would have preferred to pit his mind against an enemy's human brain. At least there was an element of hand-to-hand combat, of pilot against pilot. In this work, you had to out-think the machine.

Within his outside estimate of thirty minutes, Major Zee had started to winch up the missile fire-unit. It was all precisely as described by Grechko, who was down in the wadi now, with Yesnov, stripping the weapons carrier of useful gadgets.

The sound of explosions accompanied their work, and the sky lit up fitfully. The thrum of the jet overhead, and the long rolls of thunder in the ravine, seemed a sufficient guarantee of *fedayeen* discouragement. Nevertheless Ruthi had insisted on covering them with her Soviet Kalashnikov. She stood above them on the ledge, legs apart, pointing the snout across the gully. There was blood on her bare arms: the blood of the Arab and the blood of Mosheko the Jewish mechanic. Behind her, Golden called out, "How much longer?"

"We're ready to go." Zee stopped cranking the manual winch. "Give me a hand."

They wrestled chunks of metal into the Sikorsky's hull. The launcher was surprisingly light: the missiles were easily manhandled. Ruthi strapped the last piece into place and returned to her station on the ledge. She could hear Yesnov and the Russian puffing up the slope.

Inside the helicopter, Mosheko gave instructions for what he called "twitching" the engine starter. The damn thing was capricious, he said, and then he fell into a fit of coughing. Blood welled out of his mouth.

Major Zee glanced at the doctor who shook his head and snapped the cap from a tube of morphine. He tried to put the needle into a vein in Mosheko's arm. The little mechanic pushed him away with surprising strength. "It's like this, you see," said Mosheko. . . .

They were all the same: mechanics, gunners, tank-men. Some-times it seemed to Major Zee that every soldier had his own secret way of doing things. Once, doing duty as a forward air-controller, he'd spent an agonizing day on a mine-sweeping in-fantry-carrier. The gunner had improvised a mounting from movie-camera equipment to cushion the shock of bumpy terrain, enabling him to keep his sights fairly steady. It was this particular gunner's own gadget and he guarded it like a military secret. And now here was Mosheko, coughing his life up, disclosing his own unique way of starting the flaming engine!

But it was not so much the self-starter that worried Mosheko. There was a rotor-speed governor that controlled the transient drop of revs-per-minute during takeoff. Long after the engine sputtered and then settled into its accustomed rhythm, he lay in the litter and watched the vibrating metal over his head. He heard the muffled clunk of closing doors and felt the slight rise in cabin pressure against his eardrums. He was aware of Doctor Golden balanced over the body of the Syrian, washing the man's intestines with hot water and cotton, Ruthi helping him, the pair of them like a pair of mechanics rebuilding a car as they put back the purple coils, a task in which they had been interrupted. The shadow of the Russian fell across the mechanic's face and for a moment he saw the puzzled expression there.

Then Yesnov was holding his hand.

The Sikorsky shook with the quickening revolution of the rotor blades. Mosheko knew every creak and rattle. He felt the hull shift under him like a restless hippo struggling to its feet. The floor heaved. Now the next three seconds became critical. The rotor-speed governor, an Israeli version so minified that it weighed less than three pounds, fed from a powerpack and was easily overlooked. Yet in these three seconds it carried through its printed circuits the seeds of life for seven tons of metal and fuel. If it performed, the Sikorsky's blades would recover their stable revolutions and tug them all onward and upward. Mosheko held his breath, urging the machine to take the fence as if all these tin limbs and wire tendons could gather together to rise up; as if they were a fragment of that frequent dream when his arms became wings. He knew the moment this heap of cold metal surged with fluids and resurrected itself and became a bird again. He closed his eyes and released his breath, and the blood flooded his throat and he choked on it.

Aaron got the brief message. The Sikorsky was airborne.

The last of another volley of missiles had exploded too close for comfort. The thud still resonated through his spine. Behind him, Talik muttered and switched channels as the operators guided the missiles.

A last run down the valley would draw fire away from the helicopter, giving it time to rise vertically to maximum height and dash to safety. Aaron took the Phantom on a course calculated to hypnotize the missilemen: straight and level, at medium altitude. The first of a new batch of missiles streaked out of the dark. Another two minutes of dodging quarter-ton warheads of high explosive loomed ahead. Another two minutes of dueling with mechanical brains. If they were mechanical. A machine was made of dead matter; brains were made of living matter. The frontier between dead and living was muddled; and perhaps the brains of the missiles were married to men of blood and bones on the ground beneath too cleverly to be outwitted. Never mind. Talik would be recording just as conscientiously as he had traced the telephone circuits.

We'd make a great pair of bank robbers, thought Colonel Aaron, a second before the bang. The Phantom shuddered and a fire warning light flashed on, indicating serious trouble in one engine. MAYDAY! The distress call was automatic.

"I'm not ejecting," Talik said coolly, anticipating the order. "Not until I know you will. It's probably a wire torn loose. . . ."

"Probably." Aaron's voice was dry. He went through all the proper procedures. The light still burned. The missiles continued to come up at them. "Don't swallow your cork," he murmured and put the Phantom into a steep dive.

There was really no alternative. Talik would never eject without him. And Aaron would never eject if there was any chance of bringing the Phantom home. It was best to hit the deck, under the range of the big *tilim,* and risk the new off-the-shoulder missiles. It was not much of a gamble. Nobody ever survived an inflight explosion.

17

RETURN TO MASADA

The children flocked like starlings, their chatter filling the dark orchards on the high ground near Jerusalem. A fine crop of pinkish-yellow apricots had to be snatched from the pincers of a snap-frost.

Were the children in danger? The question had to be asked before any mobilization of schools for an emergency harvest; and again, as now, while the children gathered.

Captain Naomi relayed the question from her post in the Citadel to the chiefs assembled in the desert. The time was three hours after midnight, approximately 04:50 on the back-timing scale. There was no immediate reply.

Her blood was stirred by the awfulness of the times. A child should not have to fear the dark because of men. Not on a night like this,

> when creeping murmur and the poring dark
> Fill the wide vessel of the universe.

What brought such words to mind? She sat in a pool of light, dimmed as much for economy as for security, and felt herself back in the cockpit, as once Jacob had been, as Aaron was even now.

Yet she alone had the vantage point too of the child she once had been, perched in the watchtower above the farm-school of Ben Shemen. Here in the Citadel she watched in the same silence the busy motions of friend and foe. The watchtower had seemed a safe place to the child. The cockpit had enclosed the girl in a world she could control. Here in the Citadel she was a woman, freshly aware of the scars left by childhood, physically scarred by the hazards of flight, but nevertheless a woman at the quiet heart of the battlefields. The child in the tower had amused herself in the silent watches, repeating lines from the plays which gave Ben Shemen its theatrical reputation. Every year they did Shakespeare. She wasn't sure, she didn't immediately recall, the time and place of an English king called Harry. But the words were plain now as they had been then: From camp to camp, through the foul womb of night,/The hum of either army stilly sounds. . . . Fire answers fire, and through their paly flames/Each battle sees the other's umber'd face./Steed threatens steed. . . . piercing the night's dull ear. . . ./The armourers, accomplishing the nights,/With busy hammers closing rivets up,/Give dreadful note of preparation.

She was startled by the intercom's stridency. She answered *"Ken!"* and the squawk-box shrilled back: no risk of rockets or shells; no guerrillas reported by the patrols; Red Alert in force on the Syrian front; nevertheless delay the children.

Naomi slid one leg across the other, leaned on the desk, focused on "Number of enemy aircraft destroyed—Number of ours lost, damaged, U/S [unserviceable] due to ops—Pilots missing . . . Please enter figures where appropriate."

Why was it taking so long? Security, Intelligence, all said the children were safe. So why this delay among the chiefs on the base in the Wilderness of Zin? Mobilization of children was not something lightly to be dismissed. It gave them a share in building the nation; made them aware of the struggle to draw nourishment from the soil. When danger threatened the crops, the schools were put on alert. If action was needed, before storm or frost struck, all manner of vehicles might be pressed into service and the children would spill from their homes in the way their fathers tumbled into milk-vans or wagons and buses to rush to the front. It was their land to defend, sons and daughters too.

The land once meant everything to Naomi. To watch things grow, to hold life, to draw the wet heads of half-born calves out of their mothers, to turn the soil and plant the seeds, these had comforted the girl mindful of a rootless past. She was never religious. The festivals were occasions for an almost Hellenic display of gratitude for deliverance from winter or foul weather. She had loved the ceremonial fetching of the first barley, accepting the religious significance as part of her inheritance yet always conscious that others worshiped in the same cycle. The Pharaohs of Egypt and the emperors of China blessed the fields. Shavuoth was going down to cut the first sheaves of the season, loading the carts and following them home again in rites so universal that Hindu or Buddhist, Moslem or Christian, recognized them. The land confronted her with the reality of life and the necessity of death. She no longer feared either, and from this sprang the confidence to fly. She had an aptitude for mechanical things and a natural skill. She became self-assured in the cockpit. She had seen death at the runway's end, and understood it.

"Ken!"—Let the children go, the squawk-box pronounced. She called the liaison officer, made a note in her log, and remembered that the daughter of Jacob would be among the mobilized children. Jacob's wife had died giving birth to the girl, while he was himself a flying-instructor with the fledgling air force of Uganda. She glanced down the list of schools. Children of army and air-force commanders were scattered among them, probably unknown to the men making decisions at this moment. She felt godlike, alone in the soundproof room, charting the movement

of those who lived within the fortress and provided it with sustenance and safety.

At Technion City, overlooking the port of Haifa and the hills of Galilee, men went to work on the Russian-built weapon delivered a little earlier by Major Zee's helicopter. The basic unit was a 40-pound portable launcher, a blowpipe that fired a missile which a terrorist could handle by himself. With such a weapon, the Arabs might hope to ring down a steel curtain.

The Technion was the last place to be dismayed by such a challenge. The college had been established by German Jews early in the century, high on Mount Carmel within sight of the snows of Mount Hermon. For many years it had been a center for underground Haganah operations and weapons used in the first war of 1948 were made in its workshops. The first building was financed by a Russian tea-merchant and an American philanthropist back in 1913, and its growth reflected the State's development in size, modernization, and collaboration between men and women of strangely varied backgrounds. "We are *not* religious," one of its professors had told S in what was a familiar disclaimer, but the stranger found the usual awareness of Biblical history that in other lands would have passed for "religion." The Technion covered three hundred acres where the prophet Elijah established his altar and demonstrated the supremacy of the Lord over the false prophets of Baal. A young student had explained this to S, who certainly wasn't conscious of it himself, but the same student also insisted that he hadn't a religious bone in his body.

Others, more exalted, seemed to find a similar difficulty in making these distinctions. A rousing speech on Israel's technological progress was given after the Six-Day War by the Technion's President, formerly the first chief-of-staff, Yaakov Dori: "The secret weapon with which Israel's Defense Forces won . . . was their spiritual superiority, allied to technological superiority. Then machine and man became one solid mass of steel and fire, drawing power and impetus from the spirit of the fighting man." But Dori would deny that he was an especially religious man.

Grechko was driven from the airstrip a hundred kilometers south of Haifa, through the silent streets of Tel Aviv. The Russian must have caught tantalizing glimpses of normality: the all-night sandwich bar at the Sheraton Hotel; cars lined bumper-to-bumper near the waterfront; and the pulse of rock groups in underground discotheques.

When the helicopter dropped into the Tel Aviv base, pausing there for fuel, Yesnov jumped out and commandeered the staff-car already purring out of the night to meet them. "I'll drive," Yesnov had told the girl corporal at the wheel. "You fly on with Major Zee in case he needs an extra pair of hands."

On the road, Yesnov said nothing until they were passing the zoo. "Why did you defect?" he asked casually, using Russian.

Grechko ignored the question and then said carefully, "I studied a great deal while I was among your enemies."

"You became an enemy too. Remember that!"

"You are wrong. We are educated people, we Russians. We admire achievements of a technical order. We have no money to spare for beggars and fanatical fools. We wasted our experts, our wealth, our lives even, on China. Where did it get us? It's a fool's game helping savages!"

Yesnov grunted and wheeled into headquarters.

Behind him a girl and a boy shifted their guns, enigmatic as figures in a poem by the late Israeli poet Nathan Alterman.

> Two step forth—a boy and a girl
> Clad for work and for war
> Heavy-shod and still
> Are they living or dead?
> Who knows, as they stand unmoving there.

The boy was a guard. The girl would set wheels in motion for the Russian's debriefing.

There was something in Grechko's background that Yesnov could not know, but Intelligence and this girl now did. The Russian had served in Asia, first working with the Chinese on their original nuclear-research center, later in Hanoi. He had transferred to Kazakhstan's missile range, having expressed strong disapproval of the Communist regimes in Asia. This might have no significance at all. Russia had gone through a phase of color prejudice, a sophisticated extension of the period when eight nationalities had been decimated by Stalin's order—the Crimean Tartars, the Chechens, the Ingushi, the Karachai, the Balkars, the Meskhetians, the Kalmykas of the Steppe, and the Volga Germans. The large areas emptied by those cruel deportations had been filled by Russian settlers. The girl specialized in these matters. She could quote verbatim the speech made by Khrushchev in 1956 that broke ten years of total silence, when the deported became *non-persons* belonging to *non-nations*. Khrushchev had spoken of "monstrous acts of mass deportation of whole nations." But then followed the disclosures from Peking of Russian "imperialism and racial prejudice." The girl had little confidence in any Russian change of heart. This man who claimed to be defecting, this Grechko, doubtless disliked the Arabs as heartily as he said he did. There was still an element of ancient Russian arrogance. She had a perverse loyalty to Arab culture and thought this Russian represented the technocrats who threatened in every part of the world to squeeze the individual and the artist out of existence.

Yet for all his denials of belief in God, the Russian had jotted down the prophesy of Isaiah: "The wilderness and the solitary place shall be glad for them; and the desert shall rejoice, and blossom as the rose." Why had he scribbled this into one of those old-fashioned notebooks that were kept by men of letters in another century? Nothing in his known history justified it, except

the forlornly solitary fact that he had grown up in the countryside around Kiev.

The Russians, thought the girl, have a proven record as nation-
killers. She could find no simple reason why one of them should
suddenly become an admirer of nation-builders.

The helicopter clattered across Jerusalem in the pale dawn's
light. The fingers of the wilderness, yellow and stony, clawed
their way into the city's outskirts.

Doctor Golden held the Syrian's limp wrist. Beside him, Ruthi
tended the plastic tubes and a fresh bottle of plasma. She had
returned from the cockpit with the news radioed from Haifa.
During the stopover there, the Syrian had been photographed.
Now the identification was certain. Captain Nayef was one of
the terrorist leaders in the attack on the school near Qiryat
Shmona.

Across the aisle, Mosheko's body lay naked and crumpled and
shiny with sweat.

The helicopter hesitated near the Dome of the Rock, already
catching a dim perception of light.

Doctor Golden glanced down at the sleeping city. How often,
as a pilot, had he flown over it just at such an hour when the air
was marvelously still and the honey-pink stone gleamed with an
inner glow? People always talked of going *up* to Jerusalem.
Jesus announced his intention of going *up* from Galilee. He
spoke literally. The city lay some 2500 feet above the sea and
more than 3000 feet above Galilee itself. Across the way stood
the Hebrew University on Mount Scopus, a symbolic victim of
religious hatreds. When the foundation stone was laid in 1918,
Dr. Weizmann had said, that as the sun flooded the hills with
golden light he thought "the transfigured heights were watching,
wondering, dimly aware perhaps that this was the beginning of
the return of their own people after many days." But any ex-

pression of such emotion seemed only to attract hostility, so that in 1948 the university and Mount Scopus were put under United Nations supervision. The Jews were allowed to send a convoy once every two weeks but it was out-of-bounds to all except those stationed there. When it was recaptured in 1967, the buildings had been reduced to a shambles, the laboratory equipment willfully destroyed.

Dr. Golden was startled out of these somber reflections by a large white cross made from bedsheets which was suddenly illuminated below. He put a steadying hand on the Syrian's litter as the Sikorsky began its shuddering descent. The girl crossed to Mosheko's side.

On the lawn outside the hospital, two physicians with degrees in psychiatry waited. They were accustomed to coping with fanatics: indeed, their wards were filled with Arab terrorists whose madness, real or feigned, kept them from being released to face the vengeance of Al Fatah and others. They would restore Nayef the Syrian to health and then have to decide how to judge his ravings.

"At that moment," Doctor Golden was to tell the stranger later, "I would have advised them to let him go. Return him and return the Russian. Let them both testify that we Israelis are prepared to pull down our fragile temple, Samson-like, and destroy the Philistine world along with ourselves rather than endure defeat."

But he was tired, as he readily admitted.

Major Zee was tired in a different way. He had been wearing the Sikorsky like a piece of clothing for many hours under extreme tension. Helicopters were not like airplanes in which the pilot rode along, coaxing it through the patterns prescribed by the laws of flight. A rotorcraft was an intimate part of oneself. Every movement was a response to the machine's controller: *pilot* was a misnomer, in a way, which was why many fliers spoke of "commanding the ship" when they left the cockpit of a jet for one of the big choppers. The transition from fixed-wing to rotor was not easy. One had to remember that a jet could fly hands-off whereas the helicopter was unforgiving of even a second's inattention.

Coming in, now, in front of the hospital in the dangerously shadowy light at high altitude with the sun's rays soon to slip over the Mount of Olives an hour ahead of sunrise in the bowl of Galilee, he had to skid the sluggish machine into a shallow approach across ground beyond sight. To pilots who had never flown helicopters, it looked as easy as riding a sycamore leaf. To Zee, it was more like flying a double-deck bus with the steering-wheel set high on the top deck. He worked with the unconscious skill of someone whose nerves and limbs have grown mysteriously over the years into the fibers of the machine, and though he still thought of himself as the driver of an airborne tank hanging from a sky-hook, he had become a craftsman. He could see this identification with the machine in Mosheko but not in himself. In the same way, the mechanic privately regarded Major Zee as a wizard and discounted his own trained ear for each discordancy within the machine.

The machine possessed an agility that often led military men to overestimate it. General Dayan, earlier in the year, had injured himself by jumping a little too dashingly from a hovering rotorcraft. It was true that it could climb vertically to a thousand feet and then, minus power but with some maneuvering, sink back to the precise takeoff point. It could pirouette prettily within inches of the ground or circle a point so that it always faced that point while its tail spun round. Only its commander knew how perilously it balanced at the center of many forces. Weight and altitude made a great difference, and the helicopter could not compensate by moving its wing more rapidly through the air to get the airspeed needed for flight: there was, therefore, an altitude where vertical takeoff became impossible and landing dangerous. Ship-commanders like Zee, with experience in high-performance jet fighters, could extend the so-called Dead Man's Curve: a plot showing the combinations of speed and altitude from which safe landings were almost impossible if the engine failed. There were other situations such as "settling with power" when the machine might start to sink in its own down-wash at high altitude; and from these, Major Zee had learned to escape too.

He had come out of this latest adventure a trifle more exhausted, a shade more nervously taut. These past three years had seen the helicopter used by the IAF like the fast frigates of another piratical age. A machine it might be, yet without its commander it became another useless chunk of scrap.

Zee flew his machine like a buccaneer, knowing its moods, sensing its limits as if he were one of Drake's captains trimming sail and pacing the crew before burning a Spaniard's beard. He felt his way down the last few feet, touched solid earth, measured the shift of weight from rotors to wheels. The blades were still turning when bearers stretched the Syrian and Mosheko onto trolleys and bore them into the gloom, Doctor Golden galloping at their side.

Major Zee climbed stiffly to the ground. "Well, Ruthi?"

She lit two cigarettes and handed him one. The glow revealed the lines of fatigue: his face glistened with perspiration.

"Mosheko will be fine."

"Thank God for it. I can't spare him."

They smoked in silence. They had moved away from the machine but suddenly Zee threw down the cigarette and ground it under his heel.

"You want me to check?" Ruthi asked.

"I'm sorry—you're tired."

"No, you deserve to know." She moved toward the hospital doors and then stopped. "Get rest," she said softly, arms across breast, hugging herself in the gesture of a mother. "He *will* be all right."

Zee nodded and returned to the machine. He climbed into the metallic womb and sprawled on the greasy deck, using a life-preserver as a pillow. He wondered if the Russian had defected under orders. He tried to remember if he'd left anything out of his report during the Haifa stopover. Around him the machine groaned and relaxed its iron ribs, expelling the hot smells in long vaporous breaths. He savored the old smells, not wood and canvas and tarred ropes, but airplane-dope and oil, and fuel coursing through tubes like blood vessels. Each machine had its own familiar taste and he was very fond of it. Above the hull, the rotor blades drooped in sleep.

"For what it's worth," said Jacob, "I think we have to hit them hard now, and keep hitting, round the clock, regardless of how it looks to the world outside. *We* know, and the rest of the world doesn't. There isn't time for explanations. We have to keep striking until every machine is held together by luck and string if necessary. Until every pilot clutches his eyeballs. Until we don't have a single man doing a job where a girl can function just as well . . ."

He stood in the room resembling an operating theater, over-looking the map known as The Table.

Someone said, "We depend upon others understanding our predicament. The days have gone when we could act alone, knowing ourselves to be right."

"If getting more Phantoms means that we become obedient allies—if our independence means we lose our identity to some superpower—then why fight at all?" asked Jacob.

They stood together, the chiefs and Jacob, watching the map. A solitary counter moved toward the symbol marking the base. Nothing else moved down there except the counter, shifted by a girl with a croupier's long stick. Nothing else moved on The Table between the Soviet border eight hundred miles in one direction and the new Soviet air-division base in Libya a thousand and more miles in the other direction. Nothing but the counter representing Colonel Aaron's Phantom homeward bound.

"Get the mid-field arrester gear ready for emergency landing."

The order had gone out when Aaron announced his intention of sticking with the plane. After the first automatic MAYDAY there had been a steady signal from the aircraft's Identification-Friend-or-Foe system. On the ground, men expert in the Phantom's idiosyncrasies checked and rechecked what information they could get from Aaron once he crossed the border. They were accustomed to working out such problems for pilots making maiden flights in jets, when a needless abandonment of aircraft could be prevented by advice from controllers below. The fact that the Phantom had not blown up made it virtually certain that the fire warning was due to a malfunction in the wiring, resulting from the bang. But what had caused the bang?

Circling the base now, Aaron could offer no clue. There was nothing to indicate trouble beyond that single winking light. His undercarriage was down and positively locked. What he could not see, and neither could anyone on the ground in the dim light before dawn, was the condition of his tires. When a Phantom tire exploded, it did so with a tremendous bang.

The mid-field arrester gear was designed to cope with such an emergency. A flat tire would chew itself and the wheel to pieces upon landing, so that the plane dragged itself at high speed off the runway. On board a carrier, the worst that could happen would be a bone-shaking, almost vertical thud after which the Phantom had been known to bounce into the air again. If the tail-hook had torn itself out while the plane roared up the deck and back into the air, it would be flown around the carrier and back into a spider web of nylon, the strands trapping the wings and stopping the plane with a fair chance of inflicting a good deal of damage. Yet the design of naval aircraft also presented the pilots with certain characteristics that were of great value. The Phantom offered great stability at slow speed, despite its sharply swept wings, so that it did not wallow or "Dutch roll"; and the engines provided such tremendous power that a bad landing could be corrected by a fast decision to fly around again.

Colonel Aaron had a great deal going for him as he began his gingerly descent. Not the least was the arrester-gear wire strung across the runway. His task was to put the Phantom down just short of this wire, marked by a prominent light. With his tail-hook extended, he would snatch the wire which was connected to a water-brake system to provide the powerful deceleration required.

He made his approach in the knowledge that every part of the Phantom was built for the savagery of naval operations. The wings, to fly at very slow speeds, had to be rotated to an extremely nose-high position: they were milled from large aluminum slabs and, like the rest of the machine, were made to resist the fringes of the heat barrier just beyond Mach 2.

The weakest link was the tire. In the heat of IAF operations, the tire had to survive extreme pressure on near-boiling tar for long periods of taxiing and sudden run-ups to 180 miles an hour, endure the swift transition to sub-zero temperatures, and slam back into the baking earth again, undergoing these extremes of internal pressure and temperature many times a day. Black streaks along the runways spoke of scorched rubber. Weary mechanics scrawled hangar-wall cartoons of over-inflated tires screeching for mercy.

Aaron had isolated the possibility of a burst tire from a multitude of alternative causes of potential disaster. He put the case to Talik, inviting his comment. At a time like this, Colonel Aaron was a stickler for cockpit courtesies. Being assured that his FO had arrived at the same conclusion, he slid the Phantom into the groove for whatever lay in store—a safe landing in a tangle of wire spaghetti, or a collapsed undercart and a fiery fuel-fed crash.

In one of the floodlit hangars where fitters and riggers hammered and riveted around the hulks of aircraft, where Skyhawks stood like disemboweled lobsters while their engines swung from chains, where Aaron's disabled Phantom was as much a personality as the actress Gila Almagor, where metal rang upon metal and flywheels whirred, one mechanic checked his logbooks. His job was to maintain the Phantom's ejection seats, so complicated they demanded a specialist's care. The seats were built to fling the occupants clear of a damaged plane at very high and low speeds, putting a variety of strains on the equipment. The seat must protect a man ejected into winds that could tear him apart. It must deploy its parachute only when the man had dropped to a safe height. Yet the same seat must also hurl a man high enough from ground level, and the chute must pop fast enough, to cushion the short fall. The specialist who kept such magical seats in trim saw that his latest safety inspection had been made just the previous morning. Satisfied, he joined the others drifting onto the apron where the last of the fire trucks growled between the concrete caverns.

In a nearby hospital, equipped to cocoon badly burned men, a nurse stood by the radiophone linked with the square-ended vehicle already at the runway's end and known as "the blood wagon."

A few miles away a small girl tottered sleepily into her mother's bedroom and said she'd just heard Daddy's engines.

In fact she had heard one engine. Aaron had closed down the J-79 whose fire-warning light continued to glitter. He was certain that the light was misinforming him but there was no point in taking chances. He could handle the Phantom on the remaining engine and come over the runway at a speed and in an attitude that would settle the plane firmly onto the concrete. The thing to avoid was a "floater" in which the tail hook missed the wire.

He did not want to drop heavily either. Once he started a high vertical descent rate, the plane could fall with a dangerous thud. He wanted to find a midway touchdown, firm enough to engage the wire, light enough that if he sensed a weakness in the under-carriage, he could go round again and choose to make a belly landing with all the further precautions this would involve. If he had to go round again, he must decide now if he could hope to light off the silent engine. He had done this before in an emergency. The J-79 was normally started on the ground by a mobile air turbine which blew the necessary air at a speed and in sufficient volume to rotate the Phantom's turbine blades fast enough to fire the engine. But in the urgency of a *Zanek!* he had been forced to leave the ground starter with only one engine burning. He had taken off on one engine, and when his airspeed was enough to blow a rotating wind into the dead J-79, he'd lit up with the throttle in the full afterburner position. The results were splendidly erratic but at least he'd made his interception on time. Now, eyes narrowed in order to judge his position from the runway flares, he decided against relighting in the event of a fouled attempt to get down.

The line of flares shrank and became a narrow series of dots. The first pair vanished abruptly, blocked from his vision by the Phantom's long nose held high. He was close to stalling as he swept down the runway, the wheels scarcely touching.

On either side, the unseen watchers heard the cry of pain ripped from a wheel making contact: a piercing ugly sound above the turbine's whine. There was a second screech as the Phantom slithered into the initial stage of a ground loop. At such a speed, without the arrester wire, it would never have completed the loop, folding instead into the harsh sand. But the wire sang against pulleys and water-weights. The machine groaned. A fountain of sparks sprang from the tail-hook under the small rebounding surge that drew the plane backward again. The great hook lifted up, releasing the wire with a long hiss, and tucked itself back under the tail.

Aaron closed down the remaining engine. He hated the idea of being towed the last mile. He need not have worried. A car pulled alongside. A familiar face grinned up at him. Had there ever been a time when the air-chief missed a vital debriefing?

Jacob listened while the Phantom crew gave their account. The evidence was overwhelming. The Russians were trying to close a lid over Israel.

Long ago, speaking then as air-chief, Ezer Weizman had said, "The sky is Israel's only open dimension. Altitude and range are our only strategic depth."

Jacob stared down at the big plot on The Table. We've always been small, he thought. Small communities. Citadels. Ghettos. Two thousand years ago the Romans turned the fury of an empire against the last Jewish citadel of Masada above the Dead Sea.

Flavius Josephus had told the story:

They embraced their wives and children, gave them their last kisses; and then, as if they had borrowed the hands of strangers, they executed that fatal resolve to snatch out their own hearts. All killed their wives and children as the least of all the evils they had to fear. Then each man flung himself on the corpses of his dearest and bared his throat to those picked for this hideous office. The Romans, beholding this vast number of corpses, could not tire of admiring how so many people, through so great a scorn for death, had conceived and executed so strange a resolve.

Now, each new recruit to Israel's armored units took his oath on the summit of Masada: "Never again."

Across the great map under the glass-paned balcony where Jacob waited, a shadow fell. A girl pointed her stick at Inchas, forty-eight miles northwest of Cairo. She adjusted the small black box strapped to her waist, from which ran a cord to the telex plug in her ear. The box enabled her to isolate several feeds from outlying posts. The plug prevented a clutter of noise in the room like an operating theater. Her rod hovered over the clump of counters at Inchas and then withdrew. Another stick from the other side of The Table wavered uncertainly between two other bases in the Nile delta.

The plot was coming to life. Sticks prodded counters as MiGs taxied on predawn ground tests at Gianaklis, seventy miles northwest of Cairo, and Al-Mansoura, directly north of the Egyptian capital. The movements were matched within Israel and the stranger could see in his mind's eye the cones of fire from jets that dipped and curtsied out of their bays.

The questions, the indecisions, the soul-searching agonies had solved themselves. The Russians had chosen to seal their gadfly enemy inside his tiny territory, and now with busy hammers would close the rivets up. The Security Committee's wisdom had been confirmed and the IAF must embark upon missions that would place fresh strains upon everyone. For a small and isolated state, there was no strategic depth to absorb an enemy's assault except the sky; no open dimension except the sky. The armored sky.

18

JACOB'S LADDER

The sky was open. Between Day X in Jacob's diary and a ceasefire on August 7, 1970, an estimated* 420 regular and reserve pilots flew five thousand sorties with the support of fewer than ten thousand IAF girls and men. They flew to keep the sky open. The subsequent ceasefire was hailed as an accomplishment abroad. The toll of damage inflicted on Russian-built bases, however, suggested that the pause was needed by the enemy to finish the wall to confine the Israelis.

But confinement of the small and the stubborn no longer seemed so easy. For the first time in the history of small and independent communities, lack of territory did not deny space to the defenders. The sky provided a new dimension, because the airplane turned it into a new means of defense in depth. Behind the airplane there had to be the powerful resolve of a people who refused to be crushed between the superpowers. The significance of small states such as Israel had been described to the

---

* All figures based on authoritative neutral sources. Air losses should be seen in the perspective of the terrible casualties inflicted on Israel's ground forces after the 1967 war and the 1970 ceasefire: 642 soldiers killed, 2033 wounded, representing in total nearly *one-quarter* the number of Israel's army regulars.

stranger by Conor Cruise O'Brien: "Survival as an independent
entity, is the most important contribution any country can make
in a world that tends more and more towards big monolithic
communities. It is positively bad for the human animal to conform within computerized super-states. There has to be a living
connection with an older way of life where communities were
smaller and men don't have to bother about their identity because it is something you never question. This requires independence of thought, culture, self-respect and pride in one's
own past . . ."

The brother of a pilot killed in the 1948 war understood this
need, and became one of Israel's leading archaeologists. Yigael
Yadin's father had directed scholarly attention to Masada through
the discovery of the Dead Sea Scrolls.

Since the destruction of Masada, his people had known no
homeland until the invention of the airplane coincided with that
of the kibbutz. Yigael Yadin, having done so much to foster a
concept of self-defense without benefit of buffer zones and hinterland, could remember when the kibbutz was regarded as a
microcosm of the State to come. His early days with the Haganah
resistance paralleled the development of the airplane as an instrument of personal combat.

Masada was the place where General Yadin's sense of history
best showed its value in a mini-state's survival. "You begin for
the first time, in these archaeological digs, to discover the physical reality. At Masada, the story of the Roman siege has all
manner of significance. When you dig there, you wonder if
Josephus Flavius told it right. Bit by bit, following his account,
you find a building or a wall or an object exactly as described
nearly two thousand years ago. Flavius, like the Bible, is an
archaeologist's manual."

Yadin put the flying machine to work in a classic example of
the soldier-scholar solving military problems through a sense of
history. During the 1948 fighting, he tried to break through with
his troops to a key Egyptian position blocking entry into the

Sinai. The road to this position, a town called Auja, was also swarming with Egyptian forces. In a moment of calm, General Yadin stretched in his hammock and recalled old Biblical and Roman maps that had shown another parallel road used by the armies of two thousand years ago. The ancient road was nowhere to be seen until Yadin examined the area in a small plane. From the air, the old road was plainly visible. Yadin marched his men along the route, outflanked the surprised enemy, and took the gate to the Sinai. Later, when archaeology became his all-consuming passion, he used helicopters to get at a cave near Masada among gaunt cliffs and deep canyons. From a ledge he penetrated three hundred feet deep into the rock. "In darkness, with no air and with thousands of bats, we discovered baskets with many vessels and documents, papyri, hidden by refugees from the Romans in the second revolt against Rome, which would be about 135 A.D. Imagine the excitement of putting your hands blindly into the earth and drawing out documents left by your people all that long time ago."

It is no coincidence that military leaders learned their skills from the self-defense tactics of Jewish pioneers, who in turn retained the stubbornness of Masada, and that most have a consuming interest in archaeology as a source of self-knowledge. Yadin, while still an active general, met with the Egyptian delegates during peace talks following the 1948 ceasefire. The Egyptians asked to have Beersheba returned to them. Yadin said, "Perhaps you'd like us to return the sun and the moon as well?" A pencil between his fingers bounced against the table and struck General Seif-el-Din on the head. The sudden tension was broken by another Egyptian's asking, "Why shouldn't you return the moon?" and everyone laughed. As so often, both sides recognized faint echoes of the long history they shared.

Driving back from a trip to Masada, the stranger asked the Little Lieutenant if she thought technology was coming to the aid of mini-states trying to keep their individuality at a time when great political and economic amalgamations seemed ready to swallow them up.

She saw the Hitlers and the Stalins as clumsy innovators in the art of manipulating the masses. This, she thought, was the century for dictatorship because the pressures of population made it inevitable that the multitudes would choose the least troublesome forms of government. An individual in an overcrowded community found it easier to submit rather than challenge authority, if only because he lacked the time to fight the bureaucracies that multiplied along with the growth in population. More subtle ways of manipulating the masses had been found as leaders adjusted to the new technocracies.

She did not regard digging up the recent past to be one of the healthiest of occupations. She had just read documents released by the United States government on the twenty-fifth anniversary of the American seizure of the Buchenwald death-camp. She did not want to be reminded of the efficiency with which sixty Jews a day were pushed singly down a shaft into the strangling-room, where they were garroted and hung on one of forty-five hooks that revolved through the incinerators. That was bureaucratic efficiency, though. That, she thought, was evidence of the trend in this century: a mindless obedience on the part of millions to orders.

"Wasn't the study of history necessary to recognizing these things?"

"I don't know," she said. "We're attacked for getting sentimental about the breakthrough to the Wailing Wall in 1967 and the way Dayan scribbled a prayer on a slip of paper and pushed it between the stones. I saw criticism in the foreign press. We were exploiting our 'geo-theological identity' to achieve political ends. Yet all I know is that every nation draws strength and reassurance from its cathedrals and museums, its palaces and monuments to great figures of the past. For us, for me as a *sabra*, physical proof of our existence here as a people is found in archaeology. Otherwise, our past is all in words and memories, insubstantial."

Jacob had put it differently: "We dig down to discover our identity. We reach up to find our future. For centuries our people became accustomed to having walls built around them. Aviation provided us with the means to frustrate anyone building a wall around our homeland. A way to climb upward. Aircraft became our ladder, if you like."

Jacob's ladder began to go up about the time Motti Hod's grandparents were trying to create the substantial and permanent evidence of an ancient culture that the Little Lieutenant was some day to inherit and cherish. They were pioneering near Haifa when the German gliding pioneer Otto Lilienthal was guiding with his body an engineless flying contraption remarkably like the aircraft to come. Lilienthal was killed in one of his own hang-gliders in 1896. The Wright brothers followed with a kite whose wings could be warped or twisted for control in the roll. Their Flyer in 1903 was the first piloted and powered airplane to lift itself off the ground, sustain itself in the air, and land on ground as high as that from which it had taken off.

Britain's First Sea Lord, Admiral Sir John Fisher, was at the time anticipating oil as fuel for future machines of war, and looking for cheap oil sources in regions that Britain could dominate.

In 1907 an odd-looking machine like a giant perambulator with revolving wings at the tips of two booms spluttered out of a field in France with a gentleman in a cap, breeches, and suspenders. This was Paul Cornu in his twin-rotor helicopter: the first. The baby-pram hull dangled under a structure with all the entrails exposed: in this it was like the sky-cranes of today. Here was the forerunner of a machine that would provide the future kibbutzim with their heliborne protectors.

In 1908 the source of Admiral Sir John Fisher's oil appeared to be found when British Petroleum brought in a gusher in Persia.

In 1909 the founders of Motti Hod's kibbutz at Degania took over and ran what had been Jewish National Fund farmland.

In this same year "a boy of extraordinary aptitude both for archaeology and a wandering life among the Arabs," * Thomas Edward Lawrence, bastard son of an Anglo-Irishman, aged twenty, went by foot a thousand miles through the Bible lands; and passing Motti Hod's future birthplace, commented that the sooner the Jews farmed all Palestine the better.

By 1914 the world was on the brink of a great war that would change for all time the nature of armed conflict by opening up the vast battlefields of the sky.

In the beginning of that year, Britain's agents in the Middle East, among them Lawrence, prepared for the titanic struggle ahead. The Ottoman Empire had dominated the Arab world for four hundred years. When the Turks fell into decline, France had seized Algeria and Tunisia; Britain had occupied Egypt and then the Sudan, and was creeping forward wherever weaknesses lay. Russia, established in Armenia and the Caucasian lands, sought control of Constantinople and the gate to the Mediterranean. Germany schemed, with Turkish help, to link East African forces with Berlin through Yemen. France needed Syria at any cost. Britain anticipated a need to scatter all the competition by backing an Arab revolt against what remained of Turkish power.

It was a bad time for the handful of Jews around Galilee to launch an experiment based upon the brotherhood of man.

Air fighting began when squadrons of two-seater scouts flew from Britain to France on the outbreak of World War I. Pilots and observers carried rifles or revolvers. Awkward duels took place when they ran into German aircraft on similar reconnais-

---

* The words are those of David George Hogarth, Oxford scholar, Orientalist, a man of action who used archaeology to cover his work in political intelligence "to keep Britain great."

sance missions. In the early encounters, rival aircrews potted away at each other but thought it bad form to finish off a crippled enemy. Then the machines were given guns, and fast single-seat scouts protected the reconnaissance planes. Scouts began to work in pairs when they found they were vulnerable to surprise attacks. Pairs developed into sections of four scouts, sections made up "squadrons," and squadrons added up to "wings." By 1917 there were spangled circuses of fifty machines or more.

This was the year of the Balfour Declaration: that astonishing reassurance given to the Zionists by the British government. It ranked alongside the Declaration of Independence and Magna Carta as a document to which the historian might ascribe the start of a political regime. It promised Palestine to the Jews.

Unfortunately, Lawrence of Arabia was at the same time promising Palestine to the Arabs. He was whipping up support for the Sharif of Mecca's revolt against the Turks but the image of Lawrence as a man who fought gallantly to free the Arabs is shattered by recently published documents. The true purpose of Lawrence's activities is clear from his manual for British political agents on how to handle Arabs. For example:

"Win and keep the confidence of your leader. . . . Never refuse or quash schemes he may put forward: but ensure that they are put forward in the first instance privately to you. Always approve them, and after praise, modify them, insensibly causing the suggestions to come from him until they are in accord with your own opinion. When you attain this point, hold him to it, keep a tight grip of his ideas, and push him firmly as possible but secretly so that no one but himself (and he not too clearly) is aware of your pressure."

Palestine had become the twice-promised land. The Jewish settlers knew nothing of this. They were Tolstoyan socialists, hopelessly utopian in the light of what was going on behind the scenes. They believed in simplicity and the nobility of labor.

Their hopes were buoyed by the announcement from the British Foreign Secretary, Balfour: "His Majesty's Government view with favour the establishment in Palestine of a national home for the Jewish people and will use their best endeavours to facilitate the achievement of this object. . . ."

A loosely worded promise had been made to Hussein, Sharif of Mecca, by Sir Henry MacMahon, British High Commissioner in Egypt to "recognize and support the independence of the Arabs." Since then, the British position had been that Palestine was not included in this general pledge. Nevertheless, a British government document, released from official secrecy in recent times, states a different case. Hogarth, the creator of the Lawrence-of-Arabia legend, prepared an Arab Bureau report in 1916 which said in part: "What has been agreed to, therefore, on behalf of Great Britain is: (1) to recognise the independence of those portions of the Arab-speaking area in which we are free to act without detriment to the interests of France. Subject to these undefined reservations the said area is understood to be bounded north by about latitude 37-degrees, east by the Persian frontier, south by the Persian Gulf and Indian Ocean, west by the Red Sea and the Mediterranean up to about latitude 33-degrees. . . ." In the area defined, Palestine was in a part of Syria promised to the Arabs.

A verbatim report of the British War Cabinet's meeting which reinforced this recently came to light. Lord Curzon, uttering the Foreign Office position, said on November 27, 1918, "There is first the general pledge to Hussein. . . . Palestine was included in the areas to which Great Britain pledged itself that they should be Arab and independent in the future."

Into this perfectly muddled situation, Lawrence now injected a further complication. He saw the Balfour Declaration as a way of retaining influence in Palestine through Jewish settlement. He began to work for an Arab state in Syria which would be held under British protection with Zionist money and advice. His old patron, the scholar-spy Hogarth, had seen the Sharif of Mecca to explain British policy on Zionism (if he succeeded, he knew more than anyone else). What Hogarth did not tell the Sharif, by his own later admission, was that Britain contemplated an independent Jewish State in Palestine.

The times were slippery and Hogarth was typical of them. He created Lawrence as a player in the continuous game of world politics. It was played as vigorously against friends as enemies, because today's friend was likely to become tomorrow's enemy, and vice versa. Hogarth, "a cynical and highly-educated baboon" in the eyes of one acquaintance, was (in the eyes of another) a cool operator in the Middle East, which "appealed to every romantic and lawless instinct in his nature." He was a great linguist, expert in Arab affairs, sardonic and dedicated to the idea that British was best and the best that could happen to a foreigner was to come under Britain's wing. By this yardstick, anything was forgivable.

Historians sifting through this outstandingly deranged period often fix on the nimble-witted tactics of Zionist leaders as if there was something especially unprincipled in the fancy footwork they performed to get their way.

Professor Hogarth's protégé, Lawrence, in the aftermath of World War I, now walked a new tightrope. He brought together the Arab Revolt's military leader and the future President of Israel. Emir Feisal and Dr. Chaim Weizmann, left by themselves, might have worked out some alliance. At the meetings in London attended by Lawrence during December 1918, Feisal (son of the Sharif of Mecca) gave his word that he would do everything to support Jewish demands and would declare at the forthcoming peace conference that Zionism and the Arab movement were fellow movements and that complete harmony prevailed between them.* Dr. Weizmann earlier had told Feisal that the Jews alone could help him build a strong and prosperous Arab king-

* From the Weizmann Archives, Rehovoth, Israel.

dom: "We shall be his neighbors and we do not represent any danger to him, as we are not and never shall be a great power."

The air battles of World War I were good clean fun by comparison with international chicanery. Now they were being analyzed. The sky gave a new dimension to war. Already some scientists looked toward space as the ultimate battlefield. Philosophers wondered if air-power might be a boon to small nations. Meanwhile the technology of aerial warfare had advanced at a pace few had foreseen. Multi-engined German Giants and Gothas had bombed London. Radio-telephone, later known as R/T, had been operated successfully between ground controllers and British scout-planes. Combat formations were routine. The later planes attained speeds of 200 miles an hour and ceilings in excess of 20,000 feet. Liaison between planes and armies had become easier with the use of observers, telegraphists, and a system of signals. Parachutes had just started to boost morale because for the first time a pilot stood a sporting chance of surviving the destruction of his plane.

The dogfight, too, had fixed itself firmly in the public imagination. Aces were born (and most of them died almost as quickly). Baron Manfred von Richthofen, Circusmaster of *Jagdstaffel 11*, with sixty-three victories to his credit, was shot down. His scout-squadron was renamed in his honor *Richthofen Jagdgeschwader* and a new commander was to be also its last: Hermann Göring.

Bothered by arthritis, Göring had to be content at first to be an observer in the German Air Service. But he had forced himself to learn to fly, had become the holder of the *Pour le Mérite** after twenty victories, and held together the remnants of Richthofen's hunting packs of scouts, who knew all about the long careful stalk, the up-sun ambush, and the savagery of the dog-

---

* Hermann Göring's medal was named for Frederick the Great, founder of the German Empire, who could speak only French, hence the odd title.

fight. Oberleutnant Göring may not have been himself a master of team fighting, gunnery, ambush, and decoy, but he took with him the experience needed to hone another air force, the *Luftwaffe*.

The need for ingenuity in the defense of the young Jewish settlements became apparent when Arab desperados attacked two small and isolated communities at Metullah and Tel Hai in March 1920.

Killed among the seven defenders of Tel Hai was a distinguished Zionist, Joseph Trumpeldor, who had lost an arm in the service of the Czar's armies and come from Russia to farm. He was, perhaps, the first of the Israeli army's casualties. It was a portent of a tragedy which was to become the ordinary condition of Palestine and then Israel. A paramilitary youth movement was formed in his memory: BETAR. It became the prototype of the ghetto fighters in Europe and a school for underground Jewish soldiers.

The conflict between Jews, who felt themselves a nation without a state, and Arabs, who seemed to be divided into too many states, was evident to a few observers. Richard Meinertzhagen, Chief of Intelligence to Britain's General Allenby in Palestine, wrote on March 19, 1919, to his Prime Minister in London, Lloyd George, a private and confidential letter, recently released from official secrecy:

> We are very wise to allow the Jews to establish their national home in Palestine. We have also freed the Arabs from the Turkish yoke and we cannot forever remain in Egypt. This peace conference has laid two eggs—Jewish nationalism and Arab nationalism; these are going to grow up into troublesome chickens; the Jews virile, brave, determined and intelligent; the Arabs decadent, stupid, dishonest and producing little beyond eccentrics influenced by the romance and silence of the desert. The Jews, despite dispersal, have distinguished

themselves in the arts, music, science, and gave Britain one of its distinguished Prime Ministers. *In fifty years time** both Jew and Arab will be obsessed by nationalism, . . . [which] prefers self-government, however dishonest and inefficient, to government by foreigners however efficient and beneficial. . . . Jewish and Arab sovereignty must clash. . . . My proposal is based on befriending the people who are more likely to be loyal friends—the Jews; they owe us a great deal and gratitude is a marked characteristic of that race. Palestine is the cornerstone of the Middle East, bounded on two sides by desert and on one side by the sea. It possesses the best natural harbor in the eastern Mediterranean. The Jews moreover have proved their fighting qualities since the Roman occupation of Jerusalem. . . . The Egyptians even with superior numbers are no match for an inferior Jewish army. But as modern weapons—tanks and aircraft—develop, offensive power rests more and more on human bravery and endurance. That is why I regard Egypt as Palestine's potential enemy. With Jewish and Arab nationalism developing into sovereignty and *with the loss of the Canal in 1966* (*only 47 years hence*) we stand a good chance of losing our position in the Middle East.

He showed a prescience in focusing on the Sinai peninsula, which, he reminded Premier Lloyd George, had been conquered by his chief, General Allenby. The Sinai, he wrote "places us in a position whence we can frustrate any Egyptian move to close the Canal."

Britain assumed the Mandate for Palestine in 1922, two years after Trumpeldor's death gave rise to rumors of British mischief-making for which no documentation seems to exist, and a year after the arrival as an immigrant of Mrs. Golda Meir.

Born in Kiev, the future Premier of Israel was the daughter of the carpenter Moshe Mabovitz, who moved from Russia to the United States. Golda became an active socialist whose Hebrew was Americanized and whose English has been described as

* Author's italics.

"Seventh Avenue New York." She agreed to marry another Russian Jew, Morris Myerson, if he went to Palestine with her. They married in 1917 and left for Palestine four years later. Golda (who later shortened her name to Meir) worked on a kibbutz at a time when there were still only eighty thousand Jews in widely scattered communities. This figure increased sharply after the United States government imposed quotas on immigrants to America, particularly after 1933 when the Nazis took power in Germany. Jewish migrants from Europe turned to Palestine, where the British had decided on a quota geared to the region's economic capacity. On humanitarian grounds, the figures were increased yearly so that the Jewish population numbered four hundred fifty thousand by 1939. By that time, Mrs. Meir had been through what she later called the most wretched years of her life. Diplomats dealing with her in 1970 were to say, affectionately but positively, that it was like negotiating with a fifty-year struggle for existence.

Secret air forces began with Hermann Göring and the Nazis. Few know that the Soviet Union provided them with a secret flying-school. By 1936 there was an open defiance of the Allied ban on a German air force and the Luftwaffe became official. It had a war on which to cut its teeth—Spain. It had a commander-in-chief—Hermann Göring, back from Sweden, where he was cured of drug addiction and resuscitated as a pilot.

This was the year when the Arabs precipitated in Palestine what the British called a "rebellion." The conflict cost three thousand lives in the next three years. The Jews were left to defend themselves. Many had learned in the ghettos of East Europe the techniques of communal self-defense in surroundings just as hostile. Their semiofficial defense organization, the Haganah, trained in secret.

The Jews had always been prevented by the British authorities from developing their own defenses (there were exceptions, notably the British Army Captain, Orde Wingate, but these came later). Training was conducted at night, disguised as sporting-club outings. Pistols were carried in water canteens. Grenades were hidden in loaves of bread. "The Jews in Israel in fact had to assume the burden of defending themselves against their enemies ten years before the British abandoned the Mandate and left them on their own." *

The Germans, on the other hand, had been flouting the World War I peace settlement for as long as the Haganah had been in existence: since, in fact, 1921. The German civil airline *Deutsche Lufthansa* concealed military aircrews. Gliding trained the future Nazi aces. One of Germany's best-known fighter pilots in the world war to come, Adolf Galland, trained with the Italian air force and perfected his skill on the airline route to Spain.

Not unnaturally, the techniques pioneered by Germany were watched with thoughtful interest in Palestine.

The double standard could hardly escape notice. When Göring was testing his Luftwaffe in the Spanish Civil War, Mrs. Meir had reconciled her powerful support of socialist pacifism with the need to countenance the militant Zionists. There was just too much evidence that British officialdom was moving in a direction that must spell disaster for Jewish settlers. By 1937 the British proposed a straightforward partition of the country. Neither Jews nor Arabs could accept this. And the British were now too busy preparing for the bigger menace in Nazi Germany to spare the forces to impose partition. In Spain a deliberate experiment in aerial bombardment was conducted by Hermann Göring against the market town of Guernica: and on April 10, 1937, wave after wave of German bombers attacked the defenseless area, killing sixteen hundred civilians. Göring admitted at the Nuremberg trials after World War II that Guernica was a practice target for inexperienced lads of the Luftwaffe.

There were attempts by individual Britons to help the Haganah

* Michael Howard and Robert Hunter, "The Crisis of 1967" (London: Institute for Strategic Studies).

prepare against the *blitzkrieg* tactics which Nazi Germany had perfected in winning the Spanish Civil War for Franco. A rural police force in Palestine drew on Jewish Agency advice. Thus Moshe Dayan was for a time a British police sergeant. There was Orde Wingate, who trained Jewish commandos until he was dispatched back to Britain as too great an embarrassment. By 1939 the Haganah had a permanent special force organized into commando units, the Palmach, which gave birth to the underground air force that was to become the IAF.

In 1939 the British Government adopted a policy limiting Jewish immigration. This White Paper bewildered and infuriated the Jews and did little to pacify the Arabs. In effect, seventy-five thousand Jews were to be permitted to enter Palestine during the next five years, so that their numbers never exceeded one-third the Arab population. This check on immigration came at a time when the Jewish people were suffering a persecution unprecedented in history. David Ben-Gurion, now leading the Zionists, said, "We shall fight the White Paper as if there were no war. We shall fight the war as if there had been no White Paper." The matter was suspended while Britain itself led the struggle against Hitler. By 1940 Britain was fighting in the air for survival. The Arab leaders were openly supporting Hitler. Yet British military tribunals continued to jail every Jew convicted of possessing arms. One of Wingate's midnight commandos, voluntarily attached to the British army, was imprisoned while on a training exercise.

The lunacy went on. The Arabs by 1941 were sure Britain was finished and proclaimed in Baghdad their latest holy war—against the British. Suddenly Jews who were sentenced to years in British jails for carrying arms were released the next day. David Raziel, for instance, had been sentenced to ten years for terrorism, was immediately released to fight, and was buried with full British military honors a few months later after he was killed in a raid. Moshe Dayan was let out of a British military prison to lead behind-the-line raiders.

At the end of World War II, Arab nationalism was gathering strength. Just as the white man in Asia had been discredited by Japanese victories, the Western imperialists in the Middle East had been exposed as blundering and divided.

The Jewish *Yishuv* in Palestine was the only force, however, actively fighting British imperialism. Mrs. Meir actually found herself in 1946 running the *Yishuv* (the Jewish community) after male leaders were imprisoned for blowing up all the frontier bridges in protest against the heartless and still inexplicable British restriction on Jewish immigration even in the face of the terrible emergency left in Europe's death-camps. Britain, to be sure, was catering to Arab client-states and this meant turning back the boatloads of homeless Jews flocking out of Europe's ruins. Yet it remains a mystery that nobody recognized the folly of seeking a return to the pre-1939 buccaneering days.

Thirty years after the ambivalent Balfour Declaration, Britain declared it "was not prepared to undertake the task of imposing a policy on Palestine by force of arms." The United Nations Special Committee on Palestine recommended, as a British Commission had ten years earlier, that Palestine be partitioned into a Jewish and an Arab state with economic union and an international regime for the city of Jerusalem. The frontiers left the Jewish state with a seemingly indefensible collection of territorial bits and pieces. The Arabs were hostile to a Jewish state of any kind: the United Nations proposal provoked violent riots in Syria and Iraq. Other Arab states reacted with varying degrees of intensity. The British Mandate ended on May 15, 1948.

The Jews, the People of the Book, surprised those who thought of the new State as a formal expression of an almost fanatical religious resolve. David Ben-Gurion proclaimed Israel. But nowhere in that Proclamation of Independence is there direct reference to the Almighty. The closest is a mention in the last paragraph to the Rock of Israel.

To the stranger, any attempt to summarize Israel's history is full of pitfalls. Literally hundreds of works have to be consulted. Their authors sometimes wrote with an air of infallibility and appeared not to have read each other's accounts. The god's-eye view, in books claiming to describe these events, seemed fraudulent. For instance, Sir John Glubb (otherwise known as Glubb Pasha, commander of the Arab Legion) published a version of the 1948 war which credited the Jews with a unified and efficient command, "wide-scale military training, complete modern armament, heavy mechanical equipment, expert and strong defenses." This was a dangerous view to popularize among the Arabs, who were thus encouraged to see the hidden hand of neocolonialism at work—or how else did a handful of Jews organize these superb defenses?

The stranger found, in talking with a great number of Israelis of different ages and background, that *from their point of view* the great powers (and the small ones with influence) played musical chairs with all sides during the years of unending conflict. Therefore, by whatever route they had arrived at the position they were in during 1970, they were going to have to work out their own salvation.

Elephant Moses had put it this way: "We live in an age where technology is perhaps our only reliable ally."

The stranger said, "Most liberal commentators seem to regard technology as the chief enemy of the individual. They argue that the next stage in human society will be the technocracy, where machines impose dictatorship on men."

"But look at it this way," said Elephant Moses. "We are a tiny state, yes. On the other hand, we are inventive in a century when technical innovation has permitted the big empire-builders of the past to give up territory. Britain is a group of small islands, today surviving on technical knowhow, whereas a few decades ago she would have been unable to exist without the biggest empire in history. The Dutch are more prosperous today without their Asian possessions. The French also.

"The difference is that we are a mini-state without any existence prior to 1948. This has been a curse and a blessing. A curse because we came into being when the Arab world was exploding with anger against imperialism, and we became a target through a misunderstanding of who we were. A blessing because we were forced to improvise, to make the best of little, to steel ourselves. Each war left us stronger. That doesn't mean war is good, but it made us develop fighting services that brought together people of totally different experiences. We discovered our defense in the sky and doubtless we shall find fresh technology by which to defend ourselves when the sky becomes a little crowded."

Survival of the resolute instead of survival of the strongest? This has been the argument, at least, of Israel's technical advisers to the small and equally young Afro-Asian states worried about guarding their independence and their own way of life against big-power encroachments. Technology has miniaturized the sources of power and perhaps the mini-state has the same significance for the future as the harnessing of the atom. Mrs. Golda Meir thought so. She was Foreign Minister for ten years (one of her qualifications, say some, is the meeting she had secretly in Amman with the King of Jordan in a last-minute attempt to stop him from joining the 1948 war. To escape attention, she traveled in Arab clothing).

It was Mrs. Meir who said, "The great satisfaction for me, as Foreign Minister, was the relationship we established with the new independent countries of Africa and Asia. Here were people tackling problems and facing challenges for which they had not been any better prepared than we were. It was natural that we, as Jews, would have a lot in common with them. They had their individual cultures that they were anxious to preserve, just as we have."

At the height of the 1970 crisis, Mrs. Meir had to decide upon an increase in Israel's commitment to ninety-four countries of the underdeveloped world. Some twelve thousand technicians had undergone training in Israel and almost a thousand Israelis were serving as advisers and instructors abroad. One of the most stubborn advisory missions consisted of kibbutzniks teaching commercial farming in Cambodia under Communist gunfire. This was a great burden at a time when Soviet intervention in the Middle East had so disturbed Mrs. Meir that politicians compared her with someone in the Roman Senate crying "Hannibal is at the gates!" In fact, she agreed to more advisory commitments abroad (Pakistan, gripped by a virulent anti-Semitic fever, had just successfully demanded the withdrawal of an American advisory mission of economic experts because most were Jewish). Then, receiving a doctorate in philosophy at the Hebrew University, she said, "Today, and I literally mean today, Israel faces a struggle more critical than any we have ever had to face before."

Such a cry of anguish, in Israel, was not histrionic. S had found for himself, and the view was borne out by military observers abroad, that Israeli assessments of what was happening in their region were accurate. Months before the world generally accepted the existence of Soviet SA-III missiles on the Suez Canal, an analysis of the situation was broadcast by a former Israeli intelligence chief, General Chaim Herzog:

> Doubts are now dispelled about Russian intentions with the introduction of SA-III missiles known as Goas in NATO nomenclature. What's more important, the Russians are manning them. This seems an indication that not only the Arabs but the Russians are unwilling to de-escalate the situation. . . . *If President Nasser stopped the artillery on the Canal, our air operations would cease.** The Soviet Union, in place

* An official promise, many times repeated.

of counselling moderation which would have led to a suspension of Israeli air attacks, has allowed itself to be dragged in. . . . Israel has sounded out Egypt in various ways and by bringing about what could be termed "bombing pauses" has looked for an appropriate reaction from the other side. But we've suffered casualties from the number of artillery exchanges in the past week alone, showing no inclination to respond. On the contrary, as Israeli pressure eases, Egyptian pressure increases accordingly. The Soviet action is a significant departure from past policy. This equipment is on the secret list and has not been issued to any extent—if at all— outside the Soviet Union. Where it is applied, as in East Germany, it is still manned by Soviet troops. . . . So the Egyptian war of attrition has the unqualified support of the Soviet Union. With this comes United States reluctance to supply Israel with additional planes. The Phantoms were more important for their symbolic value than their military value, which itself was considerable. The Middle East cannot be taken out of the worldwide context of US-USSR confrontation. Russia advances wherever weakness is found. . . . It is sad to see the United States unwilling to resist the Russian advance in a firm and unequivocal manner when history has shown by now this is the only hope if a policy of containment is to be pursued.

Herzog, once a senior British Army Intelligence officer, had always kept his cool. He was neither an alarmist nor a fool. His father had been Rabbi of Ireland, then Chief Rabbi in Britain and later in Israel. Chaim Herzog was himself commissioned in a famous British regiment, the Black Watch. His brother-in-law, whom he met at Cambridge University, was Abba Eban. The Foreign Minister was to say in July 1970, while the IAF was smashing the SA-III construction sites, that Israel was still prepared for free and direct negotiations with every Arab state; that peace frontiers were open for negotiation and that any question could be discussed. Herzog, in yet another role, that of military governor of the West Bank, had already taken this opportunity to start a dialogue with the million Arabs who there came under Israel's rule "to begin to create a bridge between us and the Arab world."

Herzog had learned to fly, hard on the heels of his other careers. At fifty-one, he was an active pilot. He saw the air force as an innovator. It had been bold when military rigidity might have curbed initiative and forfeited surprise. He had learned the lesson of the Battle of Britain, which began with the RAF tied to such idiotic peacetime training methods that the Luftwaffe almost got the upper hand.

Men such as Herzog saw that a tightly organized, flexible air force had a further importance. Because pilots are by nature (and by natural selection) highly individualistic, and because IAF ground crews were obliged by shortages of manpower and equipment to display ingenuity, a good air force produced the ideas which were necessary for survival.

Such an air force fitted into the concept of flexible defense forces based upon citizen soldiers. A leading military strategist had written: "The nuclear balance of terror limits the way that wars can be fought. On the ground, the methods first developed two thousand years ago now become feasible again. Ground warfare has in effect gone back to basic things: courage, imagination, speed, and surprise."

Was this enough? A few days after the 1970 ceasefire, Defense Minister Moshe Dayan reported to the Knesset that in the nighttime hours just before and after the effective moment of ceasefire at midnight, local time, August 7, Egyptian air defense contingents and their Soviet advisers had moved batteries of SA-II and SA-III missiles closer to the Suez Canal. One battery, he said, was deployed only twelve miles from the waterway. This was what all the months of daily bombardment by the IAF had been designed to prevent.

General Chaim Herzog pointed out that IAF air superiority had been the peace-keeping mission that stopped an Egyptian attack across the Canal. When the missiles were moved closer, even IAF planes on the Israeli side of the Canal became vulnerable to Soviet-built missile attacks.

Fifty years earlier, and in all the time between, appeals by settlers to buy the means to defend themselves had been largely ignored. Fifty years after the killing of Captain Joseph Trumpeldor, the one-armed farmer from the Czarist armies, three eighteen-year-old girls on holiday before joining the Israeli Defense Forces were blown apart while driving along the Golan Heights. Two boys were killed with them. It was the fifth day of the ceasefire from which Arab guerrillas exempted themselves.

The IAF carried out reprisals. For this Israel was criticized abroad. Nothing was said by the same critics about the continuation of Arab terrorism. Washington, reported *The New York Times* on August 16, 1970, was irritated in high places by the way Dayan publicized his charges of Egyptian bad faith.

The climate scarcely differed from that period when Dayan was a British police-sergeant and London played the role of the irritated patron, except that in those days it was pistols and grenades that were withheld.

A young Phantom pilot, months earlier, had discussed the readiness with which the foreign press seized upon Egyptian reports of an IAF raid, allegedly on a school. The stranger had seen aerial photographs that seemed to prove the school was in fact used as a military base. The incident, on April 8, was an isolated one. S knew, from his own observations, that the IAF took care to check and double-check the validity of targets. Premier Golda Meir herself frequently vetoed a raid if she thought there was the least possibility of needless killing or civilian casualties.

S asked the pilot how the children had been killed.

"We don't kill children," he said. "We don't kill civilians."

"How can you be sure?"

He stared at the stranger. He had a way of sitting very still.

His hands never moved when he spoke. His eyes never left one's face. He was like all the pilots S had encountered: extremely thin, pale, and about as relaxed as a Siamese cat.

"How can I be sure?" His gray eyes looked through the stranger. "Would *you* kill children?"

Then he said, "I don't like bombing. But the kind of bombing we do is not the same thing as in Vietnam. Here, if I throw bombs on an Arab artillery position, it has a positive result. It may stop shells falling on my brother or on my village. This is not bombing of an indiscriminate nature. Why is it permissible for Syrian mortars to bomb my parents or sisters, or guerrilla rockets to hit my village school bus, and wrong for us to strike at those responsible?"

The question was no more easy to answer than another question that exercised Israelis during the first days of the 1970 cease-fire:

Were they self-sufficient enough to survive the pressures from all sides?

A number of men sought new ways to make sure of it. They were committed by force of circumstance to stick with the proved policy of simplicity and improvisation. Yet the enemy now deployed equipment so complicated that the procedures were almost all automatic. "The Egyptian has to be told by the Russian expert which button to press and when," said Czareko, the base-commander who had served five years in the Soviet Air Force, whose home village near Kiev had a cemetery recording that his family had lived there six hundred years, and who remembered the shock of discovering at the age of seventeen from his best friend next door that he was, in fact, "a dirty Jew."

The machines that opposed Soviet armor were stripped to the bone. The men who handled them would decide how effective they could be. One was Czareko, who had told S, "If the others were up at five in the morning, during my time in the Russian air force, I was up at four just to prove that a 'dirty Jew' was better."

19

VOICES IN

THE COCKPIT

O, the bold aviator was dying,
And as 'neath the wreckage he lay, he lay,
To the sobbing mechanics about him
These last parting words he did say:
"Take the cylinders out of my kidneys
The connecting rod out of my brain, my brain,
From the small of my back get the camshaft
And assemble the en-gyne again."

The song heard at wartime parties to celebrate victories and deaths would be remembered more in the spirit than in the words by two former RAF pilots who tailored Israel's modern air force, General Dan Tolkowsky, who commanded the IAF at a time when it standardized on French supersonic jets, and General Ezer Weizman, who succeeded him.

Assembling the engine again, or any other part of Israel's few aircraft, had become an art in the earliest days. The stranger heard doubts expressed in 1970 by foreign air-attachés who thought the time had passed when planes could be patched, clipped, and cropped. Yet S saw abundant evidence of improvisation in a sky filled with complicated weapons.

This "can-do" attitude is easier to understand in the light of IAF experience. When Ezer Weizman shot down two RAF fighters in the 1948 war, Israeli forces had counterattacked the Egyptians and the British sent aircraft to warn Israel not to move any closer toward British installations along the Suez Canal. The warning was obscure, and the luckless RAF pilots were thought to be supporting Egyptian armies already closing upon Tel Aviv. The response of Ezer Weizman and his fellow pilots was a fiercely defensive one which left no ill-feeling on either side. Indeed, the RAF was soon thereafter training pilots recommended by Ezer Weizman.

The camaraderie among men who fly is a persistent quality. So is the inventiveness of men who service their machines. Ezer Weizman's dogfight with the RAF is no less instructive than the machine he was still flying in 1970. Both demonstrate an attitude of mind which, if it is not understood, leads a stranger to underestimate completely the kind of people the Israelis have become. His Spitfire was an example of changes that could be made in a thoroughbred fighter when, as now, it seemed little could be done by individuals to improve the performance of advanced machines. During the desert warfare of World War II, Spitfires based in Egypt were altered on the spot to catch high-flying German spy-planes. Engines were souped up, rudder bars were trimmed to cut down weight, armor plating was removed, wingtips elongated, lightweight batteries installed, armament reduced to a mere couple of 0.5-inch guns, and locally made filters and modified carburetors were introduced. Earlier, when the Spitfire needed to be flown more tightly to grapple with highly maneuverable German fighters, a simple expedient was found that made it possible for a pilot to resist the heavy G-forces that caused blood to flow from the head, resulting in a temporary blackout. A light extension to the rudder pedals allowed the pilot to bring his feet up, thus raising his knees and contracting his stomach so that he could more easily clench the stomach-muscles and restrict the blood draining toward his boots.

It is not hard to guess at the modifications that are still possible in the supersonic jets of today, although IAF pilots (reported upon by slightly dazed manufacturers in the United States, France, Britain and elsewhere) find they have to be firm, during purchasing missions, about the simplification of equipment. There is a parallel here with the experience gained by Luftwaffe pilots in the Spanish Civil War, and the lack of combat experience that led the RAF into trouble at the start of World War II. Here, for instance, is the sour comment of Air Vice-Marshal "Johnnie" Johnson, one of the RAF's top-scoring pilots, who also fought with the United States Air Force in Korea before he took over the RAF's Middle East Command:

> Everyone thought the dogfighting of the first world-war had gone for ever. Anyone who discussed it, prior to the second world-war, was an old fogey. High-speed maneuvering was impossible in the Spitfires and Hurricanes coming along, because of the effects of G on the pilot.

This, as the Vice-Marshal has several times reported, led to peacetime exercises that might be good for discipline but were useless in combat. He has described being rebuked by a senior officer for "opening the hangar doors," i.e., talking shop, over a glass of beer when the Battle of Britain was under way. Meanwhile the Germans had perfected new tactics which were to bring about the reintroduction of the forgotten principles of World War I dogfighting.

Talking with IAF veteran pilots about their reactions to foreign air forces, S was always struck by the similarity in their views with those of the enraged survivors of the Battle of Britain whose comrades had died largely because of peacetime complacency. One IAF commander, voicing a typical opinion, said, "When evaluating aircraft abroad, and in converting to foreign jets, our pilots annoy the manufacturers' test-pilots or infuriate foreign air-force instructors by continually asking 'Why?' But the question is necessary. We can't afford the luxuries that pad out peacetime service aircraft, and often—because our needs are different—we could make do with a simpler device, or substitute a weapon of our own for something that goes with the package."

The IAF's emphasis on dogfighting is often enough ridiculed by those who, echoing the fly-by-rote "experts" of thirty and more years ago, argue that modern jets impose too many strains for tight maneuvering. The stranger, listening to young instructors passing on their knowledge to cadets (often directly from the heat of battle), could only conclude they knew more on the subject than the kibitzers.

On the subject of evading the fire of an enemy fighter who jumps a disadvantaged plane, for example, here is a twenty-four-year-old IAF pilot speaking: "Kick the rudder pedal as far as it will go and push the stick to the same side and forward. You will be thrown to one side and the blood may rush into your head if you don't have an anti-G suit. This causes a red-out, the opposite of a blackout, because in this case the blood rushes to head in consequence of negative G. You will be in a spiral dive. The enemy on your tail should have fired over your head. Now, if he follows you down, he can line you up again in his sights unless you shake yourself and bring all controls back to center, then pull hard on the stick, going from red-out to blackout. You will be climbing fast and should be in a superior position to the enemy."

This was the advice used by at least one pilot flying a piston-engined aircraft surprised by a Russian-built fighter. It was typical of precautionary instruction given to all pilots—partly because they may find themselves at short notice flying a slower aircraft on liaison or spotting duties; partly because it's useful to know what tactics might be adopted by an enemy pilot in a slower machine that one has jumped oneself.

General Tolkowsky took over the IAF in 1953. He told the stranger, "When I was flying in the RAF, I never made the least

effort to find out about organization. If we'd had an inkling of
what life was on the verge of offering us, we'd have tried very
hard to pick up a few tips. As it was, each of us who were to
make up the basic elements of the Israeli Air Force went through
our own individual learning class. That's one reason why it took
time for everything to crystallize. What makes this area incredibly interesting from an air-power point of view is the configuration of geography plus climate plus history which produces the
possibility for a system of air-defense that is unique."

He was talking in the twilight of a summer's day, looking every
inch the banker, with the quiet murmur of Tel Aviv traffic penetrating into his modest and austerely furnished office. A small,
aristocratic figure, this was the man who fought deeply en-
trenched attitudes, including Moshe Dayan's own skepticism
(since, needless to say, abandoned).

"You take the Battle of Britain," he said. "There was a fortui-
tous collection of circumstances. First, Britain itself, a small
group of islands. Then the English Channel, as a waterway. The
radius of action of Spits and Hurricanes. The development of
radar . . . It all added up to a fascinating system that worked
just right.

"Israel takes us a step further in the challenge it presents. On
the one hand, it's surrounded by ground forces, which in military
terms is a bad thing. But actually, from an air-force point of
view, it's a wonderful, supreme example of how you can use limited resources with great suppleness and versatility. The air war
in the desert up to 1945 provided much of our inspiration (I got
in late—about 1942). We lapped up all the memoirs that came
out and it grew upon us in the mid-fifties that we should regard
the air force as a kind of fleet of warships in the sky. I used to
quote Admiral Mahan* to our chaps, because he woke up the
Americans to the supreme importance of sea power. He showed

---

* Alfred Thayer Mahan was an unknown United States naval captain in
1890, when he published the first of his books which were to effect a
revolution in the study of naval history "similar to that of Copernicus in
the domain of astronomy."

that sea power was far-reaching and affected the national well-being in peace and war, and he had interesting points about keeping a large reserve, for instance, and making the utmost use of ships. I wanted our chaps to see the analogy with air power, and I circulated Admiral Mahan's story about the gallant captain in the Royal Navy who distinguished himself in battle against the French in the eighteenth century and then fifteen years later, in command of a flotilla, was trapped by the French in a new maneuver. The poor fellow was court-martialed, his naval career ended. This, said Admiral Mahan, is what happens to people, however courageous, however distinguished their conduct may have been in battle—if they let X number of years elapse, the enemy arrives unexpectedly on their doorstep and they have had their chips."

Tolkowsky paused and stared at the darkening sky outside. Earlier he had paid tribute to his predecessors, including the armored-corps specialist, General Haim Laskov, who brought order to an air force built on bits and pieces of equipment and quite a number of flying adventurers. Tolkowsky had introduced a concept of air strategy:

"We had certain limits on what we could do, we had the huge emptiness of the Sinai desert across which the Egyptian armies had to come. . . . Now if we had been a sea power, we should have needed a two-ocean navy because we had Egyptians here and Syrians and their friends over there. But the sky is common property and in it we could move our units. We had to find a way of multiplying the effectiveness of these units, by speed, by making them multipurpose machines, by making positive use of what seemed at first a disadvantage, which was the way we were bunched up inside a small concentrated area at the center. We had to develop close control in order to punch out in any direction.

"I've already talked about the Englishman, F. W. Lanchester, who first thought of operational research. We extended his theories with regard to the arithmetic of firepower: there are lots of ways to juggle with it, but the principle thing is that a multipurpose aircraft can produce X results if utilized in several roles in several places during several missions in the same day. In addition, because our army is based on reserves essentially, the air force had to buy time while the ground forces got organized in the event of an attack. So we had to base the air force on a corps of regulars maintaining a very high pitch of readiness. This costs money. A lot of blood was spilled."

In 1954 the French had agreed to sell a formation of Ouragans, now the oldest jet fighter-bombers in IAF service, six Mystère 2s and twelve Mystère 4s. The cost seemed astronomical to Israeli leaders, who shied away from a strong defense system on idealistic as well as economic grounds. The French foreign ministry was also resisting the sale, and another year passed before the first Ouragans landed.

The spilled blood came from the clash inside Israel between those leaders who thought it was possible to survive with the old Spits and Mustangs until a vague future when some crisis might force them to purchase the latest in jets.

"It takes years to build readiness, you can't think of a tap that can be turned on and off," said Tolkowsky. "It's ridiculous and quite indefensible to lie low and take it easy for a few years and then when trouble strikes, decide to get busy. But to put across this viewpoint, we had to persuade the holders of the pursestrings that we had on the one hand to put money into moribund aircraft while preparing for the new ones coming off the line.

"For a time, in order to get the organizational readiness we needed, even though we weren't sure about equipment, we continually changed training programs, switched squadrons from one kind of duty to another and from one emergency base to another. . . . It was crazy, it was hard on the aircraft, it was hard on everybody, but it was one of the very few ways we could build up organizational readiness while we fought to get modern planes. We had to have our chaps ready to move in the middle of the night. We had to be able to pull in reserves at any time.

"We would respond quickly to any development on the borders, partly for the practice, but then we'd be told, 'You fellows are too quick on the draw, it's costing us money whenever you react.' That's when I quoted Admiral Mahan's story of the poor old British navy captain."

Here Tolkowsky thumped the desk, slowly and deliberately. *"You have to anticipate trouble every day of the week."*

The point finally got across in what the former IAF commander called "a peculiar way," and the general staff was finally convinced.

"In the years just before the 1956 Suez campaigns, we had a lot of commando/paratroop operations which were pursued vigorously by General Dayan, who initiated them and needed new ways to control units in hostile territory.

"We had a lot of Piper Cubs and the army chaps discovered the Cubs were fine for control on the field of battle, they were wonderful for picking up chaps who got wounded, they were great for extricating chaps who had gotten into difficulties.

"So this wonderful paradox arose. We sold the ground forces on air-power by way of the most humble little airplane of all, the Piper Cub!"

Tolkowsky adjusted the starched cuff of one shirtsleeve until it matched the other, precisely a quarter of an inch beyond the sleeve of his conservatively striped suit jacket. "We persuaded them the air force was a wonderful weapon for doing all kinds of peculiar things on very short notice. There was a classic occasion when a couple of navy chaps got in difficulties and were surrounded by hostile tribesmen. Half-a-dozen Piper Cubs landed on the beach and took them out while Motti Hod in a Mustang flew cover and took pot-shots at the Arabs.

"We could only do this because we'd got fellows crazy enough to be duty-pilot for this and duty-pilot for that, all hours of the day and night, and all weekends. These special ops were cloak-and-dagger stuff, certainly, but they became part of the routine and they got us acceptance.

"The associated problem, in persuading the brass of our legitimacy, was that we had to have our own multipurpose air-force headquarters with a staff-command all rolled into one. We needed the minimum of noise in the system. We had to be able to get direct from headquarters to the chap at the end of the runway and say, 'Get cracking!' The chiefs-of-staff said this was a load of baloney and why couldn't we all use the same headquarters and have the same Quartermaster-General deal with logistics and supplies along with everyone else's. We said that's a load of bunk. And it was General Laskov who came up with a sort of Solomon's judgment and said, 'Well, look, we'll form an integral part of the general staff, and the Quartermaster will work through an air-force counterpart who is one rank lower.'"

The French jets arrived before the 1956 Suez campaign in time to give the IAF the means to support their ground forces. The first Mystère 4s were delivered, and a formation of Vautour all-weather multimission attack bombers landed at the end of that war.

An analysis of the 1956 war by air strategists claimed it would have been better if Israel had never signed with France and Britain the Treaty of Sèvres, which forbade the IAF to cross the Canal. The view was widely held that the IAF could have destroyed the entire Egyptian air force at that time. At all events, the campaign demonstrated the effectiveness of Dan Tolkowsky's doctrine of paired aircraft as the basic unit of combat and tactical support. The second plane, or wingman, protected the first going into combat or in retreat. Combinations of paired aircraft were used, but the basic unit was one plane with another protecting his tail.

"Money was always tight and we had to demonstrate another

lesson—that it was not just false economy but downright criminal to waste time with too small a number of planes. People would say, 'You should have twelve Ouragans and I would say, No. We need eighteen on squadron and six in maintenance. The powers-that-be wanted to make a big show at the Independence Day fly-past and I said what's the use of pretending we've got something up our sleeve when we haven't. It was utter bunk, talking about doing things in stages. All we got was a false sense of security. That's how we got our two dozen Ouragans in 1955, and so on.

"All this obstinacy, this dedication on the part of men who would sacrifice anything for what they believed was necessary to good air defense, it all went back to Danny Shimshoni, an American who came here in 1948 and helped develop the technical school at Haifa and the flying-school. He started the ball rolling. Everyone saw that by simply holding on, these schools would be turning out more and more pilots, more and more technicians. . . .

"The richest period of inventiveness was around 1950–1951. I was flying to England with our ambassador at the time and I remember how he buttonholed me once we were away. He'd toured the bases and he was absolutely shattered by what he saw. In terms of numbers and crews, you see, we had practically nothing."

The stranger sat in the Spitfire squatting in a dark corner of the hangar, and overshadowed by the giants of today: delta-wing jets and sky-crane helicopters displaying their innards like medieval figures from anatomical charts of long ago. There seemed no great distance between them. The smells were much the same.

This unlined cockpit and the light metal bucket seat were just big enough to accommodate Ezer Weizman's lanky frame. In this fighter, he'd flown some of the first IAF missions. Here were the gunsight switches; here the rubber-mounted panel with the main flying instruments—turn-and-bank indicator, altimeter, airspeed indicator, artificial compass, rate-of-climb indicator, artificial horizon; to the right, oil and fuel pressure gauges, oil and radiator temperature gauges, engine-revs counter. Further right in the cockpit were the undercart selection lever and emergency hand-pump; the key for recognition signals. To the left of the panel were flap lever and flap position indicators, undercart indicator, flying position indicator, light switch, landing-light lever and air-pressure control. Below these, radio switch and channel selection buttons, throttle and pitch control levers, trim-tab knobs, and levers to control radiator flap and seat positions.

"Before taking off, the stomach's knotted. Once you're committed to an operation, the brain ticks like clockwork. You're trying to see the other chap before he sees you, before he gets tactical advantage. Everything happens very fast. Much later, when you're about to fall asleep, one vital piece of the battle pops into your mind and you come alert and suddenly it's all clear. . . ."

Voices from the past.

"I took a section of four," Ezer Weizman is saying. "Usually it was never more than two because we had only twenty aircraft serviceable during the War of Independence. It was January 7, 1949, and I flew south at seven thousand feet. We had no oxygen. Two of the others are dead now.

"That morning we'd jumped an Egyptian patrol and shot one down. Then there was a scrap with some RAF types in the Sinai. Things got confused. Our army said the RAF was bombing it. I don't know. I don't know.

"We had twenty-five pilots operational. After lunch I took a foursome and caught these RAF boys deep inside our own territory. We shot down five, Spits and Tempests. I pulled up to eighty-five hundred feet before the attack and when I was just at a very nice angle, I went in. My Number Two shot one down on the first pass. I was in a right turn and saw someone spinning into the ground. My bloke belly-landed. He was bloody annoyed.

"We left a note at the British Consulate next day saying, 'Sorry about yesterday but you were on the wrong side of the fence.'

"Our authorities were bloody mad. It wasn't a very happy day. We all got fantastically drunk that night."

Ezer Weizman was then twenty-three and within three years he was studying at the RAF Staff and Command College, where he found no evidence that the British bore any grudges.

He had served with the RAF in India until that air battle, Israel's first. He was, at the time, commanding the Negev Squadron and fliers were still considered oddballs.

When he took over from Dan Tolkowsky in 1958, he had flown all the IAF's aircraft from Messerschmidt-109s (which he ferried from Czechoslovakia) to Meteors and the range of French jets. He told S, "War is a highly emotional, highly intelligent, unfortunately human conflict. At the height of battle, you can make or break everything according to whether you think clearly or run from reality. This is where the Arabs deceive themselves. I don't want to use that terrible phrase—'Some of my best friends are Arabs'—but the fact is, if you know the Arab mentality you know at a certain point all the rhetoric and self-deception collapses and all the wild promises are seen for what they are—dreams. So they don't make good pilots. It doesn't mean they're not good human beings. We have our own limitations. We drive on the roads like madmen. We're always arguing among ourselves. But in the air, we had the sense to study our specific problems. We took help from all quarters at the start, but we had to take our own independent view of the situation. It doesn't mean telling anyone who is friendly, 'Look, to hell with you, I know better. . . .' But we had to study other air forces and then adapt to our own needs. The RAF was built to fight the Germans. The Americans built to fight the Russians later, and now everyone is organized to fight the Russians. . . . And the Russians are organized to fight the rest of the world. Nobody's organized to fight the Arabs except ourselves, and this isn't said chauvinistically, it's a reality. You fight to win. So you study your enemy. You build your morale and leadership on a comprehension of who the enemy is, and your motives in fighting him, which in our case is self-preservation.

"Now the Arabs have this problem of self-deception. They confuse words with reality. If you do this in business, you go bankrupt. If you do it with a woman in an affair, you're a flop. If you do it in battle, you're dead.

"The strike in 1967 was the net result of the ten preceding years. We finished the war in 1948–1949 as a rabble. During the period Dan Tolkowsky commanded the air force, we argued like mad. I was his Number Two for eighteen months until he recommended I take over. We studied the characteristics of the enemy we knew and we concentrated on the necessary things. We dispensed with bombers and went for long-range fighter-bombers with better strike capability. We studied everything within a radius of 500 nautical miles and decided our navigational problems were simpler than, say, from Biggin Hill [the Battle of Britain fighter base] to Berlin on the deck.

"We selected weapons that accorded with geography and climate and we avoided oversophistication. We said low-level flying was best in terrain that is mainly flat, against an enemy with oversophisticated radar."

The old Spitfire was full of echoes.

Jo-jo the Pogo Stick, former fighter pilot now hopping around in his light helicopter: "We went for Skyhawks in 1965 and the USAF said, 'You're mad!' But the Skyhawk had just enough sophistication for our needs."

Or Motti Hod, familiar with the terrain, as only a local farmer's boy could be: "The whole Sinai has been a godsend. Room for us to train in. Horizontal space to move around."

Or Dan Tolkowsky: "We don't know the extent we may change aerial-war strategy or tactics because we're in the middle of it now. Mao Tse-tung in the middle of the Long March didn't consider what principles he was formulating, although he might subsequently claim he knew all along what he was doing. But in the middle of a struggle like this, we can say only that we've stuck to a simple basic tenet—set long-distance aims and then plod towards them. It means improvisation, husbanding of resources, careful attention to getting maximum efficiency without exhausting men or materials, and weaving into the system every kind of originality."

Or Ezer Weizman again, delighting in the clean lines of the old Spit: "Johnnie Johnson, probably the greatest fighter pilot Britain produced, said something we must always remind ourselves about, here. 'Never let your successes blind you to the need to adapt to new situations.' He gave the awful example of how the RAF lacked the air superiority across France once the Luftwaffe pulled back. He said Britain built some of the best short-range fighters in the world but 'we were prejudiced by our very own experiences and thought it technically impossible to build a fighter with the range of a bomber.' It was the Mustang that saved him—the same versatile fighter we adopted and adapted later."

Voices in a cockpit. To the stranger they could be echoes from another war. The Walrus and the Carpenter had revealed themselves to S as a combination, after the Walrus's first reference to the enemy's aircraft lining up like oysters "conveniently in a row" to be eaten.

The Walrus: "Before the '67 war, people regarded city-born boys like myself as a kind of Lost Generation. We were spoiled, we didn't know the mystique of the land. After '67, I heard no more of that. The war gave us the chance to demonstrate that we just didn't like organized emotion and big displays of patriotism. The boys from the cities of Israel didn't talk much, but they flew well."

The Carpenter: "I came to Israel when I was only four or five years old. My dad was American and a small part of me always felt American—I'd say to myself in school, I'm really American. After the '67 war, I never felt that way again."

The Walrus and the Carpenter, flying together, taking turns to guard each other's tail, a pair of youngsters knocking impatiently at the door to promotion.

"We have to be ruthless about retiring the older men," Elephant Moses had said. "The air-force has to be a career, but you've got to be ready for civilian life too. That's why so many pilots continue university. . . ."

Ezer Weizman again: "Everyone got hung up on missiles in the period I was getting the Mirages. Missiles are no use in a classic dogfight, the basic 1914 and 1940 circuses. When the range is down to five hundred yards, you're back to the whites of their eyes. I had a hell of an argument with the French because I bought a lot of Mirages and hardly any missiles. I wanted cannon, and the French said, but you've got to have missiles—you're mad to go back to cannon. At the time, the RAF was buying 10,000 air-to-ground missiles from the French. Our Mystères and Mirages arrived with little knobs in the cockpit to direct the missile—the theory is you sit there and fly the bloody plane and twiddle the knob and fly the missile at the same time.

"It's all very well going straight and level. But I don't know —I don't imagine flying straight and level on a bombing run, do you? I didn't want the damn things and the knobs have never been used. People said dive-bombing's a thing of the past. And if I'd bought the missiles, nobody'd have said no. But I didn't and we developed the low-level bomb and the '67 war proved us right."

It's still Ezer Weizman's Spitfire, so the last word goes to him: "The last few years have been the tough modernization period, when we had to clarify weapons and examine ourselves in terms of time and space. We had to assume the enemy was best, and come out of every battle the better. It wasn't good enough to finish a dogfight with a bite, we had to swallow the whole meal. We didn't want pterodactyls in the air by being tied to rigid concepts. Yet we had to create order, which could be misread as rigidity.

"Time is still short for us, just as always. So we cram everything into the space envelope—fast turnarounds, hammering across short distances, using planes like slingshots so the ground crews feel they're practically there themselves. And giving every IAF man and girl the feeling of doing something special. I started the slogan *Only the best fly*. Well, some professor objected. So I changed it. *Only the unique fly*."

When the long hot summer of 1970 approached its end, the IAF was still fighting its open-ended war. Ozero was still calling Stiletto to report cobras and porcupines, for the guerrillas had never stopped their attacks on the settlements. Ruthi's father still called a stranger "Comrade" and whatever had happened to Grechko was not a matter for discussion. Ruthi's brother Yesnov was still flying several times a day, although half the sorties were made with young cadets.

Colonel Aaron was testing a new piece of equipment that might get Phantoms into the air more speedily from their QRA ready-pans. The device was adapted from the steam-catapult used to launch jets from navy carriers.

Crewmen rolled and scrambled around his Phantom, engines screaming just over their heads. The jet was straining forward against a dumbbell-shaped holdback, pulled by a catapult-bridle. The plane director, startling in orange coveralls, signaled with one hand over his head. Aaron lifted his feet from the brakes, ground crew rolled out of harm's way, engines rose to full power, and the Phantom shuddered. A fast check of the cockpit and Aaron's hand rose. Now he tensed his left arm, pushing the throttles fully forward against the new horizontal pressures to come. He pushed his head back against the headrest, waiting.

The plane director saw Aaron's hand drop to the control stick, and in turn signaled the catapult operator.

The procedure reminded Aaron of a ceremonial execution: the spectators, the busy figures sharpening and polishing and greasing. . . .

The cat fired. Everything became a blur. A beheading might be something like this.

S, the stranger, landed at Kennedy Airport in a steady drizzle. The air seemed dense with grit. There were long line-ups at the desks of the immigration men. Everyone looked tense and whey-faced.

In the taxi, too, he felt alienated. Already he missed the coziness of small cars. *"Camels eat them."* He heard an echo of the Little Lieutenant and was glad she didn't have to suffer the stifling Manhattan smog.

He stared out at children playing behind steel mesh and thought of other children swept by hot desert winds. "They're good boys," he remembered General Hod saying, "because wherever they're from, they're always close to the natural order where the quick survive."

But of course Hod was talking about nineteen-year-old pilots.

S picked up a newspaper in the hotel lobby. The August cease-fire had long ago collapsed. He read Washington's confirmation that 180 Soviet pilots were now in Egypt, which meant there were more Soviet pilots (commented a United States Air Force specialist) than there were supersonic planes in the entire Israeli air force. Twenty-five battalions of SA-IIIs, making a total of 100 launchers, were said to be entirely manned now by Russians. Some 15,000 Soviet-block military experts were also reported to be in Egypt, of whom 8000 to 10,000 were on combat assignment. "The trouble is," wrote C. L. Sulzberger in the *New York Times,* "Mrs. Meir believes a kind of Vietnam-in-reverse has already been created in the Middle East. In other words, while the United

States makes ordnance available to one side, the Soviet Union does the same for the other side—plus furnishing technicians, advisers, and actual combat troops. . . . The Israelis want Washington to deter the USSR from such direct intervention, arguing they can handle any other kind of outbreak, even if it is supported by Soviet arms and advisers, provided no Russians actually fight for the Arabs."

S got into the elevator, nose still buried in his paper. There was an unconfirmed report that a complete Russian-built missile system had been dismantled and removed by Israeli commandos.

He wondered how. Major Zee, probably, leading a flotilla of helicopters. The Walrus and the Carpenter would have been there. Doctor Golden was the sort who would back his way into such an expedition, uttering teddy-bear growls of faint protest. And the Confectioner. With Naomi or someone like her gathering the invisible strings together like a girl flying many kites.

The elevator stopped at his floor. He folded the paper, conscious of cold stares.

In a desert far away, Mosheko would be tinkering with his helicopters. Girls with flying jackets slung over their shoulders would sit at their adjutants' desks, splitting sunflower seeds or cartooning for toddlers left in the crew-rooms to be babysat. Somewhere an inquest would be in progress: a score or more pilots grilling each other: *where, how, why?*

The stranger turned before stepping into the corridor. Pale faces met his eyes: screwed mouths and foreheads glistening with indoor heat under artificial lights.

He walked away, wishing that out of the shadows might appear the inevitable guard from the Citadel: perhaps the gangling teenager he'd always thought of as Rimsky-Korsakov, with his wispy beard and solid snub-nosed automatic, who always remembered to call his chief by his first name, managing to forget the rest. Suddenly he missed them all. Corporals who behaved like colonels and generals who might look like bankers or ditchdiggers; young mothers who kept house under gumtrees between the sand-dunes; and children precociously alert to the distinctive wail of Father's jet. "The French airplane is curved like a French dame." The voice of Elephant Moses—or was it the mechanic from Nazareth?—boomed through the empty corridor and the stranger fumbled hastily with the key to his door.

The chambermaid had left the television on. S blinked at the blue glow. The volume was turned down and a fishy mouth expelled soundless words.

Two thousand seconds of silence. Surely it wouldn't come to that? Hadn't the superpowers frozen the situation—at least to the satisfaction of one side? The stranger had a sudden vision of all the heavy armor clanking to a stop while the rats nibbled under the concrete.

He turned the sound up. The fish-formed words emerged from the tube. ". . . protest lodged by Arab delegates . . . London condemned Israeli action. . . . No immediate reaction from Washington but . . . no change in the decision to postpone sale of the Phantoms. . . ."

S leaned back on the bed, his eyes on the ceiling. They were such very ordinary people: the wife at the flying-school party who wondered if they could go it alone while her teen-age daughters romped on the dance-floor; the colonels skidding on their behinds in an effort to start a Dak's engine; mechanics curled on hangar floors with exhaustion; pilots nursing a bit of soil until it grew something that might outlive themselves; the artistry of the analyst who said, "we were the first air force to utilize photo-reconnaissance on such a complete scale"; a muffled voice in the cockpit saying, "That's where Samson pulled down the temple. . . ."

At this distance, the voices could be made to sound cocksure. "What do the enemy do that's wrong? They take off." "Yes, it's true they have the fastest fighters but the only advantage this gives them is . . . in getting away." But these were the authentic voices of men with more *esprit* than spit-and-polish. They were not in fact cocky or belligerent; nor were they somber. They laughed a bit harder and worked a lot longer. All their people wanted was to be left to work out problems that were complicated enough without war or outside interference.

In microcosm they represented what all men professed to seek: a community of all kinds of individuals, from all quarters of the earth, united.

Perhaps, thought S, the truth is that in these times of mass conformity, when merely to survive we become units in a crowd, we resent people who stick stubbornly to their guns and refuse to conform and irritate everyone by saying things we don't especially want to hear. The television newscast featured a military analyst who thought Israel was kicking up too much fuss and the papers littered around the bed echoed the sentiment and suddenly S longed for the straight talk of a place where he had never really felt a stranger at all. He remembered a front-page headline in The London *Sunday Times* when the August truce began to collapse: U.S. IRKED BY ISRAELI PROTESTS. The report coincided with Tisha b'Av, the day of fasting that marks the destruction of the Holy Temple in Jerusalem. Captain Naomi had gone finally to confront reality in the children's village where she was raised, on Tisha b'Av.

Jacob had gone with her, that same Jacob, whose instinct for danger had prompted him to keep a calendar in which Day X had proved eventful and tragic. It had been his own daughter who was among the schoolchildren mobilized for the fruit-picking expedition near Jerusalem: his own daughter who had been partially blinded by an exploding rocket.

S remembered the first time he had recognized that if he was to comprehend the true nature of Israel, he would have to listen to Jacob fumbling at the locks of memory. He remembered again the generals looking crumpled and forlorn at the place where yet another child had died in the flames of hate. And remembered . . .

Never until the mankind making
Bird beast and flower
Fathering and all humbling darkness
Tells silence the last light breaking
And the still hour
Is come of the sea tumbling in harness

And I must enter again the round
Zion of the water beads
And the synagogue of the ear of corn
Shall I let pray the shadow of a sound
Or sow my salt seed
In the least valley of sackcloth to mourn

The majesty and burning of the child's death.
I shall not murder
The mankind of her going with a grave truth
Nor blaspheme down the stations of the breath
With any further
Elegy of innocence and youth.

Dylan Thomas had written the lines about another child's death
by fire, the victim of a mass compulsion to destroy. The Welsh-
man would have felt, in this other place and time, no stranger.

INDEX

Al Fatah, 244, 286
Algeria, 73, 80, 140
Allenby, Edward H., 306–307
Almagor, Gila, 118, 292
Al-Mansoura, 295
Alterman, Nathan, 283
Arab League, 68
Arab Legion, 312
Arafat, Yasser, 80
Atoll missile, 119, 127, 130
Austers, 8, 197
Avrech, Mira, 50
Avro CF-100, 91

B-17s, 202
Baath party, 241
Balfour Declaration, 302, 303, 311
Ball, George, 139, 144
Bar-Lev, Haim, 21, 74, 76, 77, 134, 135, 187, 189
Bar-Lev Line, 76, 254–55
Battle of Britain, 13, 231, 316, 321, 323, 331
Beaufighters, 201, 202
Beersheba, 255, 298
Beit She'an, 158
Ben-Ari, Mordechai, 180–81, 194–95
Ben-Gurion, David, 69, 182, 192, 201, 203, 310, 311
Ben Shemen, 235–37, 280
BETAR, 306
Blowpipe missile, 156
B'not Ya'ako, 250
Boelcke, Oswald, 107, 108
Brezhnev, Leonid, 185
Brin, Jacob, 198–99
BTR-40 armored personnel carrier, 239
Burma, 85

Cabinet Security Committee, 21, 39, 50
Cessna Skywagon, 179, 183

China, 14, 80, 168, 186, 248, 258, 284
Clark, E. G., 80
Cornu, Paul, 300
Couve de Murville, Maurice, 266
Curtis 46s, 200–201
Curzon, Lord, 303
Cyprus, 181
Czechoslovakia, 29, 68, 147, 197, 202–203

Dakotas, 195, 198, 214–16, 237, 337
Daphné submarine, 32
Darwin, Jackie, 216
Dassault, Marcel, 105, 265–67
Dassault, Serge, 266
Dayan, Moshe, 21, 24, 51, 65, 71, 74, 79, 135, 137, 182, 204, 258–259, 287, 299, 310, 311, 316, 317, 323, 326
DC-4, 203
DEFA Type 552 cannon, 32
Degania, 190, 198–200, 301
De Gaulle, Charles, 265, 266
Delfin jet-trainers, 73
Desert Air Force, 215
Dori, Yaakov, 282–83
Douglas Skyhawk, 59

Eban, Abba, 138, 315
Egypt, 39, 53, 70, 73, 74, 76, 79, 134, 139–42, 148, 185–87, 198, 228–29, 253, 298, 301, 315, 335; Air Force, 11, 12, 69, 72, 140
Ein Gev, 121
El Al Airlines, 64, 180, 194, 202
Elazar, "Dadu," 115
El Quneitra, 161

F4U-Corsair, 102
Faisal, King, 67, 242
Feisal, Emir, 304
Feron, James, 79

Fiat fighters, 234
Fisher, John, 300
Fouga-Magisters, 111, 128, 129, 132, 171, 191, 265
France, 15, 18, 29, 68, 72, 101, 105, 140, 148, 233, 265–67, 301, 325, 327, 333
Furies, 202

Gaddafi, Muamar, 73
Galland, Adolf, 309
Gaza, 94, 95, 158
Germany, 161, 301, 308–10
Gianaklis, 295
Giants, 305
Girls' Agricultural College, 65
Gloster Gladiator biplanes, 68, 193
Glubb, Sir John, 312
Gneisenau (ship), 232
Goa missiles, 139, 140, 314
Goebbels, Joseph, 148
Golan Heights, 23, 74, 98, 112–15, 119, 129, 145, 158, 317
Golani Brigade, 161
Göring, Hermann, 305–306, 308, 309
Gorshkov, Serge, 73
Gothas, 305
Great Britain, 29, 31, 67–68, 70–71, 181, 194, 201, 233, 301–304, 309–311, 327, 332
Guernica, 309

Haganah, 193, 194, 197–98, 204, 282, 297, 308–10; Air Service, 199, 200
Haifa, 64, 158
Harrier Vertical Take-Off jet, 33
Harvards, 8, 148, 198, 202
Hebrew University, 285–86, 314
Herzl, Theodore, 230–31
Herzlya, 21, 25–26, 49, 166
Herzog, Chaim, 314–16
Hippos, 122
Hitler, Adolf, 13, 14, 31, 38, 50, 67, 86, 146, 181, 310
Hod, General Mordechai (Motti), 8, 9, 11–13, 15, 19, 36–37, 39, 43–44, 47–48, 68, 75, 77, 82, 91, 120, 137, 149, 152, 154–55, 162, 170, 180–83, 187–200, 202–203, 205, 212, 221, 232, 258–59, 300, 301, 326, 331, 335
Hogarth, David George, 303, 304
Hornets, 78
Huang Hua, 186
Hunter Mark-9s, 73

Hurricanes, 87, 216, 321, 323
Hussein, Sharif of Mecca, 302–304

Ilyushin Il-28 jet bombers, 73, 126
Immelmann, Max, 93–94, 95, 104
Institute for Strategic Studies, 70, 72, 113, 137, 145, 147
Iraq, 73, 74

J-79 turbojets, 42, 142
Jaffa, 28, 80
Jane's All the World's Aircraft, 101, 120
Japanese Self-Defense Agency, 213–214
Jerusalem, 22, 57, 64, 68
Jewish Agency, 310
Jewish Brigade, 38, 193
Jewish National Fund, 199, 301
Johnson, Johnnie, 321, 332
Jordan, 39, 70, 74, 79, 141
Josephus, Flavius, 294, 297

Kagan, Benjamin, 68, 228
Kazakhstan, 242–43, 284
Keefer, G. C., 67
Khrushchev, Nikita, 284
Kollek, Teddy, 201
Korea, 107, 108
Kozlonsky, Pinchas, 202
Krishevsky, Dr., 232
Krohn, David, 180

Lanchester, F. W., 126, 324
Laskov, Haim, 204, 232, 324, 327
Lawrence of Arabia, 67–69, 301–304
Lebanon, 39, 70, 79
Lehmann, Siegfried, 235
Lehrs, Johannes von, 148
Libya, 73, 140, 267, 290
Luftwaffe, 13, 67, 306, 308, 309, 316, 321, 332

M61 Vulcan cannon, 41
Mabovitz, Moshe, 307
McDonnell Douglas Corporation, 45
McIntyre, Ian, 110
MacMahon, Sir Henry, 303
Magister jet-trainers, 73
Mahan, Alfred Thayer, 323–24, 326
Malaysia, 70–71
Malta, 100
Mandate for Palestine, 307
Mandrake, 43, 46–47, 126
Mankowitz, Wolf, 126
Mao Tse-tung, 13, 14, 144, 186, 332

Masada, 120, 294, 297–98
Matra missiles, 119, 125, 266
Me-109s, 99, 202
Megiddo, 66
Meinertzhagen, Richard, 306
Meir, Golda, 52, 71–72, 74, 97, 135, 137–38, 144, 187, 257, 307–308, 309, 311, 313–14, 317, 335
Messerschmidts, 32; Messerschmidt-109s, 8, 111, 330
Meteors, 41, 204, 330
Metullah, 306
MiGs, 12, 33, 58, 74, 82, 98, 105, 122, 191, 212, 222, 246, 295; jet-trainers, 73; MiG-15 fighter-bombers, 73; MiG-17 fighter-bombers, 73, 102–104; MiG-17 jet-fighters, 73; MiG-19 jet-fighters, 73, 229; MiG-21, 48, 79, 103, 104, 106, 107, 118–20, 124–26, 129–32, 141, 187, 229, 266; MiG-21 jet inter-ceptors, 73; MiG-21 (Mongol version), 140; MiG-21C, 140; MiG-21D, 140; MiG-21J, 127, 128, 140
Milling, Crawford, 34
Mil Mi-2 helicopter, 209
Mirages, 18, 19, 105, 118, 119, 122–125, 127, 140, 267, 272, 333; fighter-bombers, 33; MfJs, 265; Mirage 3, 73, 100–102, 104, 266; Mirage 3C fighter-bombers, 72; Mirage-3CJ, 101, 141, 265; Mirage 3E, 73; Mirage 3J, 125; Mirage 5, 72, 73
Mosquitoes, 215
Mount Scopus, 285–86
Mustangs, 8, 32, 86, 88–89, 99, 325, 326, 332
Myerson, Morris, 308
Mystères, 148, 266, 333; Mystère 2, 325; Mystère 4, 325, 327; Mystère 4A, 72, 265

Nahalal, 65
Nasser, Gamal Abdel, 37, 40, 68, 69, 71, 79, 120, 134, 185–86, 255, 258, 314
Negev, 68, 182
Negev Squadron, 330
Nigeria, 147, 232
Nixon, Richard M., 40, 52, 74, 78, 80, 138, 144
North Atlantic Treaty Organization (NATO), 267, 314

O'Brien, Conor Cruise, 297

Orloff, Hanna, 153
Ottoman Empire, 67, 301
Ouragans, 64, 72, 148, 265, 325, 328

Pakistan, 314
Palestine Liberation Front, 14
Palestinian National Council, 146
Palmach, 69, 310
Pearson, Lester B., 69
Phantoms, 33, 39–41, 43–45, 49, 61, 65, 72, 81–83, 85, 86, 89, 90, 118, 121, 125, 175, 185, 187, 212–14, 223, 224, 238, 244, 246–47, 260, 268–73, 277–78, 289–93, 315, 317, 334, 337; F-4B, 45; F-4E, 261–65; F-4 Phantom Mach 2, 141; Phantom 2, 245
Piper Cubs, 8, 249, 251, 263, 326
Pompidou, Georges, 266
Popular Front for the Liberation of the Occupied Arab Gulf, 258
Pratt & Whitney engines, 62, 142
Purim, 79–80

Qiryat Shmona, 21–22, 39, 158, 285
Quai d'Orsay, 266
Quick Reaction Alert force, 39

Rabin, Ambassador, 53
Raziel, David, 310
Raznikov, General, 124
Rees-Mogg, William, 137
Rehovot, 256
Rice-Davies, Mandy, 49
Richthofen, Baron Manfred von, 305
Rosengard, Gersham, 196
Rothschild, Lord, 146
Royal Air Force, 13, 34, 67, 72, 108, 193, 232–35, 259, 316, 320, 321, 329–30, 332, 333
Royal Armored Corps, 194
Royal Australian Air Force, 101
Rudnick, Eleanor, 201

S-12 Barlock search-radar unit, 74–75
SA-II missiles, 141, 157, 175, 177, 223, 224, 274, 316
SA-III missiles, 36, 52, 79, 139, 157, 174, 187, 314–16, 335
Sabers, 108
Sapir, Pinchas, 232
Scharnhorst (ship), 232
Security Committee, 58–59, 75, 97, 115, 137, 254, 257, 295
Seif-el-Din, General, 298

Black Sea

U.S.S.R.

Ankara ◉

TURKEY

SYRIA

Baghd

IRAQ

Mediterranean
Sea

LEBANON

Beirut ◉   ◉ Damascus

Jerusalem ◉   ◉ Amman

ISRAEL

JORDAN

◉ Cairo

SAUDI ARABIA

EGYPT

Suez Canal

Nile River

Red Sea

Miles

0   100   200

Kennedy/Karl